Frank Palmer ~~~~~~~~ ~~~~~~~~~ a typological
roles, such as Agent, Patient, Beneficiary, and ~~~~~~~~~~
relations, such as Subject, (Direct) Object and Indirect Object,
which are familiar concepts in traditional grammars. It describes
the devices, such as the Passive, that alter or switch the identities
between such roles and relations. A great wealth of examples is
used to show that the grammatical systems of the familiar
European languages are far from typical of many of the world's
languages, for which we need to use such terms as 'Ergative' and
'Antipassive'. Professor Palmer provides an elegant and consistent framework within which grammatical roles and relations
may be discussed, combining a great clarity of discussion and
evidence from an enormous number of the world's languages.

CAMBRIDGE TEXTBOOKS IN LINGUISTICS

General Editors: J. BRESNAN, B. COMRIE, W. DRESSLER,
R. HUDDLESTON, R. LASS, D. LIGHTFOOT, J. LYONS, P. H. MATTHEWS,
R. POSNER, S. ROMAINE, N. V. SMITH, N. VINCENT

GRAMMATICAL ROLES AND RELATIONS

In this series

P. H. MATTHEWS *Morphology* Second edition
B. COMRIE *Aspect*
R. M. KEMPSON *Semantic theory*
T. BYNON *Historical linguistics*
J. ALLWOOD, L.-G. ANDERSON, Ö. DAHL *Logic in linguistics*
D. B. FRY *The physics of speech*
R. A. HUDSON *Sociolinguistics*
J. K. CHAMBERS and P. TRUDGILL *Dialectology*
A. J. ELLIOTT *Child language*
P. H. MATTHEWS *Syntax*
A. RADFORD *Transformational syntax*
L. BAUER *English word-formation*
S. C. LEVINSON *Pragmatics*
G. BROWN and G. YULE *Discourse analysis*
R. HUDDLESTON *Introduction to the grammar of English*
R. LASS *Phonology*
B. COMRIE *Tense*
W. KLEIN *Second language acquisition*
A. CRUTTENDEN *Intonation*
A. J. WOODS, P. FLETCHER and A. HUGHES *Statistics in language studies*
D. A. CRUSE *Lexical semantics*
F. R. PALMER *Mood and modality*
A. RADFORD *Transformational Grammar*
M. GARMAN *Psycholinguistics*
W. CROFT *Typology and universals*
G. G. CORBETT *Gender*
H. J. GIEGERICH *English phonology*
R. CANN *Formal semantics*
P. J. HOPPER and E. C. TRAUGOTT *Grammaticalization*
J. LAVER *Principles of phonetics*
F. R. PALMER *Grammatical roles and relations*

GRAMMATICAL ROLES AND RELATIONS

F. R. PALMER

PROFESSOR EMERITUS
DEPARTMENT OF LINGUISTIC SCIENCE
UNIVERSITY OF READING

CAMBRIDGE
UNIVERSITY PRESS

Published by the Press Syndicate of the University of Cambridge
The Pitt Building, Trumpington Street, Cambridge CB2 1RP
40 West 20th Street, New York, NY 10011–4211, USA
10 Stamford Road, Oakleigh, Melbourne 3166, Australia

First published 1994

Printed in Great Britain at the University Press, Cambridge

A catalogue record for this book is available from the British Library

Library of Congress cataloguing in publication data

Palmer, F. R. (Frank Robert)
Grammatical roles and relations/F. R. Palmer.
  p.   cm. – (Cambridge textbooks in linguistics)
Includes bibliographical references and indexes.
ISBN 0 521 45204 X (hardback). – ISBN 0 521 45836 6 (paperback)
1. Grammar, Comparative and general. 2. Typology (Linguistics)
I. Title. II. Series.
P201. P32 1994
415–dc20   93-15563   CIP

ISBN 0 521 45204 X hardback
ISBN 0 521 45836 6 paperback

To Aidan, Frank, Edward and Jack

CONTENTS

Contents

Contents

ACKNOWLEDGEMENTS

I wish to thank Nigel Vincent, Masayoshi Shibatani and an anonymous (but identifiable?) referee, for reading the first draft of this book, pointing out errors and offering many very helpful suggestions. Although I have not accepted all the advice given, I am sure that they have helped me to produce a better book, but they are, of course, in no way responsible for any remaining errors or shortcomings.

NOTATION AND
ABBREVIATIONS

In addition to the usual conventions for the use of italics, quotation marks and asterisks, the following notation is used.

In the text

Initial capitals	grammatical roles and grammatical relations
SMALL CAPITALS	lexical items ('lexemes')
- hyphen	conjunction of role and relation
= equals sign	two roles identified as a single relation
/ oblique	alternative terminology or alternating items
+ plus sign	sequential elements in a construction

In the inset examples

SMALL CAPITALS	grammatical categories
- hyphen	morphemic boundary in the language material and corresponding division in the gloss
+ plus sign	combined categories in the gloss represented by a single element in the language material

To a very large extent, the transcriptions, glosses and translations are those of the original authors, although some of the abbreviations used in the glosses have been changed for consistency. A list of abbrevations is given below; others are explained in the text.

ABL	Ablative	ANIM	Animate
ABS	Absolutive	ANTIP	Antipassive
ACC	Accusative	AOR	Aorist
ACT	Active	APPL	Applicative
AGR	Agreement marker	ART	Article
AGT	Agent(ive)	ASP	Aspect

AUX	Auxiliary	MASC	Masculine
BEN	Beneficiary	MID	Middle
CAUS	Causative	NOM	Nominative
CIRC	Circumstantial	NONPAST	Nonpast
CL	Classifier	OBJ	Object
CLIT	Clitic	OBL	Oblique
COMPL	Complement	PART	Partitive
CONT	Continuous	PASS	Passive
DAT	Dative	PAST	Past
DECL	Declarative	PAT	Patient(ive)
DET	Determiner	PERF	Perfect/Perfective
DIR	Directional	PL	Plural
DO	Direct Object	POSS	Possessive
DS	Different Subject	POTEN	Potential
ELAT	Elative	PREP	Preposition
EMPH	Emphatic	PRES	Present
ERG	Ergative	P/P	Past/Present
FEM	Feminine	PRET	Preterite
FOC	Focus	PROG	Progressive
GEN	Genitive	PTCP	Participle
HAB	Habitual	PURP	Purposive
HUM	Human	REFL	Reflexive
IMP	Imperative	REL	Relative
IMPERF	Imperfect/Imperfective	SG	Singular
IMPL	Implicative	SS	Same Subject
INDIC	Indicative	SUBJ	Subject
INF	Infinitive	TOP	Topic
INSTR	Instrumental	TNS	Tense
IO	Indirect Object	TRANS	Transitive
LOC	Locative		

1
Introduction

As the title suggests, this book is a typological study of grammatical roles, such as Agent, Patient, Beneficiary, and of grammatical relations, such as Subject, (Direct) and Indirect Object, which are familiar concepts in traditional grammars; in addition it is concerned with the devices, such as the passive, that alter or switch (or 'remap' – see 1.1) the identities between such roles and relations. It will be apparent, however, in a typological study, that the grammatical systems of familiar languages are not typical of many of the languages of the world, and that the traditional terminology is inappropriate, as will be seen in the need to use such terms as 'Ergative', 'Absolutive', 'Antipassive' etc.

It should, nevertheless, be possible to suggest a consistent and reasonably simple overall framework within which such issues may be illustrated and discussed (though nothing is very simple in language). Yet very few attempts to do so have been made, and even fewer have been at all successful. The main aim of this book is to provide such a framework and to illustrate within it some of the typological characteristics of different languages. As such, it will not contain a great deal of theoretical discussion, though theoretical issues cannot be wholly ignored, for the framework must rest on certain theoretical assumptions and observations. One simple point, however, should be made: a typological study is concerned with similarities and differences between languages, and does not rest upon the assumption that there are universal (and identical) features across languages (see Palmer 1986: 2–3 and, for a more detailed theoretical discussion, Croft 1991: 1–32).

Many of the issues to be considered are interrelated and each cannot, therefore, easily be discussed independently in a logical sequence. For that reason the aim of this first chapter is to give a brief account of the main typological categories and to introduce much of the terminology that will be needed. This will form a basis for the more detailed discussion in later chapters.

A major problem is that there is, unfortunately, great confusion in the use of terminology by different writers, and even a lack of appropriate terminology for some quite important general concepts. As far as possible, traditional or widely accepted terms will be used, though some new terms are required and, inevitably, some of the decisions about terminology will not meet with universal approval.

1.1 Predicates and arguments

A traditional view (and one that is implicit in much of modern theoretical linguistics) divides the sentence into two parts, subject and predicate. Thus in the sentence below *the boy* is the subject and *chased the dog* is the predicate:

The boy chased the dog

The subject is notionally 'what is being talked about' and the predicate 'what is said about it'. The adoption of this subject-predicate analysis of the sentence is clearly shown in Chomsky's *Syntactic structures* (1957: 26), where the first rule is:

S → NP + VP

This states that the sentence consists of a noun phrase and a verb phrase, which correspond closely to the traditional subject and predicate.

An alternative view (and one that is more useful for the purposes of this book) holds that the sentence consists of a predicator and one or more arguments (or 'terms' – see below); in the sentence above, the predicator is *chased* and there are two arguments, *the boy* and *the dog*; notionally, the predicator expresses the relationship (here the act of chasing) between the arguments (here the boy and the dog). On this view, the structure of this sentence, would be:

Argument – Predicator – Argument

Or in terms of NPs and VPs (with VP used, in a different sense, to indicate only the verbal element):

NP – VP – NP

For a typological study, the two most basic assumptions (or, perhaps, observations) are, first, that the concept of predicate structure is applicable to all languages, and, secondly, that the arguments both (i) differ in their semantic relationships to the predicator and (ii) are clearly distinguished from one another through grammatical marking. Thus in the sentence above the distinction between the two arguments is shown by the word order. Switching the positions of two arguments would alter the semantic relationship of the arguments to the predicator and produce a quite different sentence:

> The dog chased the boy

A further assumption for a typological study is that the arguments can be identified semantically across languages, and it seems to be the case that, for most of the two-argument structures, one can be identified as 'Agent' (notionally the one who performs the action) and the other as 'Patient' (the one who undergoes the action). However, the ways in which the distinction between Agent and Patient are marked grammatically in different languages are varied. In particular, word order is not always relevant, as it is in English; moreover, where word order is important, it is not always the case that the Agent precedes the Patient.

Agent and Patient, thus identified by various grammatical features in individual languages and across languages in terms of similarity of meaning, are examples of what are here called 'grammatical roles'. The concept of 'grammatical relations', involving 'Subjects', 'Objects', etc. and the less familiar notions of 'Ergative' and 'Absolutive' will be discussed later (1.3.2, 1.4.2).

Two other terminological points may be made here. First, for the grammatical characterization of a sentence (or part of it) the term 'construction', rather than 'structure', is generally used (see Matthews 1981: 2), and will be used here from now on. Secondly, 'term' rather than 'argument' will be used to identify NPs that are not specifically identified as either roles or relations.

There is no determinate number of terms that may be marked grammatically, but two constructions can be regarded as the most basic, those with a single term and those with two terms, with the roles of Agent and Patient, as in English.

> The boy smiled   (the boy)
> The boy chased the dog   (the boy, the dog)

These constructions are traditionally referred to as 'intransitive' and 'transitive'. There are, however, other terms that are often marked grammatically, particularly those with the roles of 'Beneficiary', 'Instrumental' and 'Locative'. These may occur together with the single term of the intransitive and the two terms of the transitive construction. However, the single term of the intransitive and the two terms of the transitive are obligatory elements of the constructions, (so that the constructions are defined by their presence), while these other terms are optional. This can be seen from the impossible and possible sentences:

> *Saw the dog
> The boy chased the dog with a stick/in the garden

One further issue that will be the concern of this book is that there are, in many languages, pairs of sentences which differ grammatically in the marking of the arguments, but with very little change of meaning, e.g.:

> The boy chased the dog
> The dog was chased by the boy

Traditionally, these are 'active' and 'passive' respectively. In the passive, the Patient has the grammatical status given to the Agent in the Active, while the Agent has acquired an altogether different status (marked by the preposition *by*). The passive can, then, be considered to be a device that 'remaps' the roles (Klaiman 1991: 11).

1.2 Grammatical roles

It was established in the last section that, to begin with, this book is concerned with grammatical roles, which, like all typological categories, are defined both in terms of language-specific grammatical features and, across languages, by similarity in meaning. Before considering the further issue of grammatical relations more needs to be said about these roles.

1.2.1 *Grammatical and notional roles*

In purely notional terms, it is possible to identify a large number of roles that are played by the terms of a predication. These are sometimes referred to as 'semantic roles', but the less precise term 'notional roles' is to be preferred, especially since Klaiman (1991: 11) uses the term 'semantic roles' for the grammatical roles of this book.

Perhaps the best-known attempt to approach the problem of the roles in this way is that of Fillmore's 'case grammar' as set out in his 'Case for case' (Fillmore 1968); a revised and augmented set of such 'cases' (Fillmore 1971: 376) is:

Agent, the instigator of the event

Counter-agent, the force or resistance against which the action is carried out

Object, the entity that moves or changes or whose position or existence is in consideration

Result, the entity that comes into existence as a result of the action

Instrument, the stimulus or immediate physical cause of the event

Source, the place from which something moves

Goal, the place to which something moves

Experiencer, the entity which receives or accepts or experiences or undergoes the effect of an action

A similar list is given by Radford (1988: 373): Theme (Patient), Agent (Actor), Experiencer, Benefactive, Instrument, Locative, Goal, Source. Andrews (1985: 69–71) proposes Agent, Patient, Directional (Source/Goal), 'Inner' Locative, Experiencer, Recipient, Theme, Causer, Instrumental, 'Outer' Locative, Reason, Circumstantial Comitative and Temporal.

There are three problems with such notional roles. First, like all such notional features, they cannot be defined in any precise way, with the result it is not always possible to apply them unambiguously. Secondly, it is always possible to suggest more distinctions, so that there is, in principle, no limit to the number of possible roles. Thirdly, they are often partly based on the grammatical distinctions noted in languages, as is obvious in Fillmore's list, and so are not truly notional.

These notional roles cannot, however, be wholly ignored (as may be seen from 1.2.3), but it is important to understand the relationships and the differences between them and the grammatical roles. There are four points.

First, notional roles may be seen as the exponents or realization of the grammatical roles, or as being expressed by these roles. Alternatively, the grammatical roles may be seen as the 'grammaticalizations' (or, for some scholars) the 'grammaticizations' of the notional roles (see Palmer 1986: 3–7).

Secondly, grammatical marking is essentially language-specific, whereas notional or semantic characterizations are applicable to any or all languages; grammatical roles, therefore, are determined for any one language by their grammatical marking, but can be compared across languages (typologically) in terms of the notional roles that they express.

Thirdly, since grammatical roles are defined by their grammatical form, they are clearly identified and limited in number (particularly within a single language, but also typologically), whereas notional roles are far from clearly

5

defined, and there can be no clear determination of their number. Thus Agent, Patient, Beneficiary, Instrumental and Locative are the five most important grammatical roles, but the number of notional roles to be defined rests largely on the judgement of the investigator.

A fourth and very important point is that there is seldom, if ever, a one-to-one correlation between notional and grammatical categories. Thus, nouns typically refer to physical objects, but while *fire* is a noun, fire is not a physical object. Nevertheless, there is a large group of nouns that clearly refer to physical objects, nouns such as CHAIR, TREE, HORSE or BOOK, and it is this set of nouns that establishes the relation between the grammatical class and the reference to physical objects. These are the typical or 'prototypical' nouns and reference to physical objects is the prototypical feature of nouns.

In the same way, it is clear that there is no precise correspondence between the two types of role. A familiar illustration of this is the fact that in English and many other languages the grammatical role Agent subsumes not only the notional role of agent, but also the notional roles of perceiver and experiencer, as well as other such roles, as in (see 1.2.3 and 2.1.2):

> The girl saw the accident
> They like cherries

Yet the notional roles of agent and patient are the 'prototypical' roles associated with the two grammatical roles of Agent and Patient.

It may seem a little unfortunate that the same terms 'agent' and 'patient' are used for both the grammatical and the notional rules, and it might have been better if other terms such as 'Actor' and 'Goal' had been used for the grammatical terms (see Whistler 1985: 243). Foley and Van Valin (1984, 1985) talk of 'Actor' and 'Undergoer'. However, 'Agent' and 'Patient' are now well established, and the proliferation of terminology would only lead to confusion, and there, moreover, would be a need to make terminological distinctions for Beneficiary, Instrumental, Locative and their prototypical notional roles. In fact, no confusion need arise. As has already been the practice in this book, grammatical roles will be indicated with initial capitals, while notional roles will not – 'Agent', 'Patient', etc. vs. 'agent' and 'patient' etc.

1.2.2 Types of marking

As will be seen later, grammatical marking is essentially a feature of grammatical relations, but this rests upon the prior identification of the roles, which must, therefore, be considered first. Such marking can be illustrated, for the grammatical roles of Agent and Patient, from transitive, active sentences of English. Basically, there are three types of marking.

(i) Word order – the Agent precedes, the Patient follows, the verb in declarative sentences:

> The boy hit the man) (the man hit the boy

Other languages have different word order. In many languages both Agent and Patient precede the verb (the predicator), e.g. Tigrinya (Ethiopian Semitic, personal research):

> bärhe nə-məsgənna   ḥarimu-wo
> Berhe ANIM-Mesgenna hit + 3SG + MASC-3SG + MASC
> 'Berhe hit Mesghenna'

(ii) Morphology – in the case of pronouns only (except for *you*) there are different forms:

> I hit him) (He hit me

In many other languages, nouns as well as prounouns are morphologically marked for case, the case of the Agent being the nominative and the case of the Patient, the accusative, e.g. in Latin:

> Puer   hominem planxit.   Homo   puerum   planxit
> boy + NOM man + ACC he hit   man + NOM boy + ACC he hit
> 'The boy hit the man'   'The man hit the boy'

(iii) Agreement with the verb in terms of number with present tense of full verbs:

> The boy hits the man) (The boys hit the man

(There is also marginal agreement in terms of person in English, in that the first person pronoun *I* is also followed by *hit*, not *hits*.) In some languages, e.g. French and German, there is person and number agreement in all tenses, and in others, e.g. Tigrinya, there is agreement in terms of gender as well as number for both Agent and Patient:

> bärhe nə-'astir   ḥarimu-wa
> Berhe ANIM-Astir   hit + 3SG + MASC-3SG + FEM
> 'Berhe hit Astir (woman's name)'

7

'astir nə-bärhe ḥarima-tto
Astir ANIM-Berhe hit + 3SG + FEM-3SG + MASC
'Astir (woman's name) hit Berhe'

Other roles are marked grammatically in some languages, particularly Beneficiary, Instrumental and Locative (see 2.5 and also 2.6). The corresponding notional roles in other languages are marked by prepositions (e.g. English *to*, *with* and *in*). There is a problem with treating these prepositions as grammatical markers, because there are many different prepositions, so that, if prepositions in general are taken to be markers of grammatical roles, there would be a different role for each preposition. However, since they are of interest for typological comparison and especially because they are involved in issues of promotion and demotion (1.4.1), they cannot be entirely ignored, but will be treated as 'peripheral' grammatical roles.

These roles are marked by case in some languages. Thus Latin indicates Beneficiary and Instrumental by the dative and ablative cases:

Brutus   Marcello   librum   dedit
Brutus + NOM Marcellus + DAT book + ACC gave
'Brutus gave a book to Marcellus'

Brutus   Marcellum   gladio   occidit
Brutus + NOM Marcellus + ACC sword + ABL killed
'Brutus killed Marcellus with a sword'

However, as with most case systems, case in Latin (there are six cases) does not always mark grammatical relations.

1.2.3 *Agent and Patient*

It will become apparent that Agent and Patient are the two most important grammatical roles in a typological study. They form the basis of the distinction between transitive and intransitive sentences, in that in their active form transitive sentences must always contain both an Agent and a Patient, while for intransitive sentences there is a single obligatory term. This distinction is determined by the verb, the predicator, and traditionally verbs themselves are described as 'intransitive' or 'transitive', depending on which structure they require. Thus JUMP and LAUGH are normally intransitive, requiring single terms, while HIT and KILL are transitive, requiring both Agents and Patients. Many verbs are both intransitive and transitive, but with a difference in meaning, e.g. OPEN (*The door opened/He opened the door*) and RUN (*He ran in the race/He ran the competition*). Agent and Patient are also essential to the distinction between 'ergative' and 'accusative' systems (1.3) and are the terms most typically involved in devices such as the passive and antipassive (1.4).

The cross-linguistic identification of Agent and Patient depends ultimately on the notional roles with which they are associated. There is no precise correlation between these roles and the notional roles of agent and patient, though these are the prototypical roles that makes the identification possible (1.2.1). There is an extended discussion of this issue in 2.1.2, but it is useful to illustrate briefly some of the ways in which the grammatical roles fail to match the notional ones.

For instance, in English and many other languages, perceivers function as Agents, as in:

> The girl saw the accident

Yet it is obvious that perceivers are not agents, for perceivers are in no sense causers or instigators of the perception; on the contrary, it would seem that the thing perceived is more like the cause.

There are also striking contrasts both within and across languages in the choice of Agent and Patient. Thus FEAR selects the being who is afraid, while FRIGHTEN selects the cause of the fear as the Agent:

> Most men fear death
> Death frightens most men

Equally, the same sequence of events may be described by either of the following two sentences:

> John sold the book to Bill
> Bill bought the book from John

In neither case can the choice of Agent be explained in terms of simple notions of agent and patient.

More strikingly, there are differences across languages. Compare the English sentence below with its Italian translational equivalent (Lepschy and Lepschy 1977: 177, 194):

> They like cherries
> Gli piacciono le ciliegie

Introduction

The English sentence is transitive with an Agent *they* and a Patient *cherries*, but the Italian sentence is intransitive with *le ciliegie* ('cherries') as the single obligatory term and *gli* ('to them') as a Beneficiary (but see 2.5).

For simplicity Agent and Patient will sometimes be referred to by the single letters A and P. For the single argument of instransitive sentences the symbol S will be used, although it is better to consider this S as standing for 'single (argument)', as Huddleston (personal communication) suggests, rather than as 'subject', as suggested by Dixon (1979: 59ff.), which is misleading, since the term 'subject' is traditionally used not only for S, but also for A.

Dixon (1977b: 402) and Foley and Van Valin (1985: 301) call Agent and Patient the 'core constituents' of transitive sentences. However, a term is needed to include not only A and P, but also the single term S of the intransitive, and 'core roles' would seem to be appropriate. The other grammatically important roles, which occur equally in transitive and intransitive sentences, are termed 'oblique'.

1.2.4 *Other grammatical roles*

Only three other roles appear to be of importance typologically, the oblique (1.2.3) roles of Beneficiary, Instrumental and Locative. A full account of them depends, however, on issues relating to grammatical relations (see 2.2 and 2.5).

The most important of these is that of Beneficiary. Notionally, Beneficiaries refer generally to animate beings indirectly affected by the action with a possible distinction between the notional roles of recipient and beneficiary. These two roles are marked by the prepositions *to* and *for* in English, but also by word order, as in:

> The boy gave a book to the girl
> The boy gave the girl a book
> The boy bought a book for the girl
> The boy bought the girl a book

Marking by preposition is an indication of merely peripheral roles, but marking by word order may be taken to indicate the (single) grammatical role of Beneficiary. In Latin, Classical Greek and many other languages the dative case may be taken to mark the Beneficiary (but see 2.3).

Instrumentals and Locatives are most clearly indicated in less familiar languages. Both can be illustrated from Kinyarwanda (Bantu, Kimenyi 1988:

10

367–9), with pairs of examples very similar to those for the Beneficiary in English:

> Umugóre a-ra-andik-a   ibarúwa n'iíkarámu
> woman   she-PRES-write-ASP letter   with pen
> 'The woman is writing a letter with a pen'

> Umugóre a-ra-andik-iish-a íbarúwa íkarámu
> woman   she-PRES-write-INSTR-ASP letter pen
> 'The woman is writing a letter with a pen'

> Umwáalimu a-ra-andik-a   imibáre ku kíbáaho
> teacher   he-PRES-write-ASP maths   on blackboard
> 'The teacher is writing maths on the blackboard'

> Umwáalimu a-ra-andik-á-ho   ikíbáaho   imibáre
> teacher   he-PRES-write-ASP-on blackboard maths
> 'The teacher is writing maths on the blackboard'

The extent to which there are other roles is discussed in 2.7.

1.3   Grammatical relations

As mentioned in 1.2.2, it is grammatical relations rather than grammatical roles that are marked by formal features. This section and the next (1.4) explains why.

1.3.1   *Accusative, ergative etc.*

In English and many other languages, the single argument of an intransitive sentence (S) has the same grammatical marking as the Agent of an active transitive one (A), as shown by:

> He smiles   They smile
> He likes them   They like him

The three features discussed in 1.2.1, word order (preceding the verb), morphology (*he, they*, rather than *him, them*) and agreement with the verb (with -*s* for *he*, without -*s* for *they*), clearly establish the identity of S with A, and the term 'Subject' is traditionally used to refer to these two roles so identified, the other term, P, being called the 'Object'.

11

Introduction

There are, however, languages in which the single argument (S) is identified not with the Agent (A), but with the Patient (P) of the active transitive sentence. A striking example that has been extensively quoted in recent years is the Australian language, Dyirbal (Dixon 1979: 61, cf. Dixon 1972), as seen in:

> ŋuma   banaga-ɲu
> father + ABS return-PAST
> 'Father returned'
>
> yabu   banagu-ɲu
> mother + ABS return-PAST
> 'Mother returned'
>
> ŋuma   yabu-ŋgu buɽa-n
> father + ABS   mother-ERG see-PAST
> 'Mother saw father'
>
> yabu   ŋuma-ŋgu buɽa-n
> mother + ABS father-ERG see-PAST
> 'Father saw mother'

Dyirbal has a morphological case system; the two cases relevant to the discussion here are the absolutive, which is unmarked (no suffix) and the ergative, marked with suffix *-ngu*. In the examples above, the S of the intransitive sentence is in the (unmarked) absolutive case, while in the transitive sentences P, which precedes A, is similarly marked as absolutive, but A is marked with the ergative case ending *-ngu*. In the terminology of a language such as English, it would seem that the 'subject' of the intransitive sentence is identified with the 'object', not the 'subject', of the transitive. However, this is a misleading way of stating the facts: such terms as 'subject' and 'object' are inappropriate here (unless they are redefined – see 1.4.2).

Languages such as Dyirbal are often referred to as 'ergative' languages; well-known examples of such languages are Basque and Eskimo. Languages such as English are called 'accusative'. It is better, however, for reasons given below, to refer to systems rather than languages as 'ergative' or 'accusative'. In an accusative system S is identified with A (S = A), while in an ergative system it is identified with P (S = P).

The identity of S with A in English and other accusative languages is also reflected in the syntax. There are certain specific syntactic possibilities which are restricted to Subjects (S = A). For instance, in English, Subjects, but not Objects, can be omitted (or 'deleted') in the second clause of coordinate

12

constructions, if they are coreferential with the Subject of the first clause, e.g. (with the omitted Subject shown in brackets):

The boy ran away and [the boy] chased the dog

It is not possible to omit the Object in a similar way:

*The boy ran away and the dog chased [the boy]

In Dyirbal (Dixon 1979: 62–3), by contrast, it is grammatically identical roles of S and P that can similarly be omitted (see 4.1.1 for a fuller explanation):

ŋuma   banaga-ɲu   yabu-ŋgu   buṟa-n
father + ABS returned-PAST mother-ERG see-PAST
'Father returned and Mother saw [Father]'

A quite different variation from the pattern of either accusative or ergative systems is found where the single argument of intransitive sentences is marked in the same way as the Agent with some verbs and as the Patient with others (usually depending on whether the single argument is notionally an agent or not) and with a few verbs may be marked either way (see 3.5). S, that is to say, may be identified either with A or P, and it is, therefore, reasonable to distinguish two kinds of S, S_A and S_P, so that the identification is of S_A with A and S_P with P. One of the earliest examples to be discussed in some detail is E. Pomo (California, McLendon 1978: 1–3) as illustrated by:

xá·s-u·là·   wí   ko·kʰóya
rattlesnake-AGT 1SG + PAT bit
'The rattlesnake bit me'

há·   mí·pal   ša·k'a
1SG + AGT 3MASC + SG + PAT killed
'I killed him'

há·   c'e·xélka
1SG + AGT slip
'I'm sliding'

wí   c'e·xélka
1SG + PAT slip
'I'm slipping'

('AGT' and 'PAT' indicate the morphological distinction of 'agentive' and 'patientive', which can be regarded as case markers like 'nominative',

13

'accusative' or 'ergative', 'absolute'.) Such languages (or systems) may be called 'agentive'.

There is a further possibility – that S, A and P are all different; this too is attested (see 3.4). (Provided A and P are distinguished (see 2.1.2), these are the only four possibilities – S = A, S = P, S = both A and P, S = neither.)

Finally, there is one important caveat. Some languages are ergative in one respect, but accusative in another; a language may even have ergative noun morphology (S and P have the same marking on the noun), but accusative verbal agreement (S and A have the same markers on the verb) (see 3.2), or there may be variation in terms of tense or another grammatical category (see 3.3). Moreover, the syntax does not always correlate with the morphology (2.5, 4.2, 4.3, 6.5, 6.6.3). Strictly, we ought not, therefore, to talk about 'ergative languages', 'accusative languages' etc., but about 'ergative systems' and 'accusative systems' etc. within languages. Similar arguments hold for 'agentive systems'.

1.3.2   *Roles and relations (i)*

The fact that S is identified with A in accusative systems but with P in ergative systems makes it necessary to make a clear distinction between 'grammatical role' and 'grammatical relations'. For the identities S = A and S = P are different concepts from the roles of S, A and P; S, A and P are grammatical roles, but S = A and S = P are grammatical relations.

In accusative languages the grammatical relations are traditionally called 'Subject' and 'Object', S = A being the Subject and P the Object, and this is the terminology adopted here. Like grammatical roles, grammatical relations are indicated by initial capitals, though occasionally 'subject' and 'object' without initial capitals may be used, as in the next paragraph, when the terms are not being used in the strict sense in which they are generally used in this book.

There are, unfortunately, no names like 'Subject' and 'Object' in general use for the corresponding grammatical relations (S = P and A) in ergative systems. Many scholars have retained the terms 'subject' and 'object', even for ergative systems, but this can lead to confusion, because the terms can be, and have been, used in two conflicting ways. The traditional association of 'subject' with Agent might suggest that the term should be used for A (the argument marked as ergative), and this is the way in which it is most commonly used; but it can be argued, conversely, that the term is best applied to the relation that involves identification of S with another role, i.e. to S = P, especially if it has syntactic features associated with it (see 3.3 and Comrie 1988: 11). Neither solution is satisfactory, since both would lead to curious and confusing terminology: if A is identified as the subject, it would follow that intransitive sentences have objects but no subjects, while if S = P is identified as the subject, the Agent would be the object and the Patient the subject in transitive sentences, which would seem quite perverse.

There is a simple solution to this problem of the appropriate terminology for grammatical relations in ergative systems, to parallel 'Subject' and 'Object' in accusative ones. It is to use the terms 'Ergative' and 'Absolutive' for A and S = P respectively, taking the names of the two relations from the cases which mark them. It has been objected that this is to confuse case with grammatical relation, and would be like calling Subjects 'Nominative' and Objects 'Accusative'. That is not a convincing argument, because the two sets of terms are traditionally already available for accusative systems, but there are, as yet, none for ergative systems. No confusion need arise: cases may be designated 'ergative' and 'absolutive', relations 'Ergative' and 'Absolutive', the initial capitals clearly showing the difference. Support for the use of case names for the relations comes from the fact that there is a similar problem with the oblique relations. There is a similar solution – to use the case names (see 1.4.2).

It is sometimes useful to have a single set of terms for both accusative and ergative systems. The relation involving combined roles (Subject S = A in accusative systems and Absolutive S = P in ergative systems) will be called the 'primary' relation, and the other (Object P in accusative systems and Ergative A in ergative systems), the 'secondary' relation. In practice, however, these will generally be referred to in this book as 'primary terms' and 'secondary terms'; no ambiguity arises since 'primary' and 'secondary' are used only of grammatical relations.

It could be argued that, in agentive systems, no distinction need be made between role and relation. Here the identities are $S_A = A$ and $S_P = P$, but these seem to correspond directly with the notional roles of agent and patient, and it might be argued that they can, therefore, be identified with the grammatical roles of Agent and Patient, grammatical role and relation here being indistinguishable. This argument is valid as long as the system is being looked at in isolation, but not if considered typologically. Typologically, Agent and Patient are the two essential roles of transitive constructions, and it is the identification of them with S that establishes the grammatical relations. $S_A = A$ and $S_P = P$ are, then, grammatical relations;

suitable names for them are 'Agentive' and 'Patientive'. The grammatical roles are S_A, S_P, A and P.

The term 'grammatical relation' has been used because, in one theoretical approach, arguments are considered to have a logical-type relationship to the predicator, and this is expressed in such terminology as 'subject/object of the verb'.

1.4 Passive and antipassive

1.4.1 *Promotion and demotion*

Many languages have pairs of sentences such as:

The policemen have caught the thief
The thief has been caught by the policemen

Traditionally, these are referred to as 'active' and 'passive' sentences respectively. The simplest, and now widely accepted way of dealing with the grammatical relationship between two such sentences is to treat the first, the active sentence, as basic, and the second, the passive, as derived from it by a set of formal rules. In the active sentence, the Agent (*the policemen*) is marked as the Subject and the Patient (*the thief*) as the Object, both by word order and the agreement of the Subject and the verb. In the passive sentence it is the Patient that is marked as the Subject, while the Agent has peripheral status (marked by a preposition), or can be omitted altogether. Treating the relationship between the two types of sentence in terms of the derivation of the passive from the active, it may be said that this involves (a) the 'promotion' of the (secondary) Patient-Object in the active sentence to the status of (primary) Subject in the derived, passive, sentence, (b) the 'demotion' of the Agent-Subject to the status of a peripheral term (or its deletion) and (c) marking of the verb as passive (see 5.1 for more discussion). The terms 'promotion' and 'demotion' assume a hierarchy of primary and secondary relations, with all other relations being lower on that hierarchy.

Similar examples from Tigrinya (Ethiopian Semitic, personal research) and Gilbertese (Micronesian, Keenan 1985: 245) are:

Məsgənna nə-Məḥrät ḥärimu-wa
Mesgenna ANIM-Mehret hit + 3SG + MASC-3SG + FEM
'Mesgenna hit Mehret'

Məḥrät bə-Məsgənna tä-ḥärima
Mehret by-Mesgenna PASS-hit + 3SG + FEM
'Mehret was hit by Mesgenna'

E kamate-a te   naeta te   moa
it kill-it   the snake the chicken
'The chicken killed the snake'

E kamate-aki te   naeta (iroun te   moa)
it kill-PASS   the snake (by   the chicken)
'The snake was killed (by the chicken)'

In Tigrinya, the Subject is marked by agreement with the verb and the Object by agreement with the verbal suffix (Tigrinya marks masculine/feminine gender in both). In Gilbertese, the active/passive distinction rests solely on the passive marking of the verb and the demotion of the Agent to peripheral status.

In some languages, it is not only the Object/Patient, but also other, oblique, terms that may be promoted. Thus Malagasy (Keenan 1972: 172–3) has a passive which promotes the Object/Patient to Subject, but another voice, the 'Circumstantial', that promotes the Beneficiary and the Instrumental, which are marked as peripheral roles by prepositions in the basic, active, sentences:

Nividy   ny vary ho an'ny ankizy   ny vehivavy
Bought + ACT the rice for the   children the woman
'The woman bought the rice for the children'

Novidin'   ny vehivavy ho an'ny ankizy   ny vary
Bought + PASS the woman   for the   children the rice
'The rice was bought by the woman for the children'

Nividianan'   ny vehivavy ny vary ny ankizy
Bought + CIRC the woman   the rice the children
'The children were bought the rice by the woman'

Nividianan'   ny vehivavy ny vary ny vola
Bought + CIRC the woman   the rice the money
'The money was used to buy the rice by the woman'

In accusative systems the primary term (Subject) is S = A and the secondary term (Object) is P, and it is the primary term that is demoted (or deleted) and it is generally (but not always, as the Malagasy examples show) the secondary term that is promoted with passivization. In ergative systems, however, the

17

primary term is the Absolutive S = P and the secondary term is the Ergative
A, so that it is not surprising that, in some of them at least (see 3.2), it is the
Agent-Ergative that is promoted and the Patient-Absolutive that is demoted.
An example from Dyirbal (Dixon 1979: 61, 63) is:

> yabu   ŋuma-ŋgu bura-n
> mother + ABS father-ERG see-PAST
> 'Father saw mother'

> ŋuma   buṛal-ŋa-ɲu   yabu-gu
> father + ABS see-ANTIP-PAST mother-DAT
> 'Father saw mother'

In these examples 'father' is promoted from the status of secondary term
Ergative (marked by the ergative case) to primary term Absolutive (marked
by the absolutive), while 'mother' is demoted from primary term Absolutive
(marked by the absolutive) to the status of an oblique term, (marked by the
dative, the usual mark of the Beneficiary).

For this type of promotion/demotion the term 'antipassive' (Silverstein
1976) is used. The basic sentence may, as in accusative systems, be called
'active', the derived sentence being 'antipassive'. This antipassive is clearly the
counterpart in an ergative system of the passive in an accusative one.

1.4.2   *Roles and relations (ii)*

It was argued in 1.3.2 that the identification of S with A in
accusative systems and of S with P in ergative systems points to the need to
distinguish grammatical relations from grammatical roles. But there is
another, no less important, reason for making this distinction.

Grammatical roles such as Agent and Patient are essentially linked to
(prototypical) notional roles. When, therefore, the Patient is promoted, by
the passive, to the grammatical status held by the Agent in the active
sentence, it does not thereby 'become' an Agent, but still retains its role of
Patient. This is clear from the sentence discussed in 1.4.1:

> The thief has been caught by the policemen

Here *the thief* has been promoted to Subject, the relation held by the Agent in
the active, but it is still the Patient and has not 'become' the Agent (and the
Agent *the policemen* is still the Agent).

The traditional language of accusative systems avoids the possible confusion by using the term 'Subject' for both the A in the active sentence and the promoted P in the passive, as well as 'Object' for P in the active sentence. It can then be said the Object becomes the Subject, or better, that it is promoted to Subject. Since Subject and Object are grammatical relations, not roles, it can be seen that the grammatical roles, Agent and Patient, are unchanged, but that their status as grammatical relations is changed by passivization. (Similar considerations hold for Beneficiary and Locative when they are promoted to Subject (1.4.1), but see below for the problem of terminology.)

The Patient, then does not 'become' the Agent, but is still the Patient, even though it is also the Subject. Moreover, it is not even correct to say that it is the Patient that 'becomes', or is promoted to, Subject by the Passive. What is promoted is the Object, for promoted Objects are not always Patients, as can be seen from the discussion in 6.6: in some languages Beneficiaries and Locatives are promoted to Object, and these Objects (which are not, therefore, Patients) are promoted to Subject. Passivization involves Objects, not Patients. This has important consequences for the terminology to be used throughout this book. Discussion of passives and antipassives is necessarily in terms of grammatical relations. In basic, active sentences, however, roles and relations are not different, and either set of terms could be used – 'Subject' or 'Agent', 'Absolutive' or 'Patient'. In practice, it is simpler and more consistent to use the names of the relations (especially the familiar 'Subject' and 'Object'), except where the issue of role is important (as in the early sections of chapter 2).

There is a similar situation in those ergative systems that have antipassives. Here, the Agent is promoted to the status held by the Patient in the basic sentence, and it equally cannot be said that the Agent becomes the Patient, but, rather, that the Ergative, the secondary term, is promoted to the Absolutive. With antipassives, moreover, the Oblique roles are also involved in that the Patient-Absolutive may be demoted to the status held by the Beneficiary, Locative or Instrumental. An example of demotion to Instrumental can be found in Chuckchee (Siberia, Kozinsky et al.: 1988: 667) – see 7.3:

> ətlʔa-ta   məčəkw-ən təni-nin
> mother-ERG shirt-ABS   sew-3SG + 3SG + AOR
> 'The mother sewed the shirt'
>
> ətlʔa   ine-nni-gʔi   məčəkw-a
> mother + ABS ANTIP-sew-3SG + ABS shirt-INSTR
> 'The mother sewed the shirt'

Introduction

Demotion to Locative seems less common, but an example is given for Yidiny (Australia) by Dixon (1977a: 110) – see 7.1:

> ŋayu   balmbiɲ   wawa:l
> I + NOM grasshopper + ABS see + PAST
> 'I saw the grasshopper'

> ŋayu   balmbi:-ɲɖa   wawa:ɖiɲu
> I + NOM grasshopper + LOC see + ANTIP + PAST
> 'I saw the grasshopper'

There is a problem with terminology, however, in that 'Instrumental' and 'Locative' are names of the grammatical roles, and, clearly, the Patient is not demoted to the role of Instrumental or Locative; its role is unchanged, but there is a change in its grammatical relation. What is needed, then, is a set of terms to indicate the grammatical relations held by Instrumental and Locative in the basic sentences. No obvious terms are available and multiplication of invented terminology is unhelpful. In practice, little confusion will arise if the same terms are used for both roles and relations, and that will be the practice followed here; to say that the Patient-Absolutive is demoted to Instrumental is to be taken to mean that the argument with the role of Patient (the Absolutive) is assigned, by the antipassive, to the relation of Instrumental.

The Patient-Absolutive may also be demoted to the status of the Beneficiary, but here there is an opportunity to use a different term for the grammatical relation. In accusative systems the term 'Indirect Object' is used as the relation that corresponds to the Beneficiary, but that term is not suitable for ergative systems, since 'Object' is not appropriate to them either. The term 'Dative' is available; like 'Absolutive', 'Ergative', 'Instrumental' and 'Locative', this is taken from the name of the associated case, but distinguished from it by the initial capitals. The term is equally applicable to accusative systems, instead of, or alongside, 'Indirect Object'. An example of the Dative involved in demotion is an alternative to the Yidiny sentence quoted above:

> ŋayu   balmbi: nda   wawa:ɖiɲu
> I + NOM grasshopper + DAT see + ANTIP + PAST
> 'I saw the grasshopper'

Since Dative, Instrumental and Locative are oblique roles the corresponding grammatical relations can equally be termed 'oblique'. Similarly, where demotion is to a peripheral role (as in English, where the demoted Agent is marked with the preposition *by*), the relation can be termed a 'peripheral relation'. Indeed, it is important to note that demotion is always to an oblique or peripheral relation, never to a secondary relation (unless the inverse systems of 8.2 are treated in terms of passive or antipassive), though deletion is also possible, and quite common.

1.5 Other issues

Most of the issues that are to be considered in this book have been mentioned, often very briefly, in this chapter, although the discussion will, inevitably, introduce others that are related to those under discussion, notably promotion to object (6.6) and incorporation (7.5). There are, however, two rather different matters that are dealt with in the last two chapters, both of them concerned with issues of 'role-remapping'.

Chapter 8 considers two types of system that have something in common with the voice systems of passive and antipassive, but do not fit either very closely and may have to be dealt with separately.

Chapter 9 deals with the causative, which can be seen as a device that introduces a new argument to the relation of Subject and demotes the original Subject (A or S), as in Tigrinya (Ethiopian Semitic, personal research):

Məḥrät mäṣḥaf rə'iya
Mehret book   saw + PAST + 3SG + FEM
'Mehret saw the book'

Məsgənna nə-məḥrät   mäṣḥaf 'a-r'iyu-wa
Mesghenna ANIM-Mehret book   CAUS-see + PAST + 3SG + MASC-3SG + FEM
'Mesghenna showed Berhe the book'

2
Roles and relations

Most of the basic points concerned with roles and relations were made in the previous chapter. This chapter looks at them in more detail.

2.1 Agent and Patient

There are two issues concerning the roles Agent and Patient, first, the question whether they are universal, and, secondly, their relation to the meaning-based notional roles.

2.1.1 *The universality of the distinction*

It might seem to be obvious that all languages must make a grammatical distinction between different roles such as that of Agent and Patient, because, if there are two arguments with a predicator, it is essential to know which role is played by each of the two arguments. If, for instance, we are talking about someone hitting someone else, we need to know who does the hitting (the agent) and who was hit (the patient), and it is precisely that distinction that is communicated by the formal markers of Agent and Patient (1.2.2). Without such identification, it might be thought, communication would be impossible. Are there, then, languages that do not make the distinction at all, i.e. that do not grammaticalize basic notional roles such as agent and patient?

It is unwise to maintain that there cannot possibly be such languages, for it is dangerous to speculate about what must be in language, and all too often what appears to be an 'obvious' fact about language turns out to be merely a feature of English and familiar (usually European) languages. There is always a danger of looking for (and 'finding') grammatical categories that do not exist in the language being investigated, and, similarly, it is now generally accepted that the attempt to impose the categories of Latin upon English was a mistake. There are languages in which neither tense nor number is marked grammatically. Theoretically, then, it might be possible for a language to lack any grammatical marking of the roles.

It has, in fact, been suggested that there is at least one language that does not regularly make a clear grammatical distinction between the two basic arguments of a sentence. For Lisu (Lolo-Burmese) Li and Thompson (1976: 472) claim that 'even the grammatical relations Agent and Patient cannot be identified'; this claim is based on Hope 1974, supplemented by information supplied to them by him. The following sentences are both ambiguous in terms of agency:

> làma nya ánà khù-a   (p. 15)
> tigers TOP dog bite-DECL
> 'Tigers bite dogs'/'Dogs bite tigers'

> ánà xə   làma khù-à
> dog NEW TOP tigers bite-DECL   [NEW TOPic]
> 'Tigers bite dogs'/'Dogs bite tigers'

There is no formal marking here to indicate the different roles played by 'people' and 'dogs'. All that is marked grammatically in these sentences is the topic, with a special marker for 'new topic', which indicates what the speaker is 'talking about', so that the first sentence could be interpreted as either 'It is tigers that bite dogs' or 'It is tigers that dogs bite', and the second as 'It is dogs that bite tigers' or 'It is dogs that tigers bite'.

Li and Thompson point out that this disregard of agency does not greatly impair the communicative functions of the language for several reasons. First, the context provides clues. Secondly, semantics and pragmatics will disambiguate, as can be seen in the example they quote (not in Hope):

> làthyu nya ánà khù-a
> people TOP dog bite-DECL

> ánà nya làthyu khù-a
> dog TOP people bite-DECL

It will normally be assumed that the sentences above mean 'Dogs bite people', not 'People bite dogs', because people do not usually bite other creatures. Thirdly, there are lexical selectional restrictions, such that 'burn' must have inanimate Patients so that 'person dog burn' (with either meaning) would be ungrammatical. Nevertheless Li and Thompson further support their claim that Agent and Patient are not systematically distinct by presenting a number of sentences (all involving subordination) that are similarly ambiguous –

'The people saw the buffaloes hoeing the field'/'The buffaloes saw the people hoeing the field', 'Dogs are difficult for tigers to eat'/'Tigers are difficult for dogs to eat', 'Dogs want to eat tigers'/'Tigers want to eat dogs'. As with the first sentences there is a device for marking the topic that gives two different sentences in each case, but none for the Agent or Patient.

Unfortunately, an inspection of Hope's work suggests that, in a very important type of sentence, one that refers to a past action and with definite and specific Agent and Patient, an animate Patient is always followed by the particle that is glossed 'TO' as in:

    ása nya zànwe lǽ syɨ-a   (p. 37)
    Asa TOP child TO put to bed-DECL
    'Asa put the child to bed'

    ása nya ŋwa lǽ khwu-a
    Asa TOP me TO call-DECL
    'Asa called me'

In this type of sentence then Agent and Patient appear to be clearly marked. Admittedly, inanimate Patients are unmarked, and the 'TO' particle also occurs to mark the Beneficiary:

    ávæ̀ nya khɔ́sa dzà-a   (p. 34)
    pig TOP corn eat-DECL
    'The pig is eating corn'

    ása nya ávæ̀ lǽ khɔ́sa tsá-a
    Asa TOP pig TO corn give-DECL
    'Asa gave the corn to the pig'

This, however, does not detract from the point that Agent and Patient can be grammatically distinct in Lisu. The inanimate Patient does not need to be marked because the semantics disambiguates (and possibly also because the verb requires an animate Agent), while using the same marking for both animate Patients and Beneficiaries is a characteristic of a number of other languages (see 2.4).

Probably, the correct claim about Lisu is that it is sparing in its marking of grammatical roles, though it has a device for doing so when it is really important, and it should be remembered that even English does not always mark the distinction between Agent and Patient, as in the once often-quoted *the shooting of the hunters*, which may refer to the fact that the hunters did the shooting or that they were shot. It is worth noting that in Lisu the instrument

and the (inanimate) patient also are not formally distinguished (and either
can be omitted) as in:

> ása nya tshàbu tshɨdwù tí-a   (p. 35)
> Asa TOP salt   pestle   pound-DECL
> 'Asa pounded the salt with a foot-pestle'

But, of course, this is unlikely to lead to ambiguity.

Theoretically, it might be possible for a language to distinguish between
two arguments grammatically, but not to base the role distinction on the
notions of agent and patient. There are two possibilities. The first is that the
distinction is based on some other notional contrast, but it is difficult to
envisage what this might be, and there is no evidence for it. The second is
that the roles are determined wholly by the choice of lexical verb. Thus, given
markers (1) and (2), for a two-term system, *John* might be marked as (1) and
Bill as (2) in *John hit Bill* and *John thrashed Bill*, but with the contrasting
meanings 'John hit Bill' and 'Bill thrashed John'. This is not wholly far-
fetched, for it is, in fact, the situation with verbs such as FEAR and FRIGHTEN
where only the choice of verb determines whether the Subject is the one
causing or suffering from the fear. A similar situation holds for LIKE, if
contrasted with its Italian counterpart (1.2.1 and 2.1.2); given the notion of
liking, it is not possible to predict which term will function as Subject.
However, this kind of situation is restricted to non-action verbs; if it applied
to all verbs, it would make a language much more difficult, if not impossible,
to learn, and, again, is not attested.

Finally, there is a rather different possibility that does in fact occur: a
language may have grammatical markers for other notional contrasts. But
these 'sub-roles' seem always to be in addition to, not instead of, the
distinction made by Agent and Patient; there is a discussion of these in 2.7.

2.1.2 *Notional roles*

It has been argued (1.2.1, 1.2.3) that Agent and Patient are
prototypically defined in terms of the notions of agent and patient. A slightly
different way of looking at their relationship is in terms of causation, the
Agent being essentially the cause or 'initiator' of the action and the Patient
the one directly affected by it or its 'endpoint' (see Croft 1991).

This notion of causation makes it possible to extend the notion of agent
beyond that of animate beings acting in a deliberate fashion. For while with
many verbs of action, such as HIT, KILL, BREAK, it is clear that there is usually

a deliberate act by an animate being, this is not always so, for one can be hit or killed, and something can be broken, by a falling tree or a storm. Moreover, the causal relationship is not necessarily wholly physical: with verbs such as PERSUADE, ORDER and WORRY, the Patient is affected mentally rather than physically. Croft (1991: 167) following Talmy (1976: 107–8), suggests that if purely physical causation (by a physical object) is distinguished from volitional causation (by a mentally aware agent) as physical vs. mental, both initiator and endpoint may be seen as either physical or mental, so that there are four causation types. All of these possibilities can be accounted for in terms of Agent and Patient, if these are (prototypically) defined in terms of cause.

This view of Agent and Patient and the causal relation can be extended to verbs of state in such sentences as:

> The earth attracts the moon
> The king rules the country

It is reasonable to see the earth and the king as the source or cause of the state that affects the moon and the country.

There are, however, many verbs for which the Agent and Patient seem to have little correlation with notional agents and patients and no clear causal relation between them. One particularly important set of verbs is that of the verbs of perception, particularly those representing the five senses:

> John saw the accident
> Mary heard the cry for help
> I (can) smell something burning
> I (can) taste garlic in this soup
> I (can) feel something sharp here

The notional roles involved here are those of perceiver and perceived, and it has been noted that, in almost all languages, perceivers function as Agents and the perceived as Patients. There are a few possible exceptions to this. In Tabassaran, a language of the Caucasus (Kibrik 1985), which is discussed in detail in 3.6.2, perceivers with 'look at' are marked not as Agents but as Patients in the morphological system of the noun, while with 'see' they are marked as Beneficiaries in both the morphology of the noun and verbal agreement.

Since the cause of the perception would seem to be the thing perceived rather than the perceiver, it may seem strange that it is perceivers that are treated as Agents, although the idea that the thing perceived is the cause is probably a very modern idea based on scientific knowledge, and not, therefore, very relevant. There is, however, another feature that is important, that of animacy. Agents are generally animate beings, and there is, for that reason, often a close association between agency and animacy (see also 2.2). Since with these verbs the notion of agency or cause is not very strong, and since they refer to characteristics that are wholly restricted to animates, it is not surprising that animacy is the criterion used for determining the Agent. There is a similar argument for verbs of cognition such as UNDERSTAND and REMEMBER.

There is a different situation with verbs of emotion, such as 'like', 'fear' etc., whose two arguments may be notionally described as experiencer and experienced. Here there is a clear notion that the thing experienced is the cause, but the experiencer is normally animate. It is not surprising that there is considerable variation, both within languages and across languages, in the roles assigned to the experiencer or the thing experienced. Thus (see 1.2.3), English may be compared with Italian (Lepschy and Lepschy 1977: 194):

> They like cherries
> Gli piacciono le ciliegie

The term chosen as Agent is the experiencer (*they* in English, but in Italian the construction is intransitive and the thing experienced (*le ciliegie* 'cherries' functions as S (but there are problems – see 2.5). The contrast is seen more clearly if stated in terms of Subjects rather than Agents: the experiencer is the Subject in English but the thing experienced is the Subject in Italian. English has a similar verb, PLEASE, that treats the item experienced as Agent-Subject (the construction is transitive in English), and has pairs of verbs such as FEAR and FRIGHTEN that make opposite choices. Croft (1991: 214–15) gives examples from four different languages (English, Russian, Lakhota and Classical Nahuatl) of the verbs that are, in his terminology, 'experiencer-subject' and 'experiencer-object'; he argues that the experiencer-object verbs are causative and that 'the stimulus causes the experiencer to enter the mental state', while the experiencer-subject verbs are purely stative, and that 'the experiencer is characterized as simply being in a mental state regarding the stimulus'. This seems to be appropriate for many verbs, especially where there are pairs within a language such as FEAR and FRIGHTEN (and, perhaps, LIKE and PLEASE), but it does not explain the difference between the English and Italian examples above, which are translational equivalents.

Another feature that may determine the choice of Agent is perspective or point of view, the entity that is in perspective being marked as Agent. This helps to explain the contrast between:

> John sold the book to Bill
> Bill bought the book from John

Here both John and Bill are animate beings, and both may be thought of as having 'done something' that affected the other. The choice depends on whether it is John's part or Bill's part in the action that is of concern to the speaker. Similar pairs of verbs are LEND/BORROW and, in British English, LET/RENT.

There are many other problems and issues, not all of which can easily be resolved. There is the contrast between OWN and BELONG:

> He owns this house
> This house belongs to him

It may be the animacy feature that favours OWN (as A-Subject) and perspective that favours BELONG (as S-Subject), although Croft (1991: 251) sees BELONG as the 'normal counterpart' of the 'reverse verb' OWN, as he does for OCCUPY as compared with CONTAIN. His argument for the latter verbs is that it is normal for the 'figure' (the thing located) rather than the 'ground' (the location) to function as Subject. This notion of a 'reverse verb' is, perhaps, more obviously appropriate with verbs such as RECEIVE, where the Agent is clearly the entity affected by the action rather than its cause. With such verbs, perspective seems to overrule the causal criterion.

Even with a single verb, there are considerable notional differences between roles that can function as Agent and Patient. Thus with OPEN, either the notional agent or instrumental can be the A-Subject, while the patient can be the S-Subject of an intransitive construction (Fillmore 1968: 25–7):

> John opened the door (with a key)
> The key opened the door
> The door opened

It is worth noting that, if the instrument is the (grammatical) Agent-Subject, the (notional) agent cannot be mentioned; there is no:

> *The key opened the door by John

Although both instruments and agents may be the cause of an action, if both are to be mentioned, the agent takes preference for the role of Agent. In many languages constructions with patient or instrumental as Subject are possible only when the Object or Instrumental has been promoted to Subject by passivization (see 5.2, 5.3), or in a passive-like construction (see 6.1).

There are similar issues that involve the Patient alone, with no change of verb, e.g. the choice of Patient in:

> He smeared the paint on the wall
> He smeared the wall with paint

Here again, there is an issue of perspective: the first sentence tells what happened to the paint, the second what happened to the wall.

Patients are also not always notional patients. Some verbs have Patients that are essentially locative:

> He entered the house
> He left the house

With other verbs, there are notional differences in the Patients that may even cause ambiguity, as in:

> He painted the palace

This may either mean that he put paint on the palace or that he painted a picture of the palace, in the one case merely altering the appearance of another entity, in the other actually creating a new one. Other issues concerning Patients are raised in 5.2. However, as argued in 1.2.1, there is probably no limit to the notional distinctions that can be made, and it is no part of this book to pursue that issue further.

2.2 Subject, Object and animacy

In a number of languages there are restrictions on the kind of NP that may function as Subject (not merely as Agent, since often the Subject of the passive is involved). Thus Kuno (1973: 30) states that in Japanese transitive verbs normally require animate Subjects. Sentences such as the following are not possible (although this may not be wholly true for younger speakers):

> *taihuu ga mado o kawasita
> typhoon SUBJ window OBJ broke
> 'The typhoon broke the window'

> *zidoosya-ziko ga teenager o korosita
> traffic accident NOM teenager ACC killed
> 'An accident killed the teenager'

In Korean, according to Song (1987: 74–6), this restriction affects the passive Subject, which 'has to be, in general, animate and conscious'; this is illustrated by the pairs of sentences (the second of each pair is unacceptable):

> John-in ki sakwa-lil mŏg-ŏssta
> John-TOP the apple-ACC eat-PAST
> 'John ate the apple'
>
> *ki sahwa-nin John-ege mŏg-hi-ŏssta
> the apple-TOP John-DAT eat-PASS-PAST
> 'The apple was eaten by John'
>
> ŏmŏni-nin ai-ege/lil   yag-il   mŏg-i-ŏssta
> mother-TOP child-DAT/ACC medicine-ACC eat-CAUS-PAST
> 'The mother gave medicine to the child'
>
> *yag-in   ai-ege   mŏg-hi-ŏssta
> medicine-TOP child-DAT feed-PASS-PAST
> 'The medicine was given to the child'

Yet a passive is possible if 'child' is promoted to subject (see also 5.3):

> ai-nin   ŏmŏni-ege yag-il   mŏg-hi-ŏssta
> child-TOP mother-DAT medicine eat-PASS-PAST
> 'The child was given medicine by the mother'

It has been suggested that, for some languages, the issue is not one of simple animacy, but a hierarchy or scale of animacy or of agency. According to this, the choice of Agent or Patient as Subject, and thereby the choice of an active or passive construction, depends on the requirement that the argument that is the higher on the hierarchy must be the Subject. Thus Dixon (1979: 85) has a scale of 'potentiality of agency':

> 1st person pronoun > 2nd person pronoun > Demonstrative-
> 3rd person pronouns > Proper nouns > Human common
> nouns > Animate common nouns > Inanimate common
> nouns . . .

Croft (1991: 155), quoting Dixon and Silverstein (1976), refers to a similar scale as an 'animacy hierarchy', but animacy and potentiality of agency seem to be almost one and the same thing. The involvement of person as well as animacy in the hierarchy is illustrated from Quiché (Mondloch 1978: 59), where the Subject must be higher on the hierarchy in the passive, by the impossibility of:

*š-kun-aš   lē yawaþ   w-umal
PAST-cure-PASS the sick one 1SG + POSS-by:
'The sick one was cured by me'

However, neither agency nor animacy seem to be relevant to distinction in terms of person; Massayoshi Shibatani (personal communication) suggests that 'empathy hierarchy' or 'relevance hierarchy' might be preferable, and the former will be used here.

This empathy hierarchy is relevant to many other features that are discussed in this book. Most importantly, it is crucial to the inverse systems of 8.2, which could, in fact, be interpreted in terms of passivization with severe restrictions on Subjects in terms of the hierarchy. It may also explain the promotion of Datives, rather than Patients, to Subject by passivization in Japanese, for these are normally animate, while Patients are frequently inanimate (2.3.3, 5.3). It is also involved in the 'split' ergativity systems (3.3.2), where some nominals (those higher on the hierarchy) seem to follow an accusative-type morphology, while the others follow an ergative pattern, and there is also some evidence of it in some of the languages with agentive systems (3.5.3).

2.3 **Beneficiary-Dative**

The third-most important role to be identified typologically is that of Beneficiary, which prototypically refers to entities, usually animates, that are indirectly affected by the action of the verb (1.2.4). Its most familiar use is that usually referred to in traditional grammars as the 'Indirect Object', where it is the third term in a three-term construction (the others being Agent-Subject and Patient-Direct Object).

2.3.1 *Basic uses*

The Beneficiary-Dative is easily illustrated in a language with case such as Latin, where the nominative marks the Agent-Subject, the accusative the Patient-Object and the dative the Beneficiary-Dative, as in the example given in 1.2.2:

Brutus   Marcello   librum   dedit
Brutus + NOM Marcellus + DAT book + ACC gave
'Brutus gave Marcellus a book'

This is an invented example. An attested example is:

> Quid mihi   istaec   narras?   (Ter. *Hec.* 5. 2. 18)
> why 1sg + DAT these things you tell
> 'Why do you tell me these things?'

Languages that do not have case systems usually mark beneficiaries and similar roles with a preposition, e.g. French and English:

> John gave the book to Mary
> Jean a donné le livre à Marie

As argued in 1.2.2 prepositions may be taken as markers of peripheral roles, so that, on this evidence, Beneficiary is a peripheral role in French and English, but French also has personal pronouns that provide evidence for the full grammatical status of Beneficiary:

> Jean lui a donné le livre
> 'John gave him the book'

There are problems, moreover, with the English sentence given in the translation; these are discussed in 6.6.3.

The notional roles most commonly associated with such Beneficiaries are beneficiary and recipient, although they sometimes include other roles in which the relevant entity is indirectly affected. In German, for instance, the dative case is used not just for the person to whom something is given or sold, but also the person from whom something is bought, as in:

> Ich habe meinem   Freund   das Haus abgekauft
> I   have my + DAT friend (+ DAT) the house bought
> 'I have bought the house from my friend'

It is also used with a variety of verbs, such as RAUBEN 'to rob', ABNEHMEN 'to relieve', ZUMUTEN 'to expect of', such uses being described by grammarians as 'the dative of advantage' or 'the dative of disadvantage' (cf. Hammer 1983: 272–3). It can even be used in a sentence such as (suggested by Masayoshi Shibatani, personal communication):

> Mir   ruscht   die Hose
> 1sg + DAT slipped down the trousers
> 'My trousers slipped down' ('The trousers slipped down on me')

Other uses of the dative case are discussed in grammar books of Latin and Classical Greek, including, for instance, in certain contexts, direction towards. It may be that not all of these uses should be seen as examples of the Beneficiary, or it might be argued that the term 'Beneficiary' is too specific to cover all these uses; a possible alternative might be 'Goal' (Croft 1991: 157), but that could lead to confusion, since that term has been used in the past to refer to Patient-Object. One feature, however, that is closely associated with many of the uses, and particularly those of the Indirect Object proper, is that of animacy, usually human. Generally one gives, tells, buys etc. something to or from some other person.

A problem arises from the fact that there are two-term constructions in which one term is clearly the Agent-Subject, while the other has dative marking. Thus in Latin there is a set of verbs, which are regularly followed by the dative case, verbs such as IMPERO 'order', PAREO 'obey' and PERSUADEO 'persuade', e.g.

> Mihi, ne abscedam, imperat   (Ter. *Eun.* 3. 5. 30)
> 1SG + DAT that not I go away he orders
> 'He orders me not to go away'

It would, of course, be possible to argue that the second terms are Patient-Object and that it is an idiosyncracy of these verbs that they mark Patient-Object in the dative case, but it is more reasonable to treat them as Beneficiary-Dative for three reasons: (i) because the formal marking ought not to be ignored, (ii) because they are usually animate, like Indirect Objects (see 2.3.3) and (iii) because the patients are less directly (at least, not physically) affected by the action (see below and discussion in 2.3.2).

There appears to be a contrast between the use of the dative and the accusative (marking Beneficiary and Patient) in Hungarian (as interpreted by Hopper and Thompson 1980: 267), the dative being used to indicate that the patient is less affected by the action. Hungarian has a prefix *meg-* which they gloss 'perfective'; they argue that with the prefix the 'object is totally affected', but without it the object is not totally affected as in:

> A   gazda meg-verte az   inasokat
> the boss PERF-beat the apprentices
> 'The boss beat the apprentices'

> A   gazda verte az   inasokat
> the boss beat the apprentices
> 'The boss would beat the apprentices'

The first, but not the second, implies that all the apprentices were beaten on a specific occasion. With some verbs the dative is used even if the perfective prefix is not present, to show that the patient is not fully affected:

> meg-segit valaki-t
> PERF-helps somebody-ACC
> 'He helps somebody'

> segit valaki-nek
> helps somebody-DAT
> 'He helps somebody'

Being less fully affected is not quite the same as being indirectly affected, but similar uses of the Dative are discussed in the next section.

2.3.2   *Promotion and demotion*

There are languages in which Beneficiaries are involved in passivization and similar devices, and it is this that clearly establishes the need to recognize the Dative as a grammatical relation, as distinct from the grammatical role of Beneficiary. Thus, in Malagasy the Beneficiary-Dative/ Indirect Object, as well as the Patient-Object, may be promoted to Subject by passivization; an example from Malagasy that was given in 1.4.1 (see also 5.3) is repeated here:

> Nividianan'   ny vehivavy ny vary ny ankizy
> Bought + CIRC the woman   the rice the children
> 'The children were bought the rice by the woman'

The Beneficiary-Dative may also be promoted to Object, the grammatical relation usually held by the Patient (see 6.6). This can be illustrated from Indonesian (Chung 1983: 219):

> Saja mem-bawa surat itu kepada Ali
> I   TRANS-bring letter the to   Ali
> 'I brought the letter to Ali'

> Saja mem-bawa-kan Ali surat itu
> I   TRANS-bring-BEN Ali letter the
> 'I brought Ali the letter'

Datives also have grammatical status in some ergative languages in a rather different way. In Dyirbal, not only is the dative case used to indicate the Beneficiary (beneficiary and recipient), like the Indirect Object of accusative languages, but it is also the case assigned to the Patient-Absolutive when it is demoted by the antipassive. An example given in 1.4.1 is repeated here:

34

yabu   ŋuma-ŋgu bura-n
mother + ABS father-ERG see-PAST
'Father saw mother'

ŋuma   buṛal-ŋa-ɲu   yabu-gu
father + ABS see-ANTIP-PAST mother-DAT
'Father saw mother'

One function of the antipassive, with the Patient/Absolutive demoted to
Dative, is that of indicating 'reduced transitivity' (see 7.2.2). The demotion of
the patient from Absolutive to Dative suggests that the patient is less wholly
affected, and is, in a sense 'less of a patient', as in Chuckchee (Siberia,
Kozinsky et al. 1988: 652):

ətləg-e   keyŋ-ən penrə-nen
father-ERG bear-ABS attack-3SG + 3SG + AOR
'Father attacked the bear'

ətləg-ən   penrə-tko-gʔe   kayŋ-etə
father-ABS attack-ANTIP-3SG + AOR bear-DAT
'Father ran at the bear'

The same effect is achieved in Warlbiri (Australia, Hale 1973a: 336) by
demotion of the Patient without the antipassive (see 7.4):

njuntulu-ḷu npa-tju pantu-ṇu ŋatju
you-ERG   2-1   spear-PAST me
'You speared me'

njuntulu-ḷu npa-tju-ḷa pantu-ṇu ŋatju-ku
you-ERG   2-1-CLIT spear-PAST me-DAT
'You speared at me/tried to spear me'

The Dative is also involved with causatives in that the Agent-Subject is most
commonly demoted to the Dative, though it may also be demoted to the
Instrumental, as with passives. An example from French to be discussed in
9.3.1 is (Hyman and Zimmer 1976: 199–200):

J'ai   fait   nettoyer les toilettes au   général
I have made clean   the toilet   to the general
'I made the general clean the toilets'

J'ai   fait   nettoyer les toilettes par le   général
I have made clean   the toilet   by the general
'I had the toilets cleaned by the general'

In these examples the demoted Agent-Subject is demoted to a peripheral relation (marked by a preposition), but there are plenty of examples in 9.3 where the demoted term is marked by case.

2.3.3   *Animacy*

In the last two sections it has been seen that Beneficiary-Dative is often closely associated with animacy. In some languages the contrast between Patient-Object and Beneficiary-Dative/Indirect Object is actually used to make the inanimate/animate distinction.

In Spanish animate patients, but not inanimate patients, are marked with the preposition *a*, which is the usual indication of the (peripheral) Dative/Indirect Object:

> Ha   presentado su amigo a su madre
> have + 3sɢ introduced his friend to his mother
> 'He has introduced his friend to his mother'

> Ha   comprado un nuevo libro
> have + 3sɢ bought   a new   book
> 'He has bought a new book'

> Ha   comprado a un nuevo caballo
> have + 3sɢ bought   to a new   horse
> 'He has bought a new horse'

The first of these illustrates the basic uses of the two roles-relations, the second an inanimate patient marked as Patient-Object and the third an animate patient marked as Beneficiary-Dative.

There is a similar situation in Lisu (noted in 2.1.1) and in Marathi (India, Rosen and Kashi 1988: 6):

> Ti-ni   Ravi-laa pustak di-l-a
> She-ᴇʀɢ Ravi-ᴅᴀᴛ book   give-ᴘᴀꜱᴛ-ᴀɢʀ
> 'She gave Ravi a book'

> Ti-ni   Ravi-laa chal-ḷ-a
> She-ᴇʀɢ Ravi-ᴅᴀᴛ torture-ᴘᴀꜱᴛ-ᴀɢʀ
> 'She tortured Ravi'

There is, however, much more to be said about Datives in Marathi and some other languages (see 2.5 and 4.3).

There is a complication, however, in Spanish, in that non-specific animates are not preceded by the preposition:

> Busco una criada
> look for + 1SG a maid
> 'I am looking for a maid'

This means that I am looking for someone to be a maid, not for a particular woman who is already a maid, which would be expressed by:

> Busco a una criada

The Dative indicates not merely an animate, but a specific identifiable animate.

2.4 Primary and Secondary Objects

It was seen in the last section that the basic use of the Dative is to be found in the three-term construction in which the roles of Agent, Patient and Beneficiary are identified with the grammatical relations Subject, Object and Indirect Object/Dative. Such identification implies, of course, that this three-term construction differs from the two-term construction solely in the addition of the third term, the Indirect Object/Dative, the other two terms, Subject and Object, being shared by both constructions. This identification is based on formal grammatical features. In Latin, for instance, the Patient is in the accusative case, while the Beneficiary is in the dative; simple invented examples make this clear:

> Marcus librum vidit
> Marcus + NOM book + ACC saw
> 'Marcus saw the book'

> Marcus Fabio librum dedit
> Marcus + NOM Fabius + DAT book + ACC gave
> 'Marcus gave Fabius a book'

There are languages, however, in which it is the Beneficiary, not the Patient, of the three-term construction that is identified grammatically with the second term of the two-term construction, which, on the discussion so far, would be identified as the Object (but see below for a possible problem with this). This is so in Huichol (Comrie 1982: 99, 108):

Uukaraawiciizɨ tɨɨri   me-wa-zeiya
women   children 3PL-3PL-see
'The women see the children'

Nee uuki uukari ne-wa-puuzeiyastɨa
I   man girls 1SG-3PL-show
'I showed the man to the girls'

The infix *wa* here agrees with 'children' (the Patient-Object) in the first sentence, but with 'girls' (the Beneficiary), not with 'man' (the Patient) in the second.

Similarly, in Khasi (Assam, Rabel 1961: 77) it is the Beneficiary, not the Patient that has an Object marker preceding it:

ʔuu hiikay ya ka ktien   phareŋ
he   teach OBJ the language English
'He teaches English'

ʔuu hiikay ya ŋa ka ktien   phareŋ
he   teach OBJ 1SG the language English
'He teaches me English'

In Yokuts (California, Croft 1991: 246), not only is the Beneficiary identified with the Object, but the Patient is explicitly marked as not being identical with the Object by being placed in an oblique case:

'ama'   nan   wan-xo' k'exa-ni   nim
3SG + NOM 1SG + ACC give-DUR money-OBL 1SG + POSS
'He gives me my money'

A number of other examples are to be found in Dryer (1986: 815–18).

Where, as in all these examples, it is the Beneficiary, not the Patient, that is identified with the Object, it is clear that the terms '(Direct) Object' and 'Indirect Object' are inappropriate. Dryer suggests that, instead, the terms 'Primary Object' and 'Secondary Object' should be used, 'Secondary Object' referring to the Patient of the three-term construction alone, while 'Primary Object' refers to both the Beneficiary of the three-term construction and the Object of the two-term system. It is the Primary Object that is usually the marked term.

It might be argued that English, too, has Primary and Secondary Objects in the construction exemplified by:

Mary gave him a book

This can be contrasted with the alternative construction shown in:

Mary gave a book to him

The second construction clearly contains an Object and a (peripheral) Indirect Object/Dative, but in the first *him* has the same formal marking as the Object in *Mary saw him*. Here *him* would seem to be the Primary Object and *the book* a Secondary Object. This would suggest that there are two constructions, one with Primary and Secondary Objects, the other with Direct and Indirect Objects. Moreover, this seems to be confirmed by the passives (if, that is to say, passivization is evidence for Object status – see 5.2):

He was given a book (by Mary)
A book was given to him (by Mary)

There is a detailed discussion of this problem in 6.6.3.

One interesting theoretical point is made by Dryer – that the distinction between Direct/Indirect Objects and Primary/Secondary Objects is like that of accusàtive and ergative. If, to avoid begging the question, the second term of the two-term construction is represented as having a grammatical role symbolized by O, rather than P, and the terms of the three-term construction are symbolized as P and B, then Direct + Indirect Object constructions can be characterized in terms of P = O and Primary + Secondary Object constructions in terms of B = O, just as accusative and ergative are characterized as A = S and P = S respectively. In that case a name is required for the grammatical role symbolized as O. It cannot be called 'Patient', since the grammatical relation P = O implies that the roles P and O are different, and although the term 'Object' was used earlier, for convenience, it is clearly not the Object (a grammatical relation, not a grammatical role). No obvious name is available, and, since for much of the later discussion, this issue is not of great importance, none is suggested.

There are two final points. First, there are some languages that have constructions that are best interpreted as simply having two Objects that are not distinguished as either Direct + Indirect or Primary + Secondary (see 5.2). Secondly, even in languages that clearly have Direct and Indirect Objects, it is sometimes the Beneficiary-Indirect Object, not the Patient-Direct Object, that may be promoted to Subject by passivization, e.g. Korean (see 5.3). In terms of the syntax of passivization, these languages would seem to operate in terms of the Primary + Secondary construction.

2.5 Experiencers, 'modal subjects' etc.

There was a brief discussion in 1.2.3 and 2.1.2 of the English and Italian sentences:

> They like cherries
> Gli piacciono le ciliegie

The point being made was that the experiencer is the Subject in English, but it is the entity experienced that is the Subject in Italian. The status of the other term is different; they are Patient-Object and Beneficiary-Dative, respectively.

There are many languages that have very similar constructions with verbs that refer to various kinds of basically human experiences and feelings. In most cases the entity that is experienced is marked as the Subject, and the (usually human) experiencer as a Dative. Shibatani (1985: 833) notes:

> Spanish   Me   gusta la   cerveza
>   I + DAT like   the beer
>   'I like the beer'
>
> Russian   Mne   nravitsja kniga
>   I + DAT like   book
>   'I like the book'
>
> Turkish   Ban-a para   lâzım
>   I-DAT   money need
>   'I need money'
>
> Japanese   Boku ni   eigo   ga   wakaru
>   I   DAT English NOM understand
>   'I understand English'

However, Shibatani also quotes one example in which the experiencer is in the genitive:

> Bengali   aamaar tomaake caai
>   I + GEN you   need
>   'I need you'

The situation in Icelandic is a little more complicated. With 'like' the construction may be like that of Italian and the other languages (Andrews 1985: 107):

> Mér   líka   þeir
> I + DAT like + PL they (MASC + PL + NOM)
> 'I like them'

With 'need' the accusative is used, marking the needer as Object (Rognvaldsson 1982: 558):

> Mig   vantar   bókina
> I + ACC need + 3SG the book
> 'I need the book'

However, it is also possible for the verb to be in the singular even when the NP indicating the experienced entity (the potential Subject) is plural (Andrews 1985: 107):

> Mér   líkar   þeir
> I + DAT like + SING they (MASC + PL + NOM)
> 'I like them'

It is even possible for this NP to appear in the dative, so that there is no overt grammatical Subject (Andrews 1985: 102):

> Mér   líkar   vel   við   henni
> I + DAT like + SING well with her (DAT)
> 'I like her'

In this last example, it would appear that the verb 'like' is impersonal, i.e. a verb with no overt Subject, but with the experiencer still indicated as Indirect Object. The status of these examples is discussed at the end of this section. (Icelandic has a similar construction for its impersonal passives, see 5.4.)

An impersonal construction is often used for modal verbs, with what is often called the 'modal subject' (the equivalent of the experiencer with such verbs) marked as Object (in the accusative) or Dative (in the dative). Thus in Latin, the 'modal subject' is in the accusative case with *decet* 'it is fitting' and in the dative case with *licet* 'it is allowed'/'may':

> oratorem   irasci   minime decet   (Cic. *Tusc.* 4. 25)
> orator + ACC to be angry least   it is fitting
> 'It is by no means fitting for an orator to become angry'

> Licet   nemini   contra patriam ducere exercitum
>
> (Cic. *Phil.* 13. 6. 14)
>
> it is allowed no-one + DAT against country lead   army
>
> 'No-one may lead an army against his country'

In Amharic (Ethiopian Semitic, personal research) verbs of physical experience are impersonal, with the experiencer as Object:

> rabä-ɲ   däkkäma-ɲ
>
> hunger + 3SG + PAST + 1SG + OBJ   tire + 3SG + PAST − SG + OBJ
>
> 'I was hungry'   'I am tired'

There are similar constructions in Tigre (Ethiopian Semitic, personal research) with modal verbs:

> əgəl tigis   lästəhəl-äkka
>
> that you go be worthy + 3SG + IMPF-2SG + OBJ
>
> 'You ought to go'

With a Dative this verb means 'belong to':

> əlli kətab 'əlye   lästəhəl
>
> that book to me be worthy + 3SG + IMPF
>
> 'That book definitely belongs to me'

In the same language, the verb 'become' is used with an Object to mean 'should', but with a Dative to indicate 'can':

> gašša-ka   'əgəl tətkäbbət   lətgäbbə'äkka
>
> guest-your that you receive become + 3SG + IMPF
>
> 'You should receive your guest'

> əgel tətməhar 'i   gäbbe'   'əlka
>
> that you learn not become 3SG + IMPF to-you
>
> 'You cannot learn'

There are other verbs in Tigre meaning 'must', 'be convenient' etc., mostly with Direct Object.

Even more complex systems are found in two languages that are discussed in 3.6, Tabassaran and Georgian.

There has been considerable debate about the status of the terms marked with the dative case in some of the languages, particularly in Icelandic and some Indian languages. Some scholars have, indeed, argued that they, not the terms marked with the nominative case, are the true Subjects of the sentence, e.g. Andrews (1985: 101, 108), Kachru et al (1976: 86–91). (Others e.g. Rosen and Kashi 1988, have talked of 'inversion', whereby the original Subject and Object have been 'inverted' to become Dative and Subject.) The argument most used in favour of this analysis is that the term identified morphologically as the Dative often functions as a syntactic pivot (briefly mentioned in 1.3.1 and to be discussed in detail in chapter 4), and that in accusative systems it is Subjects that generally function as pivots. An example is (Rognvaldsson 1982: 470):

> þeim   líkar   maturinn og borða   mikið
> they + DAT like + 3sG the food and eat + 3PL much
> 'They like the food and eat a lot'

Here the Subject ('they') of 'eat' is omitted, but the coreferential NP in the previous clause is the one marked as Dative. Andrews (1985: 107) argues that, in the sentences with 'like', the preverbal dative-marked term (the experiencer) actually is the Subject (often referred to as the 'dative-subject') and that the post-verbal nominative-marked term is the Object. However, it will be argued in 4.3 that the notion of pivot should be kept separate from the notion of Subject so that the choice of a particular term as pivot is not evidence that it is a Subject.

The most compelling reason for not identifying pivots as Subjects is that the evidence from pivots is evidence from outside the clause in question: in the example above, evidence from the second clause is used to establish the Subject in the first. Yet the notion of Subject is one that involves relationships between terms and the predicator within the clause. There are, however, features within the clause that may suggest that the apparent Dative is, in fact, the Subject:

(i)   In some languages, there is evidence from the word order. Thus in Icelandic the unmarked word order has the Subject first (Van Valin 1991: 147).

(ii)   As was illustrated earlier, sometimes the verb agrees in terms of number with the Dative rather than the morphological Subject.

(iii) In Marathi (Rosen and Kashi 1988: 11) reflexives are generally coreferential with Subjects, yet they may be coreferential with the 'dative subject', e.g.:

> Mini-ni   Ravi-laa swataa-višayi saangitla
> Mini-ERG Ravi-DAT self-about   told
> 'Mini told Ravi about self (Mini)'

> Ravi-laa   swataa-či pistaka aavḍ-t-aat
> Ravi-DAT self-'s   books   like-PRES-PLUR
> 'Ravi likes his (own) books'

To treat these Datives as Subjects completely disregards the morphological evidence, yet the morphological evidence is important in the recognition of the accusative/ergative distinction. If evidence of this kind is used to establish Subject-hood and the morphology is ignored, then many ergative systems will be accusative. The fact, for instance, that there are ergative systems with passives (6.5) would be evidence that they are, after all, accusative. This may have some merit in an overall theoretical, syntactically based, model, but is unhelpful for a typological study.

It seems more reasonable to suggest that the constructions are partly like Subject + Object constructions, partly like Dative + Subject constructions. This is not altogether surprising: it may well be suggested that a semantic system that views experiencers etc. as being like agents influences the occurrence of syntactic features that ignore the morphology and treat them as Agent-Subject. It is relevant to note that there has been a shift in English, motivated by the semantics, from Dative + Subject constructions to Subject + Object constructions with verbs such as 'like' (see Jespersen 1909–49, III: 208–9).

However, not all the examples considered exhibit (morphological) Dative + Subject constructions. For some the construction is Object + Subject. These raise no problem: they merely mark the term indicating the experiencers etc. as Object and the other term as Subject, the direct converse of the situation in English and other languages (or like the construction with PLEASE as opposed to that with LIKE). Less easy to explain is the use of the genitive case; possibly it could be argued that this represents a new sub-role (but see 2.8).

2.6 Locatives and Instrumentals

(Notional) locatives and instrumentals are marked in English and many other languages by prepositions, and are thus peripheral roles (see 1.2.2). In some they are marked by case, e.g. the Instrumental in Latin by the ablative; yet the ablative does not uniquely mark the Instrumental, and there is no single case for the Locative. However, in a number of languages the Instrumental and, to a lesser extent, the Locative have grammatical functions which mark them as full grammatical relations. Four such functions may be noted.

First, the Instrumental (as well as the Beneficiary – see 2.3) may be promoted to Subject; an example from Malagasy that was given in 1.4.1 (see also 5.3) is repeated here:

> Nividianan'   ny vehivavy ny vary ny vola
> Bought + CIRC the woman   the rice the money
> 'The money was used to buy the rice by the woman'

Secondly, both Instrumental and Locative may be promoted to Object in Kinyarwanda (Kimenyi 1988: 367–9, see 6.6):

> Umugóre a-ra-andik-a   íbarúwa n'íikarámu
> woman   she-PRES-write-ASP letter   with pen
> 'The woman is writing a letter with a pen'

> Umugóre a-ra-andik-iish-a   íbarúwa íkarámu
> woman   she-PRES-write-INSTR-ASP letter   pen
> 'The woman is writing a letter with a pen'

> Umwáalimu a-ra-andik-a   imibáre ku kíbáaho
> teacher   he-PRES-write-ASP maths   on blackboard
> 'The teacher is writing maths on the blackboard'

> Umwáalimu a-ra-andik-á-ho   ikíbáaho   imibáre
> teacher   he-PRES-write-ASP-on blackboard maths
> 'The teacher is writing maths on the blackboard'

Thirdly, Instrumental and Locative (as well as Beneficiary – see 2.3) are the grammatical relations to which the Absolutive (Patient) may be demoted with antipassives in ergative systems. Demotion to Instrumental is illustrated from Eskimo (Woodbury 1977: 322–3, see 7.1):

> miirqa-t   paar-ai
> child + ABS + PL take care of-INDIC + 3SG + 3PL
> 'She takes care of the children'

> miirqu-nik   paar-si-vuq
> child + PL + INSTR take care of-ANTIP-INDIC + 3SG
> 'She takes care of the children'

In Yidiny (Dixon 1977a: 110, see 7.1), demotion is either to Locative or Dative:

> ŋayu   balmbi:ɲ   wawa:l
> I + NOM grasshopper + ABS see + PAST
> 'I saw the grasshopper'

> ŋayu   balmbi-ŋɟa/balmbi:nda   wawa:ɟiɲu
> I + NOM grasshopper + LOC/grasshopper + DAT see + ANTIP + PAST
> 'I saw the grasshopper'

Fourthly, in some Bantu languages, e.g. Swahili (Shepardson 1981) and Chichewa, Locatives may be preposed to the beginning of a sentence and then show subject-type agreement with the verb. Examples from Chichewa (Bresnan and Kanerva 1989: 2) are (agreement is shown by a set of classifiers, which are numbered in the glosses – note that the locative marker *ku* on the verb in the second and fourth sentences is itself a classifier, not a case marker):

> chi-tsîme chi-li   ku-mu-dzi
> CL7-well   CL7-be LOC(CL17)-CL3-village
> 'The well is in the village'

> ku-mu-dzi   ku-li   chi-tsîme
> LOC(CL17)-CL3-village CL17-be CL7-well
> 'The well is in the village'

> a-lendô-wo   a-na-bwéra   ku-mu-dzi
> CL2-visitor-those CL2-RECPAST-come-INDIC LOC(CL17)-CL3-village
> 'Those visitors came to the village'   [RECent PAST]

> ku-mu-dzi   ku-na-bwéra   a-lendô-wo
> LOC(CL17)-CL3-village CL17-RECPAST-come CL2-visitors-those
> 'Those visitors came to the village'

With constructions of this type, it would seem that the Locatives are actually promoted to Subject, but retain their locative marking both in their own morphology and in agreement with the verb. The original Subjects are, then, demoted, but there is no indication of the relation to which they are demoted. (In the theory known as Relational Grammar – see e.g. Johnson 1974 – demoted terms in general are said to lose their relational status, and to become 'chomeurs', the French term for 'unemployed people'.)

2.7 Other roles and sub-roles

The discussion so far has assumed that the typologically most relevant roles are Agent, Patient, Beneficiary, Locative and Instrumental. However, although these form a satisfactory basis for much of the typological discussion (and nothing more than that is claimed for them), there are languages in which, although the major roles are clearly marked, there are further criteria for distinguishing sub-divisions, or sub-roles, within them.

In Bikol (Philippines, Givón 1979: 154–5), sub-roles may be recognized for the Dative. This is shown in the topic system for which details are to be found in 8.1.2, in which one of the terms is marked as Topic by markers on both noun and verb. The markers on the verb distinguish sub-roles for which obvious names are 'Recipient' and 'Beneficiary' (Givón calls them 'Dative' and 'Beneficiary'). Examples are (DT = 'Dative Topic', BT = 'Beneficiary Topic'):

> marái ʔang-babáye na   na-taʔó-hán kang-laláke ning-líbro
> good TOP-woman that DT-give-DT AGT-man   PAT-book
> 'The woman to whom the man gave the book is good'
> 'The woman that was given the book by the man is good'

> marái ʔang-babáye na   pinag-bakal-án kang-laláke ning kandíng
> good TOP-woman that BT-buy-BT   AGT-man   PAT goat
> 'The woman for whom the man bought the goat is good'
> 'The woman that was bought a goat (for) by the man is good'

The distinction exists marginally in English in that only notional recipients, but not notional beneficiaries, may be promoted to Subject (but see 2.5 and 6.6.3):

> He gave John a book
> John was given a book

> He bought John a book
> *John was bought a book

There is a more striking situation in Ga'dang (Philippines, Walrod 1976). This too has a topic system and when the Patient is the Topic, there are three different markers on the verb for three types of Patient – 'affected', 'unaffected' and 'positioned':

bəkən-nu   i no gafa   (p. 29)
break + AFF.PAT-you TOP jar
'Break the jar'

si'gutan-nu   i no bafuy   (p. 30)
tie-UNAFF.PAT-you TOP   pig
'Tie up the pig'

isi'gu'-nu   i no bafuy so   ari   (p. 34)
tie + POS.PAT TOP   pig   LOC post
'Tie the pig to the post'

More problematic is the contrast in Finnish that is marked by the accusative and the partitive case (Fromm and Sadeniemi 1956: 120–1):

Liikemies   kirjoitti kirjeen   valiokunnalle
businessman wrote   letter + ACC committee-to
'The businessman wrote a letter to the committee'

Liikemies   kirjoitti kirjettä   valiokunnalle.
businessman wrote   letter + PART committee-to
'The businessman was writing a letter to the committee'

This use of the partitive has much in common with the use of the dative for 'reduced transitivity' briefly discussed in 2.3. In that case, it could well be argued that there is here another grammatical role, the 'Partitive'. However, unlike the Dative, the Partitive does not appear to be an independent role, since it never occurs together with the Patient, but only as an alternative to it. Another solution is to say that there are two kinds of Patient, one fully affected, the other not fully affected by the action, the first marked with the accusative, the second with the partitive.

Possibly similar to this is the use of the genitive case in Russian where it has a 'partitive' sense, as in:

daite   khleba
give + IMP bread + GEN
'Give me some bread'

Other roles may be indirectly indicated by constructions where there are two conflicting systems, as with 'dative subjects': the terms that are marked morphologically as Datives but function in other respects as Subjects are commonly notional experiencers, though other notional roles, including that of 'modal subject' are involved. Tsunoda (1985: 388) provides a classification of verbs with two-term constructions in terms of case marking and lists, as verbs with 'dative subjects' in Japanese, verbs of (i) knowledge, (ii) feeling, (iii) relationship and (iv) ability. If the role of the 'dative subject' is recognized as that of Experiencer, it must clearly be interpreted in a wide sense to include all the 'subjects' of such verbs. (Most of the languages considered by Tsunoda have ergative systems. These could be seen as providing further examples of 'dative subjects' for all four classes of verbs, but in a Dative + Absolutive rather than a Dative + Subject construction.) Similarly, in Tabassaran (3.6.2) there is an apparent 'dative subject' construction for 'see', which suggests the role of Perceiver. Tabassaran, moreover, has differential case marking for 'beat', 'hit' and 'look at', although in one respect these all appear to have Subject + Object constructions; these could be seen as indicating both two types of Agent and two types of Patient. The variety of case marking listed by Tsunoda for different languages suggests that many other notional roles are indirectly grammaticalized in a similar way.

2.8   Problematic constructions

There are some systems of case marking that are difficult to account for in terms of the discussion so far. Thus in Japanese with 'like' both terms are in the nominative case. Japanese has three constructions with the first term in the nominative: nominative + accusative, nominative + dative and nominative + nominative, as illustrated by (Shibatani 1982: 105):

> Taroo-ga hon-o   yonda
> Taro-NOM book-ACC read
> 'Taroo read a book'

> Taroo-ga Hanoko-ni   atta
> Taro-NOM Hanoko-DAT met
> 'Taroo met Hanoko'

> Taroo-ga Hanoko-ga   sukida
> Taro-NOM Hanoko-NOM likes
> 'Taroo likes Hanoko''

It is the status of the second term in the last example that is problematic, in that it has the marker of Agent-Subject although there is already an Agent-Subject in the construction.

In Kewa (Papua New Guinea, Franklin 1971: 62), there is a similar problem, but with the first term, which may either be marked as agentive or as instrumental:

> áá-mé   répena póá-a
> man-AGT tree   cut-did
> 'The man cut the tree'
>
> raí-mi   tá-a
> axe-INSTR hit-did
> 'The axe hit it'

Prima facie the most attractive solution for these examples is to say that the nominative in Japanese indicates that the Patient is not a 'true' Patient and the instrumental in Kewa is not a 'true' Agent, i.e. to make a distinction in terms of two sub-roles associated with Object and Subject respectively. More precisely, the problem might be solved in terms of prototypicality (see 1.2.1): it could be said that in Japanese the accusative marks a prototypical Patient-Object, but the nominative a non-prototypical Patient-Object and a similar solution can be provided for the Agent-Subject of Kewa. The main objection to this is that it allows that case does not unambiguously identify role, but, as argued in 2.5, that would remove the morphological basis for role identification which seems to be so for the overall framework. Moreoever, it might raise the question why the dative in Japanese should not be seen as the marker of a third sub-role associated with the Object rather than of the independent relation of Dative. (There are two alternative solutions. One would be to say that the Japanese and Kewa sentences have the role constructions Agent + Agent and Instrumental + Patient, but to allow some Agents as well as Patients to be Objects and some Instrumentals as well as Agents to be Subjects, so that both still have the Subject + Object construction. The other is to admit Subject + Subject and Instrumental + Object as additional relational constructions. Both solutions are quite unacceptable within the framework proposed.)

There is equally a problem concerning the relation between case marking and role in Latin. It was suggested in 2.3.1 that the arguments of verbs in Latin that have dative rather than accusative case should be treated as Agent-Subject + Dative), as the morphology suggests, rather than as having Patients in the dative case. Yet it was not so obvious that the genitive and partitive forms of Russian and Finnish (above) should equally be treated in terms of a different role (the Partitive) rather than as having Patients in the genitive and partitive. Other verbs in Latin require different cases, that do not easily lend themselves to a similar interpretation. The verb UTOR 'use' takes the ablative, the mark of an Instrumental. Notionally this makes some sense, but it seems less plausible to say that the ablative here marks the grammatical role of Instrumental, rather than saying that the Patient of UTOR is (nonprototypically) marked by the ablative case. Much more seriously, MEMINI 'remember' takes the genitive, which is normally not the marker of a grammatical role, but of the possessive, associated with the noun. Yet the genitive occurs as an apparent role marker in other languages, e.g. in Bengali (see 2.5):

> aamaar tomaake caai
> I + GEN you   need
> 'I need you'

It is arguable that the genitive indicates a distinct grammatical role, or that it indicates a sub-role associated either with the Object or the Dative.

More surprising, there is evidence that, in Homeric Greek (and in the tragedies of Aeschylus, but rarely elsewhere), the choice of case was to some degree grammatically free, but dependent on the semantics. Thus with KLÚO: 'hear', the case of the non-Subject may be accusative, genitive, dative or even nominative:

> ékluon   audé:n   (Hom. *Od.* 14.89)
> they heard sound + ACC
> 'They heard a sound'

> moú . . . ékluon   (Hom. *Od.* 15.300)
> me + GEN they heard
> 'They heard me'

> eukhoméno:i moi   ékluon
> praying + DAT me + DAT they heard
> 'They heard (complied with) my prayer'

> klúein ánalkis   (Aesch. *Pr.* 868)
> to hear feeble + NOM
> 'to be called feeble'

The accusative is generally used of the thing heard, the genitive of the person who speaks, while the dative indicates hearing with compliance or obeying (though there is some variation in the use of these cases). The nominative indicates 'being called or spoken of'; it does not, however, appear to involve a distinct argument, and so will not be considered further. Some of these differences may be seen as different meanings of the verb, but there is no clear way of distinguishing the meaning of the verb from the meaning of the case of the noun. The accusative/dative contrast raises no problem, since it can be handled in terms of Patient/Beneficiary. There is a different problem with the genitive: since it marks a difference in meaning (and is not determined by the choice of verb as in Latin) there is a reason for treating it as a separate role, or, like the partitive discussed above, as the mark of a sub-role of Patient.

There is, however, one (paradoxical) solution to all these problems – to say that there is no simple solution within any framework. Whatever overall analysis is provided some examples will be difficult to fit in except as anomalies. The only claim for a typological framework is that it allows for most of the relevant data to be presented and explained, not that it can provide unique and definitive solutions for all problems.

3
Accusative, ergative and agentive systems

3.1 Ergative marking

In the discussion of English and other languages in 1.2.2, it was seen that Agents and Patients (and, indirectly, Subjects and Objects) are distinguished in terms of:

(i)   word order,
(ii)   morphology of the noun or pronoun,
(iii) agreement with the verb.

The use of the term 'Subject' implies, of course, the identification of S and A (in active sentences), that identification being made in terms of these criteria. There are, however, languages in which S is identified with P (using the same criteria), these being generally known as 'ergative languages', though as argued in 1.3.1 (and see below) we should talk rather about 'ergative systems'.

It may be that there are languages in which ergativity is marked by word order, i.e. where S and P occupy the same position but a different one from that of A. This distinction would not be possible in languages where both A and P precede or follow the verb (and this covers very many languages of the world), because in such languages A and P have different positions only in relation to each other, but it would be possible if one of the terms preceded, and the other followed, the verb.

In 1.3.1, Dyirbal was given as an example of a language with an ergative system, ergativity being shown in the morphology of the noun: A alone is in the ergative case (with suffix *-ngu*), while both P and S are in the (unmarked) absolutive case. The use of case marking alone as a mark of ergativity is found in other Australian languages, e.g. Warrungu (Tsunoda 1988: 598):

pama-ngku kamu-ø   yangka-n
man-ERG   water-ABS search-P/P
'A man looked/looks for water'

A language that marks ergativity on the verb is Tzotzil (Mayan, Mexico, Foley and Van Valin 1985: 312):

> bat-em-ø
> go-PERF-3SG + ABS
> 'He's gone'
>
> s-max-ox-ø
> 3SG + ERG-hit-PAST-3SG + ABS
> 'He hit him'

It may be noticed that the affixes that mark agreement differ in position within the verbal complex, the ergative being a prefix, and the absolutive being a suffix. However, this difference in position is not reflected in the word order, since both Agent and Patient (in the reverse order) follow the verb.

> s-mil-ox-ø   Xan li   Petal e
> 3SG + ERG-kill-PAST-3SG + ABS John ART Peter
> 'Peter killed John'

Agreement with the verb is thus doubly marked, both by the form and the position of the affixes. Comrie (1978: 339) notes that languages with ergative marking on the verb alone are not rare, being found among North West Caucasian languages and the Mayan languages of Mexico and Central America. Examples from Quiché (Mayan, Guatemala) are:

> k-at-ka-cuku-x
> ASP-2SG + ABS-1PL + ERG-seek-ACT
> 'We seek you'
>
> k-ox-a-cuku-x
> ASP-1PL + ABS-2SG + ERG-seek-ACT
> 'You seek us'

Until recently, the language most commonly quoted as an example of ergativity was Basque, which is spoken in the western Pyrenean region of France and Spain, and is unrelated to any other known language. In Basque, ergativity is marked both by the morphology of the noun and by agreement with the verb, as illustrated by (Brettschneider 1979: 371):

> ni-k   gizona   ikusi d-u-t
> I-ERG man + ABS see   3SG + ABS-AUX-1SG + ERG
> 'I saw the man'

gizona   etorri d-a
man + ABS come 3SG + ABS-AUX
'The man came'

Here 'I' is marked as ergative both by the suffix *-k* and by the verbal suffix *-t*, while 'man' (in both examples) is marked as absolutive both by the absence of a suffix and by the verbal prefix *d-*. There is a similar situation in Greenlandic Eskimo (Woodbury 1977: 323):

aŋut-ip   arnaq-ø   taku-vaa
man-ERG woman-ABS see-INDIC + 3SG + 3SG
'The man saw the woman'

There are two reasons why we should talk of 'ergative systems' rather than 'ergative languages'. First, in some languages the features that have been considered here may point to conflicting conclusions about the accusative/ ergative distinction (see 3.2). Secondly, there are syntactic features that relate to the distinction, such that language may be said to have accusative or ergative syntax that is independent of, and often in conflict with, its characterization in terms of word order and morphology (see 4.1).

There is a final comment. It has sometimes been thought that ergative constructions are 'really' passives, since in passives P (promoted to Subject) = S. (Alternatively, but less plausibly, active sentences could be treated as antipassives in an ergative system.) The question depends on which of the two constructions is considered to be basic and which derived. In practice there is seldom a problem. In many languages the passive is specifically marked on the verb (as is the antipassive), though this does not establish which construction is basic in a language such as Latin where there is both active and passive inflection. More importantly, in the active the Agent and Patient have specific markers that are used primarily for them, e.g. nominative and accusative case, whereas in the passive the Agent is either deleted or marked as oblique or peripheral. Similar considerations hold for the antipassive. However, some ergative systems appear to have passives (6.5), and so two contrasting constructions, but these passives differ from passives in accusative systems in that, although the Agent is demoted (marked as oblique), the Patient does not acquire the relation of the Agent in the active (it still has absolutive marking). Moreover, active sentences are generally statistically more common than passive ones. If there is no promotion and demotion device (passive or antipassive), there is, of course, only one construction and no problem – either S = A or S = P.

There are some problematic and borderline cases, but generally there is no difficulty in identifying active and passive constructions in an accusative system, and for treating ergative constructions as belonging to a different system (but see 7.8 for further discussion). In some cases, however, the system cannot be clearly identified as either accusative or ergative, as with the inverse systems of 8.2.

3.2 Conflicting criteria

It is possible for a language to be ergative in terms of the morphology of the noun, but accusative in terms of verbal agreement; an example is Warlbiri, another Australian language (Hale 1973a: 309, 328), as illustrated by:

> ŋatju   ka-ŋa   puḻa-mi
> 1 + ABS PRES-1 + NOM shout-NONPAST
> 'I am shouting, I shout'

> ŋjuntuluḻu ka-npa-tju   ŋatju njanji
> 2 + ERG   TNS-2 + NOM-1 + ACC   1 + ABS see-NONPAST
> 'You see me'

> ŋatjuluḻu ka-ŋa-ŋku   njuntu njanji
> 1ERG   PRES-1 + NOM-2 + ACC   2 + ABS see-NONPAST
> 'I see you'

In these examples, the S of the intransitive and the P of the transitive sentences are in the unmarked absolutive case ('I'/'me' in the first and second and 'you' in the third), while the A is marked as ergative ('you' in the second and 'I' in the third). In terms of nominal morphology, then, Warlbiri is ergative, with Absolutives (S = P) and Ergative (A). In terms of agreement with the verb (on the tense marker), however, the S of the intransitive sentence and the A (not the P) of the transitive sentences are marked in the same way, as 'nominative' ('I', 'you' and 'I' respectively), while the P is marked as 'accusative' ('me' and 'you'). In terms of verbal agreement, then, Warlbiri is accusative, with Subjects (A = S) and Objects (P), which are in the nominative and accusative case respectively.

Warlbiri is not unique. A similar situation seems to occur in Burushaski (Pakistan, Morin and Tiffou 1988: 494, 509):

ne   hír-e   phaló   bók-i
the + MASC man-ERG seed + ABS sow + PRET-3SG + MASC + SUBJ
'The man planted the seeds'

ne   hir   yált-i
the + MASC man + ABS yawn + PRET-3SG + MASC + SUBJ
'The man yawned'

ne   hír-e   ja   a-yórtikin-i
the + MASC man-ERG I + ABS 1SG + COMPL-drag + PRET-3SG + MASC + SUBJ
'The man dragged me'

In the glosses, SUBJ and COMPL seem to be equivalent to NOM and ACC in Warlbiri; Burushaski, too, then is accusative in verbal agreement, but ergative in noun morphology.

The conclusion is clear. It is misleading to divide languages into those that are ergative and those that are accusative. Warlbiri and Burushaski have ergative noun-morphology systems, but accusative verbal-agreement systems.

3.3   Variation by grammatical category

In some languages there is a variation between an accusative and an ergative system (or some other system), the variation being determined by a grammatical category within the sentence: tense/aspect, class of NP and main/subordinate clause. This is sometimes, somewhat misleadingly, referred to as 'split ergativity' – it could equally well be called 'split accusativity'. A fourth type of variation ('depending on the semantic nature of the verb') is recognized by Dixon (1979: 80), but that is dealt with here as a distinct system (agentivity) in 3.5.

3.3.1   *Tense/Aspect*

The clearest and most striking example is where the split is determined by tense or aspect; where there is such a split, it is generally the case that a past, perfect or perfective tense/aspect has an ergative system while other tenses and aspects have an accusative system.

Thus in Samoan (Milner 1973: 635), the perfective aspect has ergative marking, with Agent marked and Patient unmarked, while the imperfective has accusative marking, with Agent unmarked and Patient marked:

> na va'ai-a   e   le   tama le   i'a
> PAST look at-PERF ERG the boy   the fish
> 'The boy has spotted the fish'

> na va'ai   le tama i   le   i'a
> PAST look at + IMPERF the boy OBJ the fish
> 'The boy was looking at the fish'

Hindi is often quoted as a language that has a similar split, and the point is made clear in the contrast between the imperfective and perfective forms illustrated by (Allen 1951: 70, with transcription modified):

> lərka   dɔrta   hɛ
> boy(MASC) run + MASC AUX
> 'The boy runs'

> lərka   billī   dekhta   hɛ
> boy(MASC) cat(FEM) see + IMPERF + MASC AUX
> 'The boy sees a cat'

> lərke-ne   billī   dekhī   hɛ
> boy(MASC)-ERG cat(FEM) see + PERF + FEM AUX
> 'The boy has seen a cat'

The first sentence is intransitive and it can be seen that the single term S ('boy') is unmarked morphologically, but agrees with the verb (in terms of masculine gender). In the second sentence, which is transitive with an imperfective verb, the Agent ('boy') and the Patient ('cat') are both unmarked morphologically, but the Agent agrees with the verb; this, then, shows an accusative system. In the third sentence, however, which is also transitive but has a perfective verb, the (feminine) Patient ('cat') is unmarked and agrees with the verb, while the Agent has a suffix which Allen calls 'instrumental', but can clearly be regarded typologically as ergative, and which does not agree with the verb; the system is clearly ergative.

Similar examples from Gujerati (Mistry 1976: 257, 245) are:

> Ramesh   pen   khərid-t-o   hə-t-o
> Ramesh (MASC) pen(FEM) buy-IMPERF-MASC AUX-IMPERF-MASC
> 'Ramesh was buying the pen'

Ramesh-e   pen   khərid-y-i
Ramesh(MASC)-ERG pen(FEM) buy-PERF-FEM
'Ramesh bought the pen'

Other languages with a similar split system are, according to DeLancey (1981: 628) to be found in Australian, Austronesian, Mayan, Indo-Iranian, Tibeto-Burman and Caucasian languages.

However, it would seem that there is seldom a simple accusative/ergative split purely in term of tense/aspect. In Hindi, for instance, in the Perfective, ergative, system, if the Patient is definite and animate, it is placed in the dative case and does not show agreement with the verb (Allen 1951: 70):

ləṛke-ne   billī-ko   dekha   hɛ
boy(MASC)-ERG cat(FEM) + DAT see + PERF + MASC AUX
'The boy has seen the cat'

Here 'cat' is dative and not in agreement with the verb. In fact with this construction, there is no verbal agreement; the masculine marking on the verb is not determined by agreement with 'boy', but is the 'impersonal' or 'neuter', not in agreement with any of the NPs.

A split in terms of tense is also found in Nepali (cf. Bandhu 1973: 32, 4/20), but, since person is also involved, this is discussed in the next section. Georgian is also quoted by some as a language with a similar split, but the situation there is far more complex, and is discussed in a separate section (3.6.1).

There are other issues relating to case marking and the ergative/accusative distinction in Hindi and other Indian languages. These are discussed in some detail in 4.3.

3.3.2 *Class of nominal*

A second type of split depends on the type of nominal in A and P position. One of the clearest examples is found in Dyirbal, where first and second person pronouns are unmarked for A and S, but marked for P, while third person pronouns and all nouns are unmarked for S and P, but marked for A, as illustrated by (Dixon 1979: 87, but cf. Dixon 1972: 50 for a slightly more complex statement):

	First and Second	Third
S	-ø	-ø
A	-ø	-ŋgu
P	-na	-ø

The first set, then, has accusative morphology, the second has ergative morphology. This split, involving first and second person pronouns versus all other nominals, can probably be related to the empathy hierarchy (2.2); there is discussion of this in 3.4.

There is a similar situation in Warrungu (Australia, Tsunoda 1988: 596), with nouns having ergative marking and pronouns accusative marking. The cases of the nouns are (quite naturally) shown as 'ergative' and 'absolutive', while those of the pronouns are 'nominative' and 'accusative', the essential difference between the two systems being that the S of intransitives is identical with the absolutive for nouns, but with the nominative for pronouns. This can be seen in:

> pama   yama-pi-n yati-karra-n   (p. 599)
> man + ABS SO-INTR-P/P laugh-REP-P/P   [REPorted]
> 'The man was laughing like that'

> pama-ngku warrngu   mayka-n yama-nga-n   (p. 599)
> man-ERG   woman + ABS tell- P/P   SO-TRANS-P/P
> 'The man told the woman so'

> ngaya   waka-n   (p. 615)
> 1SG + NOM rise-P/P
> 'I got up'

> ngaya   yina   yangka-n   (p. 599)
> 1SG + NOM 2SG + ACC search-P/P
> 'I looked for you'

The two systems can both be used in a single sentence:

> nyula   tyampa-n katyarra   (p. 606)
> 3SG + NOM find-P/P   possum + ABS
> 'He found possums'

It must be added, though, that, in both languages, this does not affect the syntax, which is fully ergative (see 4.2). In other Australian languages, however, there is a more complicated situation, and it has been argued that there is an alternative solution to that of split systems. This is discussed in 3.4.

Person is also involved in the split in Nepali, but in conjunction with tense (see 3.3.1), in that all Agents are marked as ergative in the past tense, but the third person singular alone is also marked as ergative in the nonpast. Moreover, this affects only noun morphology, agreement with the verb following an accusative pattern (see 3.2). This can be seen in (Masayoshi Shibatani, personal communication):

> mə shaw pãu-chu
> I   apple get-NONPAST + 1
> 'I get an apple'

> məy-le shaw pa-ẽ
> I-ERG   apple get-PAST + 1
> 'I got an apple'

> us-le   shaw pãu-cha
> he-ERG apple get-NONPAST + 3
> 'He gets an apple'

> us-le   shaw pa-yo
> he-ERG apple get-PAST + 3
> 'He got an apple'

3.3.3   *Main/subordinate clause*

Dixon (1979: 96–8) also notes the possibility of a split determined by the distinction between main and subordinate clauses, but adds that the information is sparse, although the best example appears to be from Shimshian (British Columbia/Alaska, Boas 1911) where subordinate clauses have an ergative system, but main clauses have either an ergative system or no marking, depending on the grammatical person of A and P.

Another language that has different marking in main and subordinate clauses is Mam (Mayan, Central America, England 1983). The main clauses have an ergative system, for both noun morphology and agreement with the verb (pp. 2–3):

> ma tz'-ok   n-tzeeq'a-n-a
> ASP 2SG + ABS-DIR 1SG + ERG-hit-DS-1SG/2SG
>   [DIRectional, DIrectional suffix]
> 'I hit you'

ma chin   ok t-tzeeq'a-n-a
ASP 1SG + ABS DIR 2SG + ERG-hit-DS-2SG/1SG
'You hit me'

ma chin   b'eet-a
ASP 1SG + ABS walk-1SG
'I walked'

ma ø-b'eet-a
ASP 2SG + ABS-walk-2SG
'You walked'

In subordinate clauses, however, both S and P, as well as A, are marked as ergative (pp. 10, 14):

n-chi   ooq' n-poon-a
ASP-3PL + ABS cry   1SG + ERG-arrive-1SG
'They were crying when I arrived'

o   chin   ooq'-a aj n-kub'   t-tzeeq'a-n-a
ASP 1SG + ABS cry-1SG when 1SG + ERG-DIR 2SG + ERG-hit-DS-2SG/1SG
'I cried when you hit me'

The situation in Mam however, does not really illustrate a different system in the subordinate clause; it shows, rather, that there is no distinguishing system – S, A and P being undifferentiated. Moreover, although this may seem a strange situation, there are examples of this lack of differentiation in subordinate clauses in quite familiar accusative languages; thus, in Latin and Classical Greek S and A (the 'subject'), as well as P (the 'object'), are in the accusative case in clauses following verbs of reporting (the so-called 'accusative and infinitive construction'). Latin examples are:

Dixit Marcum   venisse
he said Marcus + ACC to have come
'He said Marcus had come'

Narrant Romulum   urbem   condidisse
They relate Romulus + ACC city + ACC found-PERF + INF
'They say that Romulus founded a city'

3.4 Systems with three basic relations

All the systems discussed so far handle the relationship between S, A and P in terms of just two basic grammatical relations. The possibilities are: for accusative systems S = A (Subject) and P (Object), for ergative systems S = P (Absolutive) and A (Ergative) and for agentive systems S_A = A and S_P = P (see 3.5).

There are languages, however, that mark all three (S, A and P) differently. One such is Nez Perce (N.W. USA, Rude 1988: 547–8, 552):

> háana-nm pée-'wiye wewúkiye-ne
> man-ERG 3ERG-shot elk-DO
> 'The man shot an elk'

> háama hipáayna
> man   3 + NOM-came
> 'The man came'

Here it can be seen that A is marked by ergative affixes on noun and verb, P by the accusative ('DO') suffix on the noun, while S is marked solely by the nominative prefix on the verb.

In several Australian languages, it seems that some nominals follow an accusative system, others an ergative system, while yet others have distinct markers for all three roles. Thus in Yidiny (Australia, Dixon 1977a), first and second person pronouns have the same forms for S and A, while nouns have the same forms for S and P as in (pp.126, 168):

	'I/me'	'man'
S	ŋayu	wagu:ḏa
A	ŋayu	wagu:ḏaŋgu
P	ŋaɲaɲ	wagu:ḏa

This is very similar to the situation in Dyirbal discussed in 3.3.2. With some of the deictics, however, there are three forms, e.g. for the indefinite human 'who'/'someone' (p.187):

```
S        waɲa
A        waɲḍu
P        waɲḍu:ɲ
```

In Diyari (Austin 1981a: 51, 61) there are three basic cases for women's names, non-singular nouns or pronouns other than 1 and 2 singular, as in:

('person' + PL)	nom.(S)	kaṇawaṛa
	erg.(A)	kaṇawaṛali
	acc.(P)	kaṇawaṛana

Men's names and singular common nouns follow an ergative pattern:

('stick')	abs.(S/P)	piṭa
	erg.(A)	piṭali

Non-singular first and second person pronouns follow an accusative pattern:

('you' + PL)	nom.(S/A)	ura
	acc.(P)	yuraṇa

There are two ways of dealing with this variation. It can be said that Yidiny and Diyari have split systems, like those discussed in 3.2, but that the split is into three types, with an ergative, an accusative and a three-relation system. There is, however, an alternative solution: this is to say that there are three different relations for all forms of the languages, but that some of the distinctions are 'neutralized' or 'syncretized'. The three sets of forms given above can be set out in a single paradigm:

S (nom.)	kaṇawaṛa	piṭa	yura
A (erg.)	kaṇawaṛali	piṭali	yura
P (acc.)	kaṇawaṛana	pita	yuraṇa

This solution reflects the use of the terms used for the cases by Austin ('nominative', 'ergative' and 'accusative'). On this analysis Diyari has a simple three-relation system. Syncretism such as that suggested here is quite common with inflected languages; in Latin, for instance, nominative and accusative are different for some nouns (*amicus/amicum* 'friend'), but identical for others (*bellum/bellum* 'battle'); the traditional account is not that there are different systems, but that the nominative and accusative forms of *bellum* are the same.

It has been suggested (Goddard 1982) that a similar analysis could be applied to all languages that have a split system for nominals, e.g. those discussed in 3.3.2, Dyirbal or Warrungu. This, Goddard argues, uses a traditional approach to case, is the simplest explanation, accounts for most Australian languages in the same way, and is partly supported by some features of agreement. These are not, however, conclusive arguments. The case for reducing the split systems to a single three-relation system is certainly more plausible when one of the systems already is a three-relation system, as in Diyari; it is less strong when there are just two systems, accusative and ergative, as in Dyirbal. The fact that the three-relation system is wide-spread in Australian languages may be of importance in a generalized description of such languages, but less so in a typological description of the languages of the world, and the issue of simplicity is open to question.

The main objection to this solution is that it disguises the fact that there is any split at all, which is of interest for its own sake in the light of discussion about ergative and accusative systems, but may also be of relevance to issues of animacy as discussed in 2.2 and 8.2. Dixon (1979: 85ff.) argues that the animacy (or empathy – see 2.2) hierarchy suggests the greater likelihood of such first and second person pronouns functioning as agents (though this is rejected by Goddard). The argument would be that NPs that are higher on the animacy hierarchy are more likely to be agents and that there is, therefore, no need to indicate that they are Agents by specific marking (and this favours an accusative system), while those lower on the hierarchy are less likely to be agents and that there is a need to indicate, by marking, if they are Agents (and this favours an ergative system). This argument is supported by the fact that, in at least one language, which has an agentive, not an accusative or ergative, system, (N. Pomo, see 3.5.3), where the Agent is human, it is unmarked morphologically, while the Patient is marked, and, conversely, where the Agent is non-human, it is marked, while the Patient is unmarked.

Moreover, the same kind of arguments as those used by Goddard could be used wherever there are conflicting systems in a language, e.g. noun morphology vs. verbal agreement, as in Warlbiri (3.2), or morphology vs. syntax, as in Tzotzil (4.2). Here, too, it would be possible to conflate the two systems by stating separately the combined function of each S, A and P, but that would seem to be far less insightful and far more complicated than saying that there are two systems, one ergative, the other accusative.

3.5 **Agentive systems**

There are languages in which the single term of the intransitive (S) is not identical either with the Agent (A) of transitives, as in accusative systems, or the Patient (P), as in ergative systems, but varies in its marking, being sometimes identical with A, sometimes with P. An illustration of such a system in E. Pomo was given in 1.3.1. A further set of examples may be taken from Lakhota (Siouan, USA, Van Valin 1985: 365–6):

ma-yá-kté 1SG + PAT-2SG + AGT-kill	'You killed me'
ø-wa-kté 3SG + PAT-1SG + AGT-kill	'I killed him'
ni-ø-kté 2SG + PAT-3SG + AGT-kill	'He killed you'
wa-hí 1SG + AGT-arrive	'I arrived'
ma-khúže IsG + PAT-sick	'I am sick'
ya-ʔú 2SG + AGT-come	'You are coming'
ni-háske 2SG + PAT-tall	'You are tall'

The first three sentences are transitive and establish the markers for Agent and Patient. In particular, it can be seen that the agentive and patientive markers for first person are *wa* and *ma* respectively and those for second person *ya* and *ni*. The next four sentences are intransitive, and show the agentive case being used for the single arguments of 'arrive' and 'come', but the patientive with the arguments of '(be) sick' and '(be) tall'.

The term 'split intransitive' is often used to describe this type of system, but although this clearly indicates the nature of the system, it is not satisfactory because the term 'split' is used in a rather different sense in 'split ergativity' (3.3) and especially because these 'split intransitives' are often also involved in a split in this other sense (below, 3.5.3). In earlier literature such systems were referred to as 'Active', but that too is an unsuitable term in view of its use to distinguish active and passive voice. Since the terms 'ergative' and 'accusative' are used for systems which typically have ergative and accusative cases, it is reasonable to refer to this third type of system as 'agentive'.

Agentive systems are treated by Dixon (1979: 80) as a fourth type of split ergativity, in addition to those considered in 3.3, 'split according to semantic nature of the verb'. This, however, leads to a paradoxical situation, which results from the fact that in this system it is the term in the intransitive construction that varies in its marking, whereas the difference between the other two systems lies in the marking of the terms in the transitive construction. An interpretation of agentive systems in terms of split ergativity would lead to a situation in which a single transitive construction is characterized as either ergative or accusative depending on the choice of the intransitive construction with which it was compared: it would be accusative when compared with an agentive intransitive construction, but ergative when compared with a patientive one. It is obviously preferable to treat the system as a distinct type, neither accusative nor ergative, and to locate the distinguishing feature in the intransitive forms alone.

Since the two types of S are represented as S_A and S_P, the system can be characterized as involving S_A = A, and S_P = P, as compared with the accusative system S = A and the ergative system S = P, and Agentive and Patientive may be seen as the two relevant grammatical relations (see 1.3.2).

3.5.1 *Basic systems*

Examples similar to those just discussed are to be found in Guaraní (Mithun 1991: 511–13, interpreting Gregores and Suárez 1967). The Agentive and Patientive forms of the first person are identified as *a*- and *še*- respectively in:

a-gwerú aína	'I am bringing them now'
še-rerahá	'It will carry me off'

The same forms are used as alternative markers of the S of intransitive constructions:

a-xa	'I go'
še-rasí	'I am sick'

Slightly less obvious is the situation in Acehnese (Sumatra, Durie 1985: 45) where Agentive is marked compulsorily on the verb by a prefix and Patientive by an optional suffix:

ka   lôn-poh-geuh
already 1 + AGT-hit-3 + PAT
'I hit him'

67

> lôn lôn-jak
> I   1 + AGT-go
> 'I am going'
>
> gopnyan caröng(-geuh)
> he   clever(-3 + PAT)
> 'He is clever'

The choice of Agentive or Patientive S is largely determined lexically, some verbs requiring a Patientive others an Agentive S (though with considerable differences in their meanings – see 3.5.2). However, in some languages, some verbs occur with either Patientive or Agentive S, usually with a clear change of meaning. Thus in Guaraní *karú* means 'to dine' with the Agentive but 'be a glutton' with the Patientive. Similar examples may be found in E. Pomo (California, McLendon 1978: 2–3):

há· wá-du·kiya	'I'm going'
wí ʔečkiya	'I sneezed'
há· c'e·xélka	'I'm sliding'
wí c'e·xélka	'I'm slipping'

há· and *wí* are the agentive and patientive forms of the first person singular, so that 'go' is agentive (i.e. requires agentive S), while 'sneeze' is patientive; the third verb is either, being agentive when having the meaning of (actively, voluntarily) sliding, but patientive when having the meaning of (involuntarily, accidentally) slipping. There is a similar feature in Batsbi (Caucasian, Comrie 1978: 366), which has been compared with E. Pomo, where 'fall' may be either agentive or patientive:

> tχo   naizdraχ qitra
> we + PAT to ground fell
> 'We fell to the ground (not our fault)'
>
> a-tχo   naizdraχ qitra
> AGT-we to ground fell
> 'We fell to the ground (through our own carelessness)'

Where there is either agentive or patientive marking with the same verb, Dixon (1979: 80) talks of 'fluid-S marking' as opposed to 'split-S marking'.

Some languages have three forms of S, which may be characterized as Agentive, Patientive and Dative (S_A, S_P and S_D). This is true of Choctaw (Oklahoma, Heath 1977: 204):

iš-iya-h
2SG + AGT-go-PRES
'You are going'

si-(y)abi:ka-h
1SG + PAT be sick-PRES
'I am sick'

im-ačokma-h
3 + DAT-feel good-PRES
'He feels good'

This could be handled in terms of the agentive and patientive intransitives, plus an impersonal structure with the Dative, similar to those discussed in 2.5. With agentive languages, however, it might be simpler to treat this as an example of a three-way distinction, with Agentive, Patientive and Dative S.

The two-term constructions of Choctaw are even more complex, e.g. (Heath 1977: 207):

hattak-at oho:yoh(-a) ø-ø-pisa-h
man-SUBJ woman-OBL   3AGT-3PAT-see-PRES
'Man sees woman'

hattak-at oho:yoh(-a) ø-į-hiyįya-h
man-SUBJ woman-OBL   3AGT-3DAT-stand-PRES
'Man wait for woman'

hattak-at oho:yoh(-a) į-ø-nokšo:pa-h
man-SUBJ woman-OBL   3DAT-3PAT-be afraid-PRES
'Man is afraid of woman'

Here there are two distinct systems, like those discussed in 3.2. The morphology of the noun is accusative and distinguishes Agent-Subject and Patient-Object, but the marking in the verb uses all three cases, and has the combinations agentive + patientive, agentive + dative and dative + patientive (or, rather, patientive + dative, for the case markers are reversed – the dative refers to the cause, 'the woman', and the patientive to the experiencer 'the man').

These constructions have some similarity with constructions found in ergative systems, Ergative + Absolutive, Ergative + Dative and Absolutive + Dative respectively. (The first and third are quite typical transitive and intransitive constructions of an ergative system, while the second is of a less usual type (see 7.4). However, the fact that the single term of the intransitive construction may be agentive or patientive (as well as dative) means that the accusative/ergative distinction cannot be made, and that the system is clearly neither, but agentive. Nevertheless, the constructions can be treated, in a parallel fashion to those of the ergative system, in terms of the roles/relations Agentive, Patientive and Dative, to give the combinations Agentive + Patientive, Agentive + Dative and Patientive + Dative.

There is a problem, however, with some two-term constructions. In E. Pomo, with verbs such as 'love', 'hate' and 'miss', both terms are marked as patientive, e.g. (McLendon 1978: 6):

> mí·ral   wí   ma·rá
> 3SG + FEM + PAT 1SG + PAT love
> 'I love her'

Similarly, Lakhota (Mithun 1991: 517) has a number of double patientive constructions (-*ni*- and -*ma*- are the second and first person singular patientive forms):

> iyé-ni-ma-čʰeča   'I look like you'
> í-ni-ma-ta   'I am proud of you'

It is debatable whether these should be treated as Patientive + Patientive constructions, although this is what the morphology suggests, since it is generally to be assumed that in a two-term construction, the roles and relations of the terms will be different. The problem is similar to that of the Japanese construction with 'like', which has both terms marked as nominative (2.8): there is no simple solution.

3.5.2 *Meaning*

The classification of intransitive verbs as either agentive (with Agentive S) or patientive (with Patientive S) in a particular language is not wholly arbitrary, but is based, to a limited extent, on a difference of meaning; in particular, it depends on the notion of agency, the arguments of agentive verbs being more like agents and those of patientive verbs more like patients, though in some cases aspectual features are also involved. However, it is well known from other grammatical categories that there is seldom if ever, a one-to-one correspondence between grammatical class and meaning. Meaning alone does not fully, or even extensively, account for the choice of agentive or patientive marking, and languages differ in the way in which they make the distinction. The most detailed and convincing account of the semantics of the distinction yet published is by Mithun 1991.

The distinguishing feature in Guaraní (Mithun 1991: 512–14, reanalysing Gregores and Suárez 1967) appears to be one of aspect in that verbs that denote events are agentive and verbs that denote states are patientive:

a-xá	'I go'
šé-rasī'	'I am sick'

Other verbs are:

Agentive		*Patientive*	
gwatá	'walk'	kaɲí-	'be weak'
ké	'sleep'	kaneʔõ'	'be tired'
yeká	'split'	-akú	'be hot'
manó	'die'	aɲatá	'be anxious'

Yet, in these terms there is no very clear distinction between events and states; -ki-'rain' 'counts as' an event in Guaraní, but -aiviruʔi 'drizzle' as a state.

However, Guaraní is not typical, since in other languages it is agency rather than aspect that determines the distinction, agency being defined, following Foley and Van Valin (1984: 29) in terms of 'the participant which performs, effects, instigates or controls the situation'. This is clearly true of Lakhota and Central Pomo (Mithun 1991: 515–21). Thus in Lakhota the agency distinction cuts across that of aspect (event/state):

ma-wá-ni	'I walk'	(agentive, event)
wa-tʰí	'I live, dwell'	(agentive, state)
ma-wášte	'I'm good'	(patientive, state)
ma-t'é	'I fainted, died'	(patientive, event)

Yet there is an interesting difference in the way these two languages treat verbs such as 'cough', 'sneeze' etc. In Lakhota they are all agentive as in (with -wa- for first person):

wa-pšá	'I sneezed'
šuwatʰe	'I missed my aim, failed'
wa-glépa	'I vomit'
iyó-wa-ya	'I yawn'

In Central Pomo such verbs are patientive; examples with ṭo· as first person patientive marker are:

ṭoˑ ʔésʔesya	'I sneezed'
ṭoˑ daláščiw	'I missed'
ṭoˑ msátčiw	'I blushed'
ṭoˑ šyéšyew	'I tremble'

The issue here, Mithun suggests, is control: control by an agent is not an essential part of agency in Lakhota, so that verbs which are performed but not controlled are still agentive, while, in Central Pomo, control is essential, and without it, a verb is patientive.

There is, however, another feature required for patientive marking in Central Pomo, that of 'affectedness' (being affected by the situation). Inherent states by which the particant is not significantly affected are represented by agentive verbs (*ʔa-* is the first person agentive marker):

ʔaˑ ʔe qól	'I'm tall'
ʔaˑ ʔe q'dí	'I'm good'
ʔaˑ ʔe nasáy	'I'm blind'

However, with inchoatives, where, apparently, the participant is affected by the change of state, the marking is patientive. There are contrasts such as:

yém ʔe ʔaˑ	'I am old'	(agentive)
yémaq' toˑ	'I have become old'	(patientive)

Moreover, only nominals referring to humans can appear in the patientive in either transitive or intransitive constructions; all other nominals are unmarked.

Caddoan languages (Texas, Oklohoma) are rather like Central Pomo in respect of agency, control and affectedness (Mithun 1991: 525–8), but, unexpectedly, 'lose' and 'die' are agentive (*ci:-* and *-ki-* are agentive markers):

ci:-yúníhʔnah	'I lost (something)'
ha-ki-hahyúsaʔ	'we die'

Mohawk (Iroquoian, New York and Quebec) provides a far less tidy situation (Mithun 1991: 528–36). Agency seems again to be the main feature, but there are some anomalies. Verbs of performance without control are divided; some are agentive, others patientive (*-k-* is the first person agentive marker, *-wak-* the patientive marker):

wa?-k-áhsa?ke?	'I coughed'	(agentive)
wa?-k-átstike?	'I vomited'	(agentive)
wak-hnyòːtskare?	'I have the hiccoughs'	(patientive)
wa?te-wak-í?tsᶙhkwe?	'I sneezed'	(patientive)

Even more surprisingly, some verbs denoting events under control are patientive:

te-wak-hᴧ réhta?	'I yell'
wak-yó?te?	'I work'
ye-wakátye?s	'I throw (it)'

Mithun suggests that these are to be accounted for historically, with meaning change. (There is further discussion of Mohawk in 3.5.3.)

A rather different point is made by Merlan (1985), that in most of the agentive systems one of the two verb classes can be considered to be the 'specialized' class. Thus in Lakhota it is the agentive type of verb that forms the specialized class, this class being both smaller and specifiable or 'marked' semantically, whereas in E. Pomo it is the patientive type that forms the specialized class. What is surprising is that these specialized classes share the characteristic of being largely restricted to verbs relating to animates, even though they may be semantically opposites; thus 'sneeze' is found in the specialized classes of both Lakhota and E. Pomo (McLendon 1978: 3), but is in the agentive class in the first, and the patientive class in the second.

3.5.3 Variation by grammatical category

Agentivity is often not a feature of the whole language, but is restricted to, or differs with, some other grammatical category; there is, that is to say, a split.

Person is involved in Lakhota, in that only first and second person have agentive/patientive markers. In E. Pomo, however, not only is the agentive/patientive marking restricted to pronouns, kinship terms and proper names, but it is also the case that common nouns operate within an ergative system, the only marker being the ergative suffix -a (McLendon 1978: 5):

buˑráqall-a míˑp-al šáˑk'a
bear-ERG 3SG-PAT killed
'A bear killed him'

73

This is similar to the 'split ergativity' discussed in 3.3.2, the split here being agentive/ergative instead of accusative/ergative. Moreover, it can be linked with the issue of the empathy hierarchy discussed in 2.2 and 3.4. It is worth noting that, in the closely related language N. Pomo (Croft 1991: 168), the case marking of agentive and patientive is split in terms of human and non-human. With human nominals agentive is unmarked, but the patientive is marked with -*al*, while with non-human nominals the agentive is marked by *ya*', but the patientive is unmarked. This marking suggests that humans are the most natural agents and non-human the most natural patients, the most natural role being unmarked. (This was the argument used in 3.4 to account for the accusative/ergative split in languages such as Dyirbal.) Mithun (1991: 542) mentions another language, Koasati, (Kimball 1985) in which noun morphology follows an accusative pattern but pronominal prefixes on the verb show an agentive system. (The converse is true of Georgian – see 3.6.1.)

In some of the Mayan languages, the agentive/patientive distinction does not depend upon the lexical type of verb, but on aspect. Thus in Jakaltek, in the completive tense S has the form associated with P, but in the progressive the form associated with A (Craig 1976 and Nora England personal communication):

<pre>
x-ach   wayi
COMPL-2SG + PAT sleep
'You slept'
</pre>

<pre>
x-ach   hin   laq'a
COMPL-2SG + PAT 1SG + AGT embrace
'I embraced you'
</pre>

<pre>
lanhan ha   wayi
PROG   2SG + AGT sleep
'You are sleeping'
</pre>

<pre>
lanhan hach   hin   laq'ni
PROG   2SG + PAT 1SG + AGT embrace
'I am embracing you'
</pre>

In Mohawk, as was seen in 3.5.2, the distinction is mostly determined by the class of verb, but, in addition, all verbs have patientive markers in the perfect apsect (Mithun 1991: 533):

k-aht₄tye?s 'I go away' (agentive)
wak-aht₄tyu 'I have gone away' (patientive)

This is capable of explanation: since the aspectual distinction of state/event is involved in the agentive/patientive classification of lexical intransitive verbs, it is also used grammatically to distinguish perfects and progressives, which generally indicate states rather than events, from other tenses, which do not.

Other languages with agentivity dependent on both verb class and tense/aspect are discussed by Merlan (1985). A far more complex system is discussed in 3.6.2.

Rather different is the situation in Acehnese, which was shown to have an agentive system in 3.5.1. There are two verbal morphemes, which actually change an intransitive verb from patientive to agentive or from agentive to patientive (Durie 1985: 47–50). Thus *meu-* converts from patientive to agentive:

sakét   'feel pain'
meu-saként   'suffer with endurance'
seunang   '(be) happy'
meu-seunang 'enjoy oneself'

The first and third forms occur with Patientive S, the other two with Agentive S, and the morpheme is said to 'add the element of control to a basically uncontrolled root'. The converse is to be seen with the morpheme *teu-* in an example in which the otherwise agentive verbs 'go' and 'stand' are marked as patientive because of the 'subject's loss of control':

jih teu-jak teu-döng lagèe   ureueng gadöh tuwah
he DC-go DC-stand manner person lost   mind [DEcontrol]
'He is wandering about stopping and starting as though out of his mind'

However, both of these two morphemes have other functions, particularly with transitives, where, essentially, they act as intransitivizers. Thus *teu-* may indicate a completed state with no mention of the Agent:

lôn crôh pisang
I   fry banana
'I fry bananas'

pisang nyan ka   teu-crôh
banana that already DC-fry
'Those bananas are already fried'

This can be explained in terms of loss of control, but, it is less easy to explain in intransitivizing functions of the other morpheme, *meu-*, which converts a transitive verb into an intransitive neuter:

| gantung | 'hang' (trans) | meu gantung | 'hang' (intrans) |
| som | 'hide' (trans) | meu-som | 'hide' (intrans) |

It also expresses the notion of accidental action:

> bak kayèe nyan ka   meu-koh (lé lôn)
> tree wood that already DC-cut   (by I)
> 'I accidentally cut down that tree'

This is unexpected, since in the earlier examples *meu-* was shown to add an element of control, yet here is glossed in terms of decontrol. Possibly this is simply a different but homonymous morpheme, as, indeed, Durie suggests.

3.5.4 *Other types of agentivity*

It has been suggested that the distinction between agentive and patientive verbs can be made for English, such verbs as DIE and GROW being essentially patientive, while JUMP and COME are agentive. (In the context of languages such as English, however, instead of 'agentive' and 'patientive', the rather opaque terms 'unergative' and 'unaccusative' (Perlmutter 1978) are generally used.) Part of the argument for this is that the 'patientive' verbs cannot occur in the imperative or with adverbs such as *deliberately* as shown by the impossible:

> *Grow tall!
> *He deliberately grew tall.

However, this is more of a semantic than a grammatical distinction, involving a meaning-based tendency rather than a firm grammatical rule. It is possible to use DIE and GROW in imperatives, although they are not so easily contextualized: a daughter seeing her mother suffering might say *Please die*, while a parent who has told a child that certain foods will make him tall might say *Come on, eat up and grow tall!*

Another feature that has been adduced to show the agentive/patientive distinction is that in some languages certain intransitive verbs, but not others, have 'impersonal' passives (see 5.5). It has been pointed out that generally only 'agentive' verbs may have such passives. Thus, in Dutch, 'swim', but not 'drown' can have such a passive (Perlmutter 1978: 168–9):

in de zomer wordt er hier vaak gezwommen
in the summer becomes it here often swum
'There is often swimming here in the summer'

*In de zomer wordt er hier vaak verdronken
in the summer becomes it here often drowned
'There is often drowning here in the summer'

Similarly, in Italian, some intransitive verbs require the auxiliary *avere* 'have', others the auxiliary *essere* or both, to form their perfect tense (Van Valin 1990: 232):

avere		*essere*		both	
parlare	'talk'	arrivare	'arrive'	correre	'run'
piangere	'cry'	sembrare	'seem'	volare	'fly'
ballare	'dance'	affondare	'sink'	fiorire	'bloom'

The first set are, it is suggested, all activity verbs, the second all state, accomplishment or achievement verbs, while the third may be either (with a difference in meaning, which would be expressed in English by tense/aspect – *è volato* 'he has flown', *ha volato* 'he flew'. It is also noted that only the activity verbs that take *avere* may be followed by an adverbial indicating a period of time, e.g. *per un' ora* 'for an hour'; the state verbs cannot, and this is true of the state verbs of English too. Here there are similarities to two of the features discussed in the previous sections, the 'fluid' systems of 3.5.1 and the involvement of tense/aspect discussed in 3.5.3.

However, it is not wholly true that Italian uses *essere*, rather than *avere*, only with verbs of state, for *essere* is used with reflexives, which are usually activity verbs and clearly transitive, e.g. (Lepschy and Lepschy 1977: 136):

Si é lavato le mani
REFL ESSERE + 3SG + PRES washed the hands
'He washed his hands'

However, Vincent (1982: 96) suggests that the use of *essere* with reflexives has been influenced by the statistically more preponderant use of the reflexives as mediopassives (see 6.1), which are essentially intransitive and non-agentive.

On a rather different point, agentivity may be marked morphologically. Thus in Cupeño (Uto-Aztecan, Hill 1969: 349–50), there are many verbs that occur with one of two suffixes *-ine* and *-yaxe*. One of the functions of the contrast between these two suffixes is the contrast between intentional and accidental activity:

neʔen pipíqnen	'I touched it'
neʔen pipíqneyex	'I bumped into it by accident'
neʔen piwecáxnen	'I threw it down'
neʔen piwecáxneyex	'I dropped it accidentally'

Semantically, this is very like the patientive/agentive contrast. However, another function is to distinguish transitive and neuter counterparts of the same verb:

| neʔen cáwelnen keláweti | 'I shook the stick' |
| keláwet cáwelpeyex | 'The stick shook' |

Although this involves different constructions, it shares with the other function the contrast of agency/control and lack of agency/control (though with the added feature than there is no mention of any performer of the action).

The issues of control as discussed here and in 3.5.3 are very complex and varied across languages, and seem to involve many different features, including agency, 'neuter' verbs, reflexivity etc. An attempt to deal with all such issues is to be found in Klaiman 1991.

3.6 Georgian and Tabassaran

A brief account of two languages from the Caucasus, Georgian (Harris 1981, 1982) and Tabassaran (Kibrik 1985), is given in this section in order to illustrate the ways in which languages may have extensive agentive systems affecting both intransitive and transitive constructions and also, in the case of Georgian, tense/aspect, yet also have either accusative or ergative characteristics. Both have been characterized as ergative, but analysis of them in terms of agentivity provides a simpler description and avoids begging questions.

The analysis of their systems rests on a case system of three terms, which are called 'ergative', 'nominative' and 'dative' in Harris 1981 and Kibrik, though Harris 1982 replaces 'ergative' by 'active'. Since the analysis presented here involves agentivity, these will be replaced by 'agentive', 'patientive' and 'dative' respectively. (For the conventions for the verbal agreement markers see below.)

3.6.1   *Georgian*

Although it is clear from Harris 1981 that Georgian has a complicated morphology, its basic system of grammatical relations proves to be fairly simple, if unusual, when compared to the systems of more familiar languages.

An agentivity system of three terms, Agentive, Patientive and Dative, like that of Choctaw (3.5.1), seems to be clearly shown for both one-term (intransitive) and two-term constructions by the morphological marking of third person NPs in terms of the three cases, the choice of case depending on the lexical class of verb ('class' in the sense required here, not in terms of Harris' verb classes, which are morphological).

Intransitive verbs are illustrated by (Harris 1981: 40, 132):

> ninom   daamtknara
> Nino + AGT yawn + 3SUBJ + AOR
> 'Nino yawned'

> vaxṭangi   ekimi   iqo
> Vaxtang + PAT doctor be + 3SUBJ + AOR
> 'Vaxtang was a doctor'

> ṭusaɣs   šioda
> prisoner-DAT hunger + 3IO + AOR
> 'The prisoner was hungry'

Two-term verbs follow a similar pattern with three types of case marking for the first NP (1981: 1, 40, 1982: 302):

> glex-ma   datesa   simind-i
> peasant-AGT sow + 3SUBJ + 3DO + AOR corn-PAT
> 'The peasant sowed corn'

> mama   mouqva   motxroba-s nino-s
> father + PAT tell + 3SUBJ + 3IO + 3DO + AOR story-DAT Nino-DAT
> 'Father told a story to Nino'

> čems megobar-s gasaɣeb-i daḳarga
> my   friend-DAT key-PAT   lose + 3SUBJ + 3IO + AOR
> 'My friend lost his key'

(A three-term construction form is given for the second of these because neither work contains an example of a relevant two-term construction.) The marking system of these may be summarized as:

(i)   agentive   patientive
(ii) patientive   dative
(iii) dative   patientive

For ease of reference, these patterns (and those of the intransitives) will be referred to as the 'agentive', 'patientive', and 'dative' constructions.

So far the examples have shown contrasting patterns in terms of verb class. The three patterns also affect the tense-aspect system of one class of verb only, both one-term and two-term. This class is exemplified by the first sentence of each set of three above; the other verb classes have the same pattern in all tenses and aspects. Examples of variation in terms of tense/aspect are (Harris 1981: 40–1, 135, 1):

nino-m   daamtknara   (agentive)
Nino-AGT yawn + 3SUBJ + AOR
'Nino yawned'

nino   amtknarebs   (patientive)
Nino + PAT yawn + 3SUBJ + PRES
'Nino yawns/is yawning'

merab-s   turme   daumtknarebia   (dative)
Merab- + DAT apparently yawn + 3IO + PERF
'Merab apparently (has) yawned'

glex-ma   datesa   simind-i   (agentive)
peasant-AGT sow + 3SUBJ + 3DO + AOR corn-PAT
'The peasant sowed corn'

glex-i   tesavs   simind-s   (patientive)
peasant-PAT sow + 3SUBJ + 3DO + PRES corn-DAT
'The peasant sows corn'

glex-s   dautesavs   simind-i   (dative)
peasant-DAT sowed + 3SUBJ + 3IO + PERF corn-PAT
'The peasant has sown corn'

The discussion so far has been concerned with the case system, which is clearly agentive. In terms of agreement with the verb, however, the situation is different, as shown by the examples above. The system is accusative, and Harris handles it in terms of Subject, Direct Object and Indirect Object. (The glosses S, DO and IO are used in Harris 1982, but SUBJ is preferred to S here; in Harris 1981 the pronouns 'he', 'I', 'her' etc. are used as glosses.) This is clearly illustrated by the examples given above. It will be seen that with the agentive and patientive constructions, there is Subject marking for the single term of the one-term construction and for the first term of the two-term construction (the other term being marked as Object). In terms of verbal agreement then, these constructions are quite simply intransitive and transitive in an accusative system. There is, however, a difference in the case marking, the Subject (in terms of agreement) is in the agentive case in the agentive construction, but in the patientive case in the patientive construction, and, similarly, the Object is either patientive or dative. There is, then, a split like that discussed in 3.3.2, but in this case a split between agentive and accusative, instead of ergative and accusative, with noun morphology being agentive, and verbal agreement marking accusative.

With the third (dative) construction, the NP marked as dative is marked as Indirect Object in verbal agreement, while the patientive NP has Subject agreement (as argued by Harris 1981: 121–2). This is not wholly unexpected, for the lexical verbs involved are almost entirely verbs of experience or modal verbs, such as 'be hot', 'be hungry', 'love', 'remember', 'be able to': it follows the common pattern with experiencers discussed in 2.5 in which the experiencer is treated as a Dative, but placed first, while the entity experienced is the Subject, or (for intransitives) there is an impersonal Subject.

Although Georgian may seem complex, there is, it would appear, a fairly neat and consistent overall pattern, with an agentive case system affecting both one-term and two-term constructions and an accusative agreement system, these involving three classes of verb and three classes of tense/aspect. However, there are two other points worth noting.

First, some verbs with agentive Subjects may have either patientive Direct Objects or dative Indirect Objects (Harris 1982: 302):

> jariskac-ma das3lia   mṭer-i
> soldier-AGT overcome + 3SUBJ + 3DO + AOR enemy-PAT
> 'The soldier defeated the enemy'

> jariskac-ma s3lia   mṭer-s
> soldier-AGT overcome + 3SUBJ + 3IO + AOR enemy-DAT
> 'The soldier defeated the enemy'

This provides another construction (Subject + Indirect Object) with another sequence of case marking (agentive + dative), additional to those already noted; such constructions are found in other accusative systems.

Secondly, many 'affective predicates' (Harris 1982: 302) have either the agentive-Subject + Object or dative-Dative + Subject construction:

čemma megobar-ma gasaɣeb-i daḳarga
my friend-AGT   key-PAT   lose-3SUBJ + 3DO + AOR
'My friend lost his key'

čems megobar-s gasaɣeb-i daḳarga
my friend-DAT   key-PAT   lose-3SUBJ + 3IO + AOR
'My friend lost his key'

With some verbs, that is to say, there is a choice between the 'normal' transitive construction and the experiencer construction with 'dative subjects'. It is not surprising that 'lose' should be one such verb, since the human involved can be seen as both agent (without control) and experiencer.

3.6.2 *Tabassaran*

Tabassaran (Kibrik 1985) is like Georgian in that there is a complex system of case marking and an independent system of verbal agreement, but differs from it in the functions of its noun morphology and verbal agreement marking and in the fact that there is no variation according to tense/aspect.

Basically there are four types of two-term construction. With agentive terminology used for the glosses (rather than Kibrik's ergative terminology), these may be illustrated by:

čuču   či   Rurčnu   (p. 279)
brother + AGT sister + PAT beat
'Brother beat sister'

čuču   čučuz   Rivnu   (p. 281)
brother + AGT sister + DAT hit
'Brother hit sister'

če   čučuz   Rigilnu   (p. 282)
brother + PAT sister + DAT look at
'Brother looked at sister'

čučuz   či   Rarqlnu   (p. 283)
brother + DAT sister + PAT see
'Brother saw sister'

The cases of the nouns for each of the verbs exemplified are:

'beat'	agt	pat
'hit'	agt	dat
'look at'	pat	dat
'see'	dat	pat

With verbal agreement markers, the situation is different, although they can also be described and glossed as 'agentive', 'patientive' and 'dative'. These markers, however, are restricted to first and second person, and there is the complication that the pronouns themselves (not their agreement markers) do not make the agentive/patientive distinction. However, this can be resolved by comparison with the nouns, as will be shown in the examples below, where 'AGT(PAT)' and '(AGT)PAT' indicate that, although the forms are the same, their cases can be identified as agentive and patientive respectively. Compared with the examples above, the four possibilities with pronouns are exemplified by (with optional markers also shown in brackets):

uzu   uvu   Rurčun-za-(vu)   (p. 279)
I + AGT(PAT) you + (AGT)PAT beat-1SG + AGT-(2SG + PAT)
'I beat you'

uzu   uvuz   Rivun-za-(vuz)   (p. 280)
I + AGT(PAT) you + DAT hit-1SG + AGT-(2SG + DAT)
'I hit you'

uzu   uvuz   Rigilun-za-(vuz)   (p. 281)
I + (AGT)PAT you + DAT looked at-1SG + AGT-(2SG + DAT)
'I looked at you'

uzuz   uvu   Rarqlun-zuz   (p. 282)
I + DAT you + (AGT)PAT see-1SG + DAT
'I saw you'

In terms of verbal agreement, there are only three possibilities, with the same pattern for 'hit' and 'look at':

'beat'	agt	(pat)
'hit', 'look at'	agt	(dat)
'see'	dat	–

Moreover, since the pronouns themselves are not distinguished morphologically for agentive/patientive, there is no overt distinction at all between these two types of verb with pronouns, although they would be different in

terms of the morphology of nouns, as noted earlier and as suggested by the
glosses 'AGT(PAT)' and '(AGT)PAT'.

With intransitives, the single NP is in the patientive case, if it is a noun:

> či Ranu (p. 296)
> sister + PAT came
> 'Sister came'

> či aldaknu
> sister + PAT fell
> 'Sister fell'

(If these intransitives are compared with the 'beat' construction above, which
is the most typical transitive construction (see 3.6.3), the system would appear
to be ergative. The first and second pronouns provide no evidence for or
against this conclusion since they do not distinguish between agentive and
patientive.)

The verbal agreement system, however, distinguishes agentive and
patientive, but only for first and second person:

> daqun-za (p. 278)
> lay down-1SG + AGT
> 'I lay down'

> RarRun-zu
> freeze-1SG + PAT
> 'I froze'

Some verbs have either type of marking according to their meaning:

Ruʒun-za	'I remained (voluntarily)'	(p. 278)
Ruʒun-zu	'I remained (against my will)'	
aqun-za	'I fell (intentionally)'	
aqun-zu	'I fell (involuntarily)'	

This appears to exemplify a typical fluid agentivity system. Agentivity is
shown by the fact that, in the construction associated with 'beat', -za and -zu
are markers of first person Agent and Patient respectively (though the
example given has the second person form -vu). This verbal agreement
marking is not found with third person NPs, as shown by the examples of
'Sister came' and 'Sister fell' above. (With first or second persons, 'come'
would have the agentive suffix, 'fall' the patientive suffix.)

There is also a construction with the dative:

> uzuz   durXnu ḱunžu-(zuz)   (p. 278)
> 1SG + DAT learn   should-(1SG + DAT)
> ˙'I should learn'

However, it is not certain whether this should be regarded as intransitive, in view of the fact that it has a complement. It might rather be regarded as an example of the third type in the transitive pattern (like 'see'). Possibly a better example of an intransitive with a dative is with the verb 'fear':

> baliz   guč'ura dasijixan   (p. 289)
> son + DAT fears   father + ELAT
> 'Son fears father'

Here 'son' is in the dative case and 'father' in the elative, which Kibrik describes as 'of the local series meaning "around"'; if the elative is treated as the mark of a peripheral relation, the sentence is intransitive.

There is a further point. Verbal agreement with a pronoun is obligatory if it is the first NP (or the only NP of the intransitive), but optional or disallowed if it is the second, and the sequence of the agreement markers is fixed, as can be seen from the examples above. It could be argued that this established a third system, involving Subject and Object, Subjects being obligatorily marked and preceding the Objects. One point that would follow from this is that the dative + patientive pattern in Tabassaran is unlike that of Georgian or the experiencer construction of other languages, in that, in this respect, the experiencer, not the source of the experience, is marked as Subject.

3.6.3 *Semantic issues*

The meaning differences between the three cases with intransitives in Georgian and Tabassaran seem generally to be fairly simple and in accordance with the discussion in 3.5.2: agentive indicates agency and patientive affectedness, while dative identifies an experiencer. Thus in Georgian (Harris 1981: 261–7) agentive verbs include 'yawn', 'dance', 'sing', 'fight' (note that, as in Lakhota (3.5.2), 'yawn' is agentive – control is not a necessary component of agency), patientive verbs include 'break', 'fall', 'remain', 'cook', and dative verbs include 'be cold', 'be thirsty', 'feel sleepy'. In Tabassaran (Kibrik 1985: 278) agentive verbs include 'begin to cry', 'work', 'come', 'fly away', patientive verbs include 'drown', 'freeze', 'hang', 'get tired', while the single dative verb is the modal 'should'.

The meanings of the cases of the two terms in the transitive constructions cannot be wholly accounted for independently of each other, but are best discussed in terms of 'transitivity', the term being used in a notional rather than a grammatical sense: this involves degrees to which the two terms notionally represent an agent affecting a patient through the action denoted by the verb. This feature was first noted in 2.3.1 in the use of dative marking for the (notional) patient in both accusative and ergative systems. The agentive + patientive pattern obviously indicates full transitivity. This transitivity is reduced if the second term is dative (agentive + dative) and further reduced if the first term is patientive (patientive + dative), while the dative + patientive construction is the least transitive, in which there is an experiencer and something experienced. Examples from Tabassaran were given in 3.6.2. Examples from Georgian are:

agentive + patientive	'bake', 'rip', 'bend', 'lock'
patientive + dative (few in number)	'play with', 'tell', 'persuade'
dative + patientive	'love', 'hate', 'forget', 'want'

An agentive + dative construction was noted as an alternative for 'defeat'; this can be taken to represent a degree of transitivity lower than that of agentive + patientive, but higher than that of patientive + dative.

It is far less easy to give an explanation for the variation in terms of tense/ aspect in Georgian. The agentive pattern is found with the aorist and optative (second subjunctive), the patientive pattern with present, future, imperfect, conditional, present subjunctive and future subjunctive and the dative pattern with the perfect, pluperfect and third subjunctive, which are also termed 'evidentials'. If this is again a matter of lowered transitivity, the contrast between the agentive and patientive might be compared with the use of antipassives and detransitives discussed in 7.2.2 and 7.4, where an ergative (= agentive) construction is replaced by an absolutive (= patientive) one with certain aspects; moreover, the fact that the aorist has the agentive pattern may be related to the fact that where there is split ergativity in terms of tense/ aspect, ergative marking is '*always* found either in the past tense or perfect aspect' (Dixon 1979: 95). For the dative pattern, it might just be argued that the dative construction derives from the evidentiality of the relevant tenses/ aspects, evidentiality being a kind of modality. Overall, however, it is clear that there has been a considerable degree of grammaticalization in Georgian that has obscured the semantics.

The reduced transitivity or 'detransitivization' in ergative systems to be discussed in 7.2.2 and, with reference to lexically based distinctions, in 7.6 looks very similar to the phenomenon in Georgian and Tabassaran, in that generally, in ergative systems, both terms are affected, the first being changed from Ergative to Absolutive and the second from Absolutive to Dative. It is this, perhaps, that has led some scholars to treat agentive sytems such as those of Georgian and Tabassaran as ergative and to use the terms 'ergative' and 'nominative' for agentive and patientive. In the case of Tabassaran there is, in fact, justification for recognizing an ergative system for the case marking of nouns, but an agentive system for verbal agreement, though Georgian appears to have only agentive and accusative systems. However, detransitivization is also found with accusative systems (see 2.3.1) and is not, therefore an indication of ergativity. It is less apparent in accusative systems, because there can only be a change in the second term, from Patient-Object to Dative; the first term remains as Subject, because the change from Agent in the transitive to Single term in the intransitive does not alter the grammatical relation (both are Subject).

4
Syntactic relations

This chapter investigates in much more detail issues of syntax raised briefly in 1.3.1 and 3.1.

4.1 Syntactic pivots

Some of the grammatical relations, particularly the Subject in accusative languages, are involved in certain grammatical constructions. Thus, in English, if two sentences are coordinated, usually with *and*, the subject of the second is normally omitted or 'deleted', if it is coreferential with that of the first, as in (with the omitted NP shown in brackets):

The man came in. The man saw the woman.
The man came in and [the man] saw the woman.

This is only possible if both nouns are Subjects, as can be seen from the impossible sentences:

The man came in. The woman saw the man.
*The man came in and the woman saw [the man].

The man saw the woman. The woman came.
*The man saw the woman and [the woman] came in.

The man saw the woman. The boy heard the woman.
*The man saw the woman and the boy heard [the woman].

This restriction on deletion in coordination, together with similar syntactic conditions that are dealt with in more detail in later sections of this chapter, is treated in terms of 'pivot', the Subject being said to be the pivot for deletion in coordination in English. However, two NPs are involved in the coreferentiality and it may be better to refer to both of them as 'pivots', the first being the 'controller' and the second the 'target' (Foley and Van

Valin 1985: 305), though in much of the discussion the term is used to refer to the second, the target.

4.1.1 *Coordination*

The discussion in the last section gave examples of coordination in English, with the Subject of each sentence as the controller and target of the deletion. There is little more to add here, except that, since passivization promotes the Patient-Object to Subject, grammatical sentences corresponding to the impossible ones above can be formed by passivization of one or both of the sentences:

> The man came in and was seen by the woman
>
> The woman was seen by the man and came in
>
> The woman was seen by the man and heard by the boy

In these three sentences the passive Subjects (promoted Patients) function as target, controller and both respectively. Since it is the primary term, the Subject, that is the pivot in English, a language with an accusative system, it is not surprising that in a language with an ergative system, the pivot is the Absolutive (S = P in basic, active sentences), the primary term of an ergative system. This is so for coordination in Dyirbal, as shown by (Dixon 1979: 62–3):

> ŋuma   banaga-ɲu   yabu-ŋgu   buṛa-n
> father + ABS returned-PAST mother-ERG see-PAST
> 'Father returned and Mother saw [Father]'
>
> ŋuma   yaba-ŋgu   buṛa-n banaga-ɲu
> father + ABS mother-ERG see-PAST returned-PAST
> 'Mother saw Father and [Father] returned'

'Father' is deleted in the second clause of both examples; in the first example it is P, which is coreferential with the S of the first clause, while in the second example it is S, which is coreferential with the P of the first clause. P, of course, would be the Object in English, and not involved either as controller or target; it would be A and S that are involved (*Father returned and [Father] saw mother, Mother saw father and [Mother] returned*). However, if the Dyirbal sentences were translated as passives in English, they would seem to follow the English pattern ('Father returned and was seen by mother', 'Father was seen by mother and returned'). This is a natural consequence of the similarity of ergatives and passives with respect to roles and relations (see 3.1).

The sentences above cannot mean 'Father returned and saw mother', 'Mother saw father and returned', because (apart from the ergative marking of 'Mother' in the first) that would involve Ergatives as the (deleted) target in the first sentence and the controller in the second. To express such sentences in Dyirbal antipassives are needed to promote these Ergative Agents to Absolutives:

> ŋuma   banaga-ɲu   buṛal-ŋa-ɲu   yabu-gu
> father + ABS returned-PAST see-ANTIP-PAST mother-DAT
> 'Father returned and saw mother'

> yabu   buṛal-ŋa-ɲu   ŋuma-gu banaga-ɲu
> mother + ABS see-ANTIP-PAST father-DAT returned-PAST
> 'Mother saw father and returned'

The use of the antipassive in the second clause of the first sentence and the first clause of the second ensures that (Ergative) Agents are promoted to Absolutive and so made available as target and controller pivots respectively.

Since the syntax in Dyirbal involves the Absolutive, the primary term of an ergative system, it can be said that Dyirbal has 'ergative syntax', whereas English has 'accusative syntax'.

Another Australian language, however, Yidiny (Dixon 1977b: 380–1, cf. Dixon 1977a: 388–90), has ergative syntax when the coreferential NPs are nouns, but accusative syntax, when they are pronouns. Thus Yidiny has the contrasting pairs:

> ŋayu   maŋga:ɲ buɲa   wuṛa:ɲ
> I + NOM laughed   woman + ABS slapped
> 'I laughed and slapped the woman'

> ŋayu   buɲa   wuṛa:ɲ maŋga:ɲ
> I + NOM woman + ABS slapped laughed
> 'I slapped the woman and laughed'

> wagu:ḍa maŋga:ɲ buɲa:ŋ   wuṛa:ɲ
> man + ABS laughed   woman + ERG slapped
> 'The man laughed and the woman slapped him'

buɲa:ŋ   wagu:ḍa   wuɽa:ɲ   maŋga:ɲ
woman + ERG man + ABS slapped laughed
'The woman slapped the man and he laughed'

In the first pair of sentences, deletion depends on the coreferentiality of A with S and S with A (an accusative system); in particular notice that the second sentence does not mean 'I slapped the woman and she laughed', as it would have if the syntax had been ergative. In the second pair of sentences, by contrast, deletion depends on coreferentiality of S with P and P with S, and the second sentence does not mean 'The woman slapped the man and laughed'. However, Dixon (1977a: 392) states that these principles of coordination in Yidiny are ' "preferences" rather than rules'. Semantics will overrule the syntax as in:

ŋayu   buɲa   wawa:l yaɽŋga:ɲ
I + NOM woman + ABS saw   was frightened
'I saw the woman and she was frightened'

Here it was argued that this interpretation follows from the fact that a man would not be frightened of a woman.

This differential treatment of nouns and pronouns in Yidiny may, perhaps be a reflection of the fact that Yidiny has split ergativity in its morphology with the pronouns (first and second) having the same form for S and A (the nominative), while nouns have the same form for S and P (see 3.3.2 and 3.4). Yet, by contrast, Dyirbal also has split ergativity in its morphology, but is wholly ergative in its syntax.

It must be said, however, that most languages that have an ergative system in their morphology are unlike Dyirbal and Yidiny: they have fully accusative, not ergative, syntax – see 4.2.

A device that serves a function similar to that of deletion of the primary term (and may accompany it) is 'switch reference', whereby, there is a marker to indicate whether the primary terms are identical or not in the two clauses. In practice this usually seems to operate along accusative lines (Foley and Van Valin 1984: 117–19), with A = S (Subject), as in Kewa (New Guinea, Franklin 1971: 104, 108):

ní réko-a ágaa lá-lo
I stand-ss talk say-I + PRES
'I stood up and am talking'

> ní réka-no ágaa lá-a
> I stand-DS talk say-he + PAST
> 'I stood up and he talked'

Here the markers SS and DS indicate whether there is the same or different Subject. In these particualr examples this may not seem to have any great significance, since it is clear who the Subjects are, but if a third person Subject is omitted, when the previous clause has a third person Subject or Object, the marking would resolve the ambiguity; unfortunately, Franklin (1971: 106) presents only an example of the same Subject with third person and none with different Subject:

> nipú tá-ri pámua-la
> 3 + SG hit-ss walk-3SG + PRES
> 'He is hitting it while he is walking'

In another language of New Guinea, Barai, it would appear that in such cases there is both switch reference and the omission of a coreferential Subject, but with a non-coreferential Subject being marked by an independent pronoun. Foley and Van Valin (1984: 342) give as examples:

> fu juare me-na fae kira
> 3 + SG garden make-ss fence tie
> 'He made a garden and tied a fence'

> fu juare me-mo fu fae kira
> 3 + SG garden make-DS he fence tied
> 'He₁ made a garden and he₂ tied a fence'

Olson (1978: 342) is given as the reference, but the actual examples given by Olson are less illuminating, since the relevant NPs are not both third person:

> na juae me-na fae kira
> I garden do-ss fence tie
> 'I made a garden and tied a fence'

> na juae me-ga fae kira
> I garden do-DS fence tie
> 'I made a garden and he tied a fence'

Other examples of switch reference are given in 4.1.2.

There is a problematic situation in Lango (Nilo-Saharan, Uganda, Noonan 1992: 259). Here coordination seems to involve Topics rather than Subjects or any other grammatical relation, as shown by:

dákô lócá ònÈnò   tÊ   dÒk
woman man see + 3SG + PERF and then + 3SG + HAB go back + INF
'The woman was seen by the man and then (she) went back'

Topicalization, with the Topic moved to initial position is a common feature of Lango. Here the Object 'the woman' has been topicalized, and a more literal translation would be 'The woman, the man saw . . . '. It is this Topic that controls the deletion in the second clause, which does not mean ' . . . and then he went back'. It might be thought that this is not topicalization, but passivization, with 'the woman' as the passive Subject, as it is in the English translation. There are two arguments against this: first there are no markers of passive, and, secondly, for reflexives it is Subjects not Topics (or putative passive Subjects) that are the controllers (see 4.1.4). (For a brief discussion of topicalization vs. passivization, see 5.5.)

4.1.2 *Complementation*

Deletion of a coreferential Subject is also common in complement clauses, e.g. in English after verbs such as WANT, and in purpose clauses:

John wants [John] to meet Mary
*John wants Mary to meet [John]

John came there [John] to see Mary
*John came there Mary to see [John]

John remembered/liked [John] meeting Mary
*John remembered/liked Mary meeting [John]

In these constructions and in coordination both controller and target are Subjects, but with verbs such as TELL, ASK or PERSUADE, it seems that it is the Object of the main clause that is the controller and the Subject of the complement that is the target, as in:

John persuaded Mary [Mary] to wait

Here it seems best to consider that it is the second *Mary* that has been deleted; the argument usually given is that *Mary* is shown to be the Object of the main clause because it can be promoted to Subject by passivization:

Mary was persuaded (by John) [Mary] to wait

93

What is important to note is that the two NPs involved as controller and target are not both Subjects, but Object and Subject respectively; the rules for pivots do not involve Subjects exclusively.

It is not surprising that in Dyirbal it is the Absolutive, the primary term of ergative systems (P/S in the active), that is deleted, as shown by (Dixon 1979: 128):

> ŋana yabu   giga-n   banagay-gu
> we   mother + ABS tell-PAST return-PURP
> 'We told Mother to return'

Here the deleted NP is S in the subordinate clause. However if 'mother' is the Agent, the antipassive is required to promote it from Ergative to Absolutive before deletion:

> ŋana yabu   giga-n   ŋuma-gu buṛal-ŋay-gu
> we   mother + ABS tell-PAST father-DAT see-ANTIP-PURP
> 'We told Mother to see Father'

Notice that the syntax is fully ergative and that both controller and target are Absolutives (in contrast with the similar construction in English, where they are not both Subjects).

There is ergative syntax in purpose clauses also in Dyirbal. The following example shows the use of the antipassive to ensure that the target for deletion is the primary (Absolutive) term:

> ŋuma   banaga-ɲu yabu-gu   buṛal-ŋay-gu
> father + ABS return-PAST mother-DAT see-ANTIP-PURP
> 'Father returned to watch mother'

(There are no examples of 'want', which is expressed in Dyirbal by the purposive particle, with no verb of wanting and no subordination.)

Other degrees of ergativity are to be found. In Mam (Mayan, England 1983: 7–8), which also has an ergative system (but see 3.3.3), it is the controller that has to be Absolutive, if the target is to be deleted, as in:

> o   chi   e?x xjaal   laq'oo-l t-ee
> ASP 3PL + ABS go person buy-INF 3SG + PAT
> 'The people went to buy it'

> ma tz'-ok   n-q'o-?n-a   tx'eema-l sii?
> ASP 2SG + ABS-DIR 1SG + ERG-give-DS-1/2SG cut-INF wood
> 'I made you cut wood'

Here the controller is S in the first sentence, and P in the second. There can be no deletion when the potential controller is Ergative:

> ø-w-ajb'el-a   chin   aq'naa-n-a
> 3SG + ABS-1SG + ERG-want-1SG   1SG + ABS work-ANTIP-1SG
> 'I want to work'

In the first and second examples 'people' and 'you' are deleted in the second clause, but 'I' is not deleted in the third.

There are also examples of switch reference in complementation. An example from Lango (Nilotic, Noonan 1985: 81) is:

> dákó   òpòyò   ní   ècégò   dɔ́gólá
> woman remembered + SG COMP closed + 3SG + SS door
> 'The woman₁ remembered that she₁ closed the door'

> dákó   òpòyò   ní   òcègò   dɔ́gólá
> woman remembered + SG COMP closed + 3SG(+ DS) door
> 'The woman₁ remembered that he/she₂ closed the door'

Surprisingly perhaps, there is a specific marker for 'same Subject', but none for 'different Subject', the pronominal prefix being the one generally used for third person.

An interesting pair of sentences from Diyari (Australia) is given by Austin (1981b: 316) with the 'implicative' construction, which corresponds to both purpose and result clauses in other languages:

> nhulu   nganthi   pardaka-rna   warrayi thanali   thayi-lha
> he + ERG meat + ABS bring-PTCP   AUX   they + ERG eat-IMPL + SS
> 'He brought the meat for them (him and others) to eat'

> nhulu   nganthi   pardaka-ma warrayi thanali   thayi-rnanthu
> he + ERG meat + ABS bring-PTCP   AUX   they + ERG eat-IMPL + DS
> 'He brought the meat for them (others) to eat'

Here the 'same Subject' form is used when the person referred to by the Subject of the main clause is included in those referred to by the Subject of the complement. Austin adds that this 'inclusion' has been noted for a number of languages and provides a further example from another Australian language, Arabana-Wangganguru (Hercus 1976: 471)

> athu   nha   kathi   ngunhi-rra tharni-lhiku
> I + ERG you + ACC meat + ABS give-PRES   eat-PURP + SS
> 'I am giving you this meat to eat (I'm having some too)'

athu   nha   kathi   ngunhi-rra tharni-nhanga
I + ERG you + ACC meat + ABS give-PRES   eat-PURP + DS
'I am giving you this meat to eat (on your own)'

It should be noted that, in both languages, although the morphology is ergative, the switch reference system operates on accusative lines, the NPs with ergative case being treated as the same or different Subjects (see 4.2).

4.1.3   *Relatives*

A relative clause is a modifier of a noun phrase, and relativization (relative clause formation) involves referential identity between that NP and one of the NPs in the relative clause itself, although this second NP may be deleted or represented by a pronoun, often of a particular type – a relative pronoun. In English this NP may be the Subject or the Object of the subordinate relative clause, or a possessive or any NP governed by a preposition, and a relative pronoun is used or there is deletion, as in:

The man who saw me (the man – the man saw me)
The man (whom) I saw (the man – I saw the man)
The man whose book I borrowed (the man – I borrowed the
    man's book)
The man to whom I spoke/The man I spoke to (the man – I
    spoke to the man)

There are languages, however, which 'relativize on' the primary term alone, i.e. in which the coreferential noun in the relative clause must be the primary term. Thus in Malagasy (Keenan 1972: 173–4), it is possible to say:

ny   vehivavy izay nividy ny vary ho an'ny ankizy
the woman   REL bought the rice for the   children
'The woman who bought the rice for the children'

Here 'the woman' is the Subject of the relative clause. Yet it is not possible to say (literally) 'The rice which the woman bought for the children' or 'The children for whom the woman bought the rice', because 'the rice' and 'the children' are not the Subjects of the relative clause.

However, Malagasy has devices for promoting Objects and other relations to the status of Subject (see 1.4.1, 5.3), the Passive for Objects and the Circumstantial for other relations (Dative and Instrumental). These promoted Subjects can function as pivots, as shown by:

ny vary izay novidin'   ny vehivavy ho an'ny ankizy
the rice REL bought + PASS the woman for the   children
'The rice that was bought by the woman for the children'

ny ankizy izay nividianan'   ny vehivavy ny vary
the children REL bought + CIRC the woman   the rice
'The children for whom the rice was bought by the woman'

(No example of a promoted Instrumental is given, but it may be assumed that this, too, may function as a pivot to give 'The money that was-used-for-buying ('was-bought-with') the rice for the children'.

Other languages relativize only on the primary and secondary terms (the Subject and Object in accusative languages). One such is Luganda (Bantu, Keenan and Comrie 1979: 341, but see also 5.4):

ekikopo e-kigudde
cup   REL-fell
'The cup which fell'

ekikopo John ky'-aguze
cup   John REL-bought
'The cup which John bought'

It is not possible to relativize on oblique terms, e.g. on 'knife' in:

John yatta enkonko n'ekiso
John killed chicken with-knife
'John killed the chicken with a knife'

However, Luganda has verbal forms that promote oblique terms to the status of Object, as in:

John yattisa   ekiso enkonko
John killed with knife chicken
'John killed the chicken with a knife'

This permits the relativization:

ekiso John kye-yattisa   enkonko
knife John REL-killed with chicken
'The knife with which John killed the chicken'

Similarly, relativization on the Beneficiary is made possible only by the use of the verb form that promotes the Beneficiary to Object:

mukazi John gwe-yattira   enkonko
woman John REL-killed for chicken
'The woman for whom John killed the chicken'

In both Malagasy and Luganda, it will be seen, the restrictions on the type of relation that may be a pivot are compensated for by the rules of promotion. English, by contrast, does not have to use the passive in order to create pivots for relativization.

Keenan and Comrie (1977, 1979) argue that there is a hierarchy of 'noun phrase accessibility' with Subject at the top, then Objects, Indirect Objects (Datives) and so on, such that if a language can relativize on any one it can relativize on all those higher in the hierarchy – e.g. that any language that relativizes on the Object will also relativize on the Subject. The full hierarchy is given as (1977: 60):

Subject > Object > Indirect Object > Oblique > Genitive
> Object of Comparison

They provide numerous examples from different languages, but there are undoubtedly some exceptions and the thesis is not accepted by everyone (see Fox 1987). As with many typological features, the hierarchy probably indicates a strong general tendency rather than a set of exceptionless rules.

There are languages in which relativization follows an ergative pattern, although these are restricted to the few that have ergative syntax in coordination and complementation. Thus Dyirbal can only relativize on the complementation Absolutive P = S, the primary term of an ergative system. This is shown by (Dixon 1979: 128):

ŋuma   yabu-ŋgu   buṛa-ŋu duŋgara-ɲu
father + ABS mother-ERG see-REL cry-PAST
'Father whom mother saw (who was seen by mother), was crying'

To express 'Father, who saw mother', the antipassive must be used, for without it 'father' in the relative clause would be Ergative A, which is not the primary relation. The antipassive promotes this A to the primary status of Absolutive, while P is demoted to the oblique status of Dative:

ŋuma buṛal-ŋa-ŋu yabu-gu   duŋgara-ɲu
father see-ANTIP-REL mother-DAT cry-PAST
'Father, who saw mother, was crying'

In all the examples considered so far, the restriction has affected only the deleted NP. It is this NP that has to be Subject (Malagasy), Subject or Object

(Luganda, or Absolutive (Dyirbal). In Yidiny (see 4.1.1), however, both the controller (in the main clause) and the target (the deleted NP in the relative clause) are involved: both must be the Absolutive primary term (Dixon 1977b: 377–80). A typical relative clause (marked by the subordinator -*ɲunda* and occurring after the main clause) is seen in:

> wagu:ɖa maŋga:ɲ buɲa:ŋ   wuṟaɲunda
> man   laughed woman + ERG slapped + REL
> 'The man whom the woman slapped laughed'

Here 'the man' is S in the main clause and P in the second. However the antipassive is needed for both of the following:

> buɲa   maŋga:ɲ waguɖanda wuṟa:ɖiɲu:n
> woman + ABS laughed   man + DAT   slapped + ANTIP + REL
> 'The woman who slapped the man laughed'

> buɲa   waguɖanda wuṟa:ɖiɲu   maŋgaɲunda
> woman + ABS man + DAT   slapped + ANTIP laughed + REL
> 'The woman who laughed slapped the man'

The first sentence follows the same rule as in Dyirbal – the deleted NP must be Absolutive and for this the antipassive is used to promote the (deleted) A. Unlike Dyirbal, however, the antipassive is also required in the second sentence to promote A ('the woman') in the main clause; this too has to be Absolutive, not Ergative. In this sense, Yidiny is 'more ergative' than Dyirbal. In addition, if the two NPs involved are both pronouns, both equally must be Absolutive S or P, and the syntax is ergative. This may seem surprising in view of the discussion in 4.1.1, where it was seen that, for coordination, pronouns have accusative (S = A) syntax.

Austin (1981b: 326) also discusses switch reference in relative clauses in Australian languages. The situation is complicated by the fact that the 'relative' also has the sense of 'while . . . .', but the following examples from Alyawarra (Yallop 1977: 130–2) are interesting:

> antimirna aynt-ila   alkuka
> honey + ABS lie-REL + SS eat + PAST
> 'I ate the honey while lying down'

> aringkirnima   irwarinika   atntirrirr-inyja
> dog + some + ABS see across + PAST run + PL-REL + DS
> '(We) looked across at the dogs (which were) running'

As with the complementation examples (4.1.2), switch reference follows an accusative pattern (involves Subjects, not Absolutives).

There is a considerable body of literature on relatives, e.g. Peranteau 1972, Keenan and Comrie 1977, 1979, Lehmann 1984. There are many differences in relative clauses across languages, involving their position, restrictions on their occurrence, the type of relative marker or its absence, whether or not a coreferential pronoun is required or permitted in the relative clause, whether the NP may itself be expressed in the relative clause etc. (see e.g. Keenan 1985). None of these directly concerns issues of pivots or grammatical relations, and will not be discussed here.

4.1.4 *Other constructions*

There are other constructions that involve pivots, usually with the Primary term as the controller. Two will be considered here, reflexives and focus constructions.

The only rule for reflexives in English (and there are exceptions) is that the reflexive pronoun must have a coereferential NP within the same clause. This coreferential NP is often Subject or Object, but can be a peripheral relation with a preposition, including the Indirect Object with *to*:

> The boy neglected himself
> He told her about herself
> He said something to her about herself
> He took from her a picture of herself

Generally, the coreferential NP precedes the reflexive, but the reflexive can come first if it has been moved to sentence-initial position for emphasis:

> Himself, the boy neglected

In many languages only the Subject can be the controller. This is so in Korean (Shibatani 1973: 292):

> ai-nun   sonye-lul caki-uy pang-eyse cha-ess-ta
> child + TOP girl + ACC self-'s   room-LOC kick-PAST-INDIC
> 'The child kicked the girl in his room'

(In spite of the gloss 'TOPIC', Shibatani identifies the first NP as the Subject.) This cannot mean 'The child kicked the girl in her room'. The reflexive target here is a possessive; English has no possessive forms of reflexive pronouns, no **himself's* etc., but uses a simple possessive or *his own* etc. instead.

There is one interesting complication in Korean: a reflexive in a subordinate clause may refer either to the Subject of that clause or to the Subject of the main (matrix) clause:

> Kimssi-nun   ku sonye-eykey caki-uy pang-ey
> Mr Kim + TOP the girl + DAT   self-'s   room-to
> iss-u-ta-ko a   yocheng-ha-ess-ta
> be + INDIC + COMPL request-do-PAST + INDIC
> 'Mr Kim requested the girl to be in his own/her own room'

(Contrast this with the very unlikely English sentence *??He asked the girl to talk about himself.*)

Similarly, only Subjects can be controllers in Malayalam (India, Dravidian, Mohanan 1982: 566) and Hindi (Kachru et al. 1976: 87):

> raajaawə   swaṇṭam bhaaryaye nulli
> king + NOM self's   wife-ACC   pinched
> 'The king pinched his own wife'
>
> lərka əpne   ghər gəya
> boy his own home went
> 'The boy went to his (own) home'

Kachru et al. provide evidence that Direct and Indirect Objects cannot be the coreferential NPs (triggers) for reflexives. However, they also show that there are other subject-like NPs ('dative subjects', ergative NPs, and 'modal subjects' in the instrumental case), that can function as triggers (see 4.3).

In Lango also (Nilo-Saharan, Uganda, Noonan 1992: 260), the Subject is the controller for reflexivization:

> òkélò òkwàò   àlábâ pÌrÈ   kÉnÊ
> Okelo ask + 3SG + PERF Alaba about + 3SG self + 3SG
> 'Okelo₁ asked Alaba about himself₁'
>
> àlábâ òkélò òkwàò   pÌrÈ   kÉnÊ
> Alaba Okelo ask + 3SG + PERF about + 3SG self + 3SG
> 'Alaba was asked by Okelo, about himself₁,
> ('Alaba, Okelo₁ asked about himself₁')

Yet it was seen in 4.1.1 that Topics, not Subjects, are involved in coordination in Lango.

In Malagasy (Keenan 1976: 263) it is only the Subject of an active construction that may act as controller:

namono tena Rabe
killed   body Rabe
'Rabe killed himself'

The following is impossible:

*novonoin' tena Rabe
was killed body Rabe
'Rabe was killed by himself'

There is a restriction on the target in Bahasa Indonesia (Chung 1983: 223) in that only Objects may be reflexives:

saja me-lihat diri saja dalam air
1SG TRANS-see self 1SG in   water
'I saw myself in the water'

With all other grammatical relations, a pronoun plus the emphatic *sendiri* must be used:

sjahrir men-tjerita-kan sesuatu tjerira kepada dia sendiri
Sjahrir TRANS-tell-BEN a   story to   him EMPH
'Sjahrir told himself a story'

In most languages the reflexive cannot itself be an Agent-Subject. Thus English has no:

*Himself neglected the boy

This is not merely a matter of the normal requirement for the coreferential NP to come first, since the sentence is still impossible if that NP is moved to sentence-initial position for emphasis:

*The boy, himself neglected

However, in Samoan (Chapin 1970: 369), which has an ergative morphological system, the rule is only that the coreferential NP must precede the reflexive. The Agent-Ergative can precede or follow the Patient-Absolutive and it is the first that is the controller and the second the target. Compare (the ergative marker is the 'agentive' marker before the relevant NP):

sa   sogi e   Ioane ia lava
Past cut AGT John himself
'John cut himself'

sa   sogi Ioane e   ia lava
PAST cut John AGT self
'*Himself cut John'

Examples of focus constructions involving pivots can be found in Mam (Mayan, England 1983: 4–7, cf. England 1988: 532). This language has an ergative system of verbal agreement, and in unfocused constructions the verb phrase occurs initially:

a   tz-uul   xiinaq
ASP 3SG + ABS-arrive man
'The man arrived'

ma chi   kub' t-tzyu-ʔn   xiinaq qa-cheej
ASP 3PL + ABS DIR   3SG + ERG-grab-DS man   PL-horse
'The man grabbed the horses'

Focusing involves movement to sentence-initial position, but only Absolutives, not Ergatives, may be focused:

qa-cheej xhi   kub' t-tzyu-ʔn   xiinaq
PL-horse ASP + 3PL + ABS DIR   3SG + ERG-grab-DS man
'The man grabbed *the horses*'

Here the Absolutive (Patient) 'the horses' is 'focused, or given contrastive emphasis'. The Ergative (Agent) cannot be similarly focused by preposing it to initial position, but the Agent can be focused if it is first promoted to Absolutive through the antipassive (though there is also another focusing device):

xiinaq x-ø-kub'   tzyuu-n   t-e   qa-cheej
man   ASP-3SG-DIR grab-ANTIP 3SG-OBL PL-horse
'The *man* grabbed the horses'

This is true also of the focused negative:

miyaaʔ xiinaq x-ø-kub'   tzyuu-n   t-e   qa-cheej
NEG   man   ASP-3SG-DIR grab-ANTIP 3SG-OBL PL-horse
'It wasn't the man who grabbed the horses'

Similarly with the interrogative, an interrogative pronoun cannot be Ergative, so that, if the Agent is questioned, the antipassive is required to promote it to Absolutive:

    alkyee x-ø-kub'   tzyuu-n   t-e   qa-cheej
    who ASP-3SG-DIR grab-ANTIP 3SG-OBL PL-horse
    'Who grabbed the horses?'

A more general discussion of focus in Mayan languages is to be found in Aissen 1992.

4.2 Syntax vs. morphology

    It was seen in 3.2 that a language may be ergative in one aspect of its morphology (marking on the noun), but accusative in another (agreement with the verb). It is similarly possible for a language to be ergative in its morphology (noun or verb or both), but accusative in its syntax, i.e. in the choice of pivots.

In fact, there are probably very few languages that are as fully ergative as Dyirbal, with both ergative marking on the noun and ergatively determined pivots for omission in coordination and complementation and for relativization, together with the regular use of the antipassive, to overcome the restrictions.

For example, Basque has ergative morphology in both its nominal marking and agreement with the verb, but accusative syntax for omission of a coreferential NP in complementation. That Basque has ergative noun morphology and verbal agreement is shown by (Brettschneider 1979: 376, 378):

    Gizona   etorri d-a
    Man + ABS come 3SG-AUX
    'The man has come'

    gizona   ikusi d-u-t
    man + ABS see   3SG + ABS-AUX-1SG + ERG
    'I have seen the man'

Deletion of the NP in complementation is illustrated by:

    Nai   dut   neska   ikusi
    desire I have girl + ABS see
    'I want to see the girl'

    Nai   dut   gelditu
    desire I have stay
    'I want to stay'

In these last two examples the deleted NP ('I') is A in the first sentence and S in the second. Conversely, Basque does not permit the deletion of coreferential P, in the subordinate clause, as Dyirbal does; if P is coreferential with the NP in the main clause, it is represented by a pronoun and a different construction, using the subjunctive and a full (finite) subordinate clause, is required (as it would be in French or Italian):

> nai   dut,   neska-k ni   ikusi n-a-za-ø-u
> desire I have girl-ERG I-ABS see   1SG + ABS-TNS-AUX-3SG + ERG-SUBJ
> 'I want the girl to see me'

Deletion of A or S, but not P, is the mark of an accusative system.

Tzotzil (Mexico, Foley and Van Valin 1985: 313) has an ergative system of verbal agreement, but organizes deletion in coordinate sentences along accusative lines, as shown by:

> A   li   Petal e bat-em-ø   ta xobel
> TOP ART Peter go-PERF-3SG + ABS to town
> s-max-ox-ø   li   Anton e
> 3SG + ERG-hit-PAST-3SG + ABS ART Anton
> 'Peter went to town and hit Anton'

For the two verbs glossed as 'go' and 'hit', it may be observed that the Agent of the transitive 'hit' is in the ergative case (marked, in the third person by the *s*-), while the Patient is in the absolutive case (marked by *ø*), and that this (the absolutive) is also the case of the single term S with intransitive 'go'; the verbal agreement is clearly ergative. Yet, as in the English translation, the Agent ('Peter'), which is coreferential with S in the first clause, is deleted in the second clause of the coordinated structure. Deletion of the Patient is possible only after passivization:

> A   li   Petal e bat-em-ø   ta xobel max-bil-ø
> TOP ART Peter go-PERF-3SG + ABS to town hit-PASS-3SG + ABS
> yuʔun li   Anton
> by   ART Anton
> 'Peter went to town and was hit by Anton'

Deletion of A, but not of P, when coreferential with S, shows that the system is accusative; the use of the passive is further evidence of this (see 6.6).

Slightly different is the situation in Kâte (New Guinea, Anderson 1976: 14). Here a series of verbs may be coordinated, but the coreferential NP is expressed immediately before the last one, and this verb alone is marked for person agreement. Deletion is thus 'retrogressive' rather than 'progressive'. Yet the rules for deletion are again in accusative terms, as shown by:

> vale-la   be?-ko nana na-ve?
> come-PAST pig-ERG taro eat-3SG + PAST
> 'The pig came and ate taro'

> vale-la   nana na-la   be?   guy fo-ve?
> come-PAST taro eat-PAST pig + ABS sleep lie-3SG + PAST
> 'The pig came, ate taro and lay down to sleep'

The deleted terms are S (with 'came'), coreferential with A ('ate') in the first example, and both S (with 'came') and A (with 'ate'), coreferential with S (with 'lay down') in the second.

Warrungu (Australia) appears to be very similar to Dyirbal in having an ergative morphological system, generally omitting coreferential terms in coordination along ergative lines and in using the antipassive to convert A to derived S for that purpose. Yet the rules for omission in coordination are not absolutely strictly along ergative lines. In what he calls 'purposive constructions', many of which would be translated as coordinated, Tsunoda merely states that ergative patterns are far more common than accusative ones. But accusative patterns occur: an example of the omission of A = S is (Tsunoda 1988: 644):

> kalu-ø   yani-ø yuray-yuray-ø pangkarra-ø palpa-n
> mouse-ABS go-P/P quiet-quiet-ABS lizard-ABS   roll-P/P
> 'The mouse sneaked up and rolled the lizard'

Here the syntax is accusative. It would seem that in Warrungu the syntax is commonly, but not exclusively, ergative. Ergativity is not absolute, but a matter of degree.

Accusative syntax in coordination, with omission of the coreferential term, is also found with a language whose morphology is neither simply accusative nor simply ergative. As was seen in 3.4, in Diyari (Australia), part of the morphology follows an ergative pattern, part follows an accusative pattern and for part of it there are three different markers for S, A and P. Yet Diyari follows an accusative pattern, linking A and S, in coordination. One type of coordination is that expressed by 'implicative clauses' which indicate that the action resulted from the previous action. Such clauses are marked morphologically as having the same Subject (SS) or a different Subject (DS) in a switch reference system (see 4.1.1); for this purpose 'Subject' means A and S – the syntax is accusative, as illustrated by (Austin 1981a: 194):

ŋawu   ŋaḍaŋi mingi-yi wakada   ŋiŋa   ŋanda-ḷa
3sg + fem + s behind run-pres neck + abs 3sg + fem + o hit-impl + ss
'She ran behind and hit him on the neck'

There is a final theoretical point. All the examples are of languages with ergative noun morphology and/or verbal agreement, but accusative syntax. The converse, accusative morphology with ergative syntax, does not seem to occur, except where there is a split, as in Dyirbal, where the first and second person pronouns have accusative morphology, but other NPs have ergative morphology.

4.3 Pivots and 'dative subjects'

There was a discussion in 2.5 of constructions in which experiencers and 'modal subjects' are represented not as Agents-Subjects, but as Datives. It was shown there that, in spite of their morphology, these Datives often have some of the characteristics of Subjects (and are called 'dative subjects'), and it was briefly mentioned that they may also act as pivots.

Simple and clear examples of Datives as pivots are to be found in Icelandic. With coordination, the Dative may be either the controller or the target for deletion of the term in the second clause, as illustrated by (Rognvaldsson 1982: 470):

þeim   líkar   maturinn og borða   mikið
they + dat like + 3sg the food   and eat + 3pl much
'They like the food and eat a lot'

þeir   sjá stúlkuna og finnst   hún álitleg
they + nom see the girl   and find + 3sg she attractive
'They see the girl and find her attractive'

In the first sentence, the deleted NP is the nominative Subject of 'eat' in the second clause and coreferential with the Dative NP in the first. In the second, the deleted NP would have been a Dative, since 'find' requires the finder to be in the dative case (with the entity found in the nominative), and coreferential with the (nominative) Subject in the first clause.

Similarly, Datives function as pivots in complementation. Examples of Datives as controllers in Russian and Khinalug (Caucasian, Comrie, 1978: 345) are:

> mne   nado   uiti
> I + DAT necessary to go
> 'I must go'

> Hinu   pʰšä   q'izi   muxwižmä
> she + DAT bread + ABS to bake can
> 'She can bake bread'

Here the NPs with which the deleted NPs in the complement clause are coreferential are in the dative case.

One of the most detailed accounts of this feature is to be found in the account given for Hindi by Kachru et al. (1976: 86–91). Here also Datives may act as pivots, although the issue of pivots in Hindi affects grammatical relations other than Datives. Hindi, it will be recalled (3.3.1), has split ergativity according to tense; depending on the tense, the Subject of the accusative system or the Ergative of the ergative system functions as a pivot. In addition there is a construction in which a 'modal subject' is in the instrumental case. This too may function as a pivot. Four types of grammatical relation are, then, involved: Subject, Ergative, Dative and Instrumental. These are illustrated in the basic sentences:

> lərke   kitab pərh-rəha hɛ
> boy(SUBJ) book read-ing   is
> 'The boy is reading a book'

> lərke ne   kitab pərhī
> boy ERG book read
> 'The boy read a book'

> lərke ko   mā   yad   aī
> boy DAT mother memory came
> 'The boy remembered his mother'

> lərke se   kitab nə pərhi gəī
> boy INSTR book not read went
> 'The boy could not read a book'

That a Subject may act both as controller and a target is shown by:

> ram   ghər jana cahta hɛ
> Ram home to go wants
> 'Ram wants to go home'

Examples of each of the other three acting as controller for deletion in complements (but of two different complement types) are:

> lərke ne ghər jana caha
> Boy ERG home to go wanted
> 'The boy wanted to go home'

> sīta ko vəhā jane kī bat yad hɛ
> Sita DAT there going poss. matter memory is
> 'Sita remembered going there'

> ram se vəha jane kī bat bətaī nə gəī
> Ram INSTR there going poss. matter related NEG went
> 'Ram could not tell about going there'

Ergatives and Datives, but not Instrumentals, may act as targets:

> ram ne pətr likhne kī bat bətaī
> Ram ERG letter writing poss. matter related
> 'Ram told of writing the letter'

> ram ne bhūkh ləgne kī bat bətaī
> Ram ERG hunger appearing poss. matter related
> 'Ram told of being hungry'

The deleted NP (*Ram* in each case) would have been Ergative (with past tense) and Dative (experiencer with 'be hungry') respectively.

There is more discussion of similar features, e.g. of what they call 'conjunction reduction', where apparently participial forms are used as temporal clauses. Subjects may be controllers or targets, as in:

> pər ke nīce bɛth kər lərka kitab pər̥h-rəha hɛ
> tree below sitting boy book read-ing is
> 'The boy sitting under the tree is reading a book'

Ergatives may similarly act as both controllers and targets, but Datives and Instrumentals function only as controllers. There is also evidence that all the four relations discussed function as controllers for reflexivization, although, unlike the situation in English, Objects and Indirect Objects do not (see 4.1.3). It is stated, further, that there are similar features of Subjects in Punjabi and Kashmiri.

Andrews (1985: 101, 108) argues that dative-marked NPs discussed are shown by the syntax to be Subjects, and Kachru et al. similarly suggest that all the types of case-marked NPs that they considered are, indeed, Subjects.

This is not altogether helpful or convincing. For the Dative, and the Instrumental in Hindi, there are four reasons for not treating them as Subjects:

(i)   It is more sensible to distinguish two different systems, one primarily morphological, the other syntactic. Grammatical relations such as Subject are established by morphology, pivots by syntax; little is gained by confusing the two.

(ii) Grammatical relations such as Subject are best seen as terms within the clause, whereas pivots extend over more than one clause.

(iii) Confusion is inevitable when sentences with these putative Subjects also have morphologically marked Subjects, as in the Icelandic example (Andrews 1985: 107 – see 2.5):

mér   líka   þeir
I + DAT like + PL they (MASC + PL + NOM)
'I like them'

Andrews (1985: 101) actually suggests (for Hindi, where unfortunately the morphology does not distinguish Subject and Object) that with 'remember', since the (dative) experiencer is the Subject, the other term (the person remembered) is the Object, though he confesses that there is 'little positive evidence' for it.

(iv) The Datives and Instrumentals of Hindi do not have all the features of Subjects (neither acts as target for 'conjunction reduction' and the Instrumental cannot be target for deletion in complements). This makes them only partially 'Subjects': there is no problem if they are merely treated as pivots, for 'pivot' is not a unitary notion – there are usually various types of pivot within a single language.

Some scholars, e.g. Anderson (1976), have similarly argued that, even for languages with ergative morphology, if there is accusative syntax, this established the Ergative as the Subject. An obvious attraction of this proposal is that the Ergatives are Agents, like Subjects, in transitive constructions. Again the best counter-argument is that the two systems should be kept apart and that pivots should not be identified with Subjects. Moreover, there are grave difficulties in applying the argument to languages such as Dyirbal that have ergative syntax. Either such languages must be regarded as exceptional in their choice of pivots, in spite of the fact that it follows the same (ergative) lines as the morphology, or it must be said that it is the Patient-Absolutive, not the Agent-Ergative, that is the Subject, in spite of the fact that Subjects are generally Agents, even in those languages, discussed above, which have ergative morphology, but accusative syntax (see Croft 1991: 24ff. for a discussion). Clearly the suggestion that languages may have two (or more) distinct systems is preferable to an attempt to reduce them to one.

4.4 Imperatives

Imperatives are dealt with here because they appear to follow rules similar to those for pivots, in that there is deletion of the Subject (in accusative languages) as in:

> Hold the handle!
> Come in!

Dixon (1979: 112–14) suggests, however, that it is a universal property of imperatives that they have a second person pronoun that is either A or S (the grammatical roles), since with an imperative, the speaker requests the addressee to act as an agent. It follows, he suggests, that the deletion of A and S in a language is no evidence for it being either accusative or ergative.

This proves, however, not to be entirely true. It is, of course, natural that the second person pronouns (deleted or not) should be agents, but this is essentially a semantic or pragmatic constraint, not a grammatical one. The only grammatical rule in English is that the Subject be deleted, and there is no grammatical restriction on the deletion of P. This is shown by the fact that imperatives can be in the passive with passive Subjects (i.e. Patients) deleted, as in:

> Be persuaded by your friends
> Be guided by your conscience

Such passives are fairly rare and even with these there is some notion of agency, in the sense that the addressee is asked to make a decision to be persuaded or guided, but that does not affect the simple fact that the deleted NP is always a Subject, but not always A or S.

Dixon makes a similar claim for jussives, as in:

> I ordered him to go
> I told him to bring the water

111

Again, however, passive Subjects may be deleted:

> I asked you to be persuaded by your friends
> I told you to be guided by your conscience

The situation in Dyirbal, with its ergative syntax, is relevant, too. With jussives the usual role for complements applies: only the Absolutive may be deleted. This means that generally, with transitive complements, the antipassive is required, to promote the Ergative-Agent to Absolutive as in (Dixon 1979: 129 – see 4.1.2):

> ŋana yabu   giga-n   ɲuma-gu buṛal-ŋay-gu
> we   mother + ABS tell-PAST father-DAT see-ANTIP-PURP
> 'We told Mother to watch father'

The rule of deletion here affects the ergative primary relation, the Absolutive P = S, not A = S, even though it would probably be usual for the deleted term to be a notional agent.

The situation with imperatives in Dyirbal is less simple (Dixon 1972: 111). The pronoun 'you' may be either omitted or retained, and it can be either S or A:

> (ŋinda) bani
> (you)   come
> '(You) come'

> balan ḍugumbil ɲinayma
> CL   woman   marry
> 'Marry the woman'

To this extent Dyirbal does not follow the ergative pattern, but Dixon also notes that, with transitives, the antipassive may be used (though it is not obligatory and he also says (1980: 457) that it is seldom found), to promote A to the primary status as in:

> ŋinda bagul   yaṛa-gu bagal-ŋa
> you   CL + DAT man-DAT hit-ANTIP
> 'You hit the man'

Thus, it is clear that in Dyirbal deletion with jussives follows ergative lines, and there is some indication of ergativity with imperatives. It seems, therefore, that there is no absolute universal requirement for the second person of imperatives (or jussives) to be A or S and that the accusative/

ergative distinction is still applicable to imperatives in some degree and wholly to jussives.

Just as there is a natural, semantically based, tendency for the Agent of transitive sentences, rather than the Patient (with passivization), to be deleted in imperatives and jussives in languages like English, so it is natural that with intransitives, imperatives and jussives (deleting S) are most likely with 'agentive' verbs. It would be unusual to say:

> Grow tall!
> He told him to grow tall

Yet even these sentences are not wholly impossible and are, therefore, not ungrammatical (as argued in 3.5.4). Moreover, there is nothing odd about:

> Sleep well!

4.5   Pivots in an agentive system

Just as languages may have accusative and ergative syntax, theoretically they may have agentive syntax, and this seems to be the case for E. Pomo, which has an agentive morphological system (3.5.3). Coordination in E. Pomo involves both deletion of a coreferential NP and switch reference, but a condition on deletion or 'SAME' marking (see below) in the switch reference system depends upon the two coreferential NPs having the same grammatical relation, just as in accusative and ergative systems they must both be Subjects or Absolutives respectively. In an agentive system the two grammatical relations are (see 3.5) Agentive $S_A = A$ and Patientive $S_P = P$, and deletion and 'SAME' marking in E. Pomo generally require that the two coreferential NPs are both Agentive or Patientive. (Notice that both relations are involved, whereas in accusative and ergative systems only one relation, Subject or Absolutive, is involved.)

McLendon (1978: 7–8) discusses five sentences. The first pair is fairly straightforward:

> há·   kálahu-y   si·má· mérqaki·hi
> I + AGT went home-SAME went to bed
> 'I went home and then went to bed'

> há·   kálahu-qan,   mi·p mérqaki·hi
> I + AGT went home-DIFF he   went to bed
> 'I went home and then he went to bed'

In the first example there would be a coreferential S in both sentences; this is Agentive, since 'go home' and 'go to bed' are both agentive verbs. There is, therefore, deletion and switch reference marking 'SAME'. (The glosses 'SAME' and 'DIFF' are used here rather than 'SS' and 'DS' as in 4.1.1, because the category involved in not Subject.) In the second, the Agentive Ss are not coreferential, so that there is no deletion and the marking is 'DIFF'.

However, if one S is Agentive and the other Patientive, the 'DIFF' marker is used and there is no deletion, even if the NPs are coreferential. In the following examples 'take a bath' and 'come' are agentive, but 'get sick' is patientive:

> há·   xa·qákki-qan,   wi   q'a·lálṭá·la
> I + AGT took a bath-DIFF I + PAT got sick
> 'I took a bath and got sick'

> wi   q'a·lálma-qan, há·   kʰúyhi qóyuhù·
> I + PAT got sick-DIFF   I + AGT didn't come
> 'I got sick, that's why I didn't come'

Much more complex and less easy to explain is:

> mí·pal   kʰí kóx-qan   mu·ṭ'íṭ'ki-y   mu·dála
> he + PAT he + AGT shot-DIFF curl up-SAME die
> 'He₁ shot him₂ and [he₂] curled and [he₂] died'

Here there is deletion, and the rules for deletion clearly follow agentive lines: the S_P of 'curled up' and 'died' are deleted through coreferentiality with the P of 'shot'. Yet the rule for switch reference seems to follow an accusative pattern, for, in spite of the coreferentiality of the P of 'shot' and the S_P of 'curled up' (together with the predictable deletion of the latter), the switch reference marking is 'DIFF', not 'SAME'; this can only be taken to refer to the 'difference' (non-coreferentiality) of the A of 'shot' and the S_P of 'curled up'. If that is so, the syntax is accusative, depending on the sameness or difference of Subjects $A = S$; agentive syntax would have marked the Patientive P and S_P as 'SAME'. On this evidence, it seems that deletion is wholly in agentive terms, but that switch reference is partly accusative.

4.6   The syntactic role of passive and antipassive

It has already been seen that the passive and antipassive play an important role in the syntax of pivots. It was noted, for instance, in 4.1.1,

4.1.2 and 4.1.3 that the passive may be used to promote a secondary or peripheral term to the status of Subject in order to create a new pivot. Thus the Patient (the original Object) may be omitted in coordination in English once it has been promoted to Subject. Compare:

> The man came in and saw the woman
> The man came in and was seen by the woman

Passivization is essential in the second sentence to promote the Object to Subject, where it may act as pivot and be deleted, in view of the impossibility of deleting the Object:

> The man came in and the woman saw [the man]

It was also seen that in an exactly parallel, but converse, way the Agent may be promoted to the status of Primary relation of Absolutive in the ergative system of Dyirbal (Dixon 1979: 62–3), as shown by:

> ŋuma   banaga-ɲu yabu-ŋgu   buɽa-n
> father + ABS return-PAST mother-ERG saw-PAST
> 'father returned and mother saw (him) (was seen by mother)'

> ŋuma   banaga-ɲu buɽal-ŋa-ɲu   yabu-gu
> father + ABS return-PAST see-ANTIP-PAST mother-DAT
> 'Father returned and saw mother'

In the first sentence it is the Patient that is deleted, because it is the P = S, not A, that is the Primary relation. The use of the Antipassive in the second sentence promotes the Agent (originally marked by the ergative) to the status of the Absolutive Primary relation, where it may be deleted, while the Patient is demoted to the oblique status of Dative.

However, some languages do not have passive or antipassives, and so cannot promote non-Primary relations to create new pivots. Where there are rules for pivots, they are dependent, therefore, on grammatical roles such as Agent rather than grammatical relations such as Subject and Absolutive. (According to Foley and Van Valin (1984: 115ff., 1985: 305), they do not have 'pragmatic' pivots, but only 'semantic' pivots.)

A language may also have a passive yet not use it to create new pivots. This, it has been suggested, is so in many Bantu languages, e.g. Chichewa (see the discussion in Foley and Van Valin 1985: 329–31, quoting Trithart 1979). Trithart argues that the passive is used not to create pivots, but in order to satisfy hierarchical rules for the choice of Subject, the hierarchy being:

> 1st person > 2nd person > proper human > common
> human > animate > inanimate

A similar use of the passive was noted (for Korean) in 2.2. It is of relevance that coreferentiality is clearly marked in Chichewa by the fact that there are obligatory Subject and Object suffixes on the verb, and that these differ according to the many different classes of noun with which they agree. An example from Watkins 1937 (quoted by Foley and Van Valin 1985: 331) is:

> Chámkɔlέ   chá-nú   cháchí-kú·rú chí-tha:β-a
> hostage + CL6 CL6-your CL6-valuable AGT + CL6-run away-INDIC
> á-chí-gwir-á   ni mu·nthu
> AGT + CL1-PAT + CL6-catch-INDIC is person + CL1
> 'Your valuable hostage is running away and the man is catching him'

With this system of agreement, rules for pivots together with the use of the passive in order to indicate coreferentiality seem unnecessary.

5
Passive

The passive was briefly discussed in 1.4. In this chapter and the next various kinds of passives and similar constructions are examined in more detail.

5.1 The identification of the passive

A simple and obvious type of passive is illustrated by (see 1.4.1):

The policemen caught the thief
The thief was caught by the policemen

Commonly the Subject of the active sentence is omitted in the passive:

The boy was hit

Sentences such as these are referred to as 'agentless passives'. It is important to note that in English it is not possible simply to omit the Subject of the active sentence to produce:

*Caught the thief

If the Agent is not to be mentioned the passive must be used.

If the passive is a typologically valid category, it must, like all such categories, be identified (i) in terms of the meaning or function it shares across languages, and (ii) in terms of its formal marking in individual languages. (For a discussion see Palmer 1986: 2–7.) It can be said that the basic functions of the passive are the promotion of the Patient (or non-Agent) and the demotion or deletion of the Agent (but see 6.7). This does not involve the acceptance of a particular syntactic theory, but merely implies that the functions of the roles of Agent, Patient etc. in the passive can be accounted for in terms of variation from their functions in the active sentence. It is the recognition that the Agent is the Subject and the Patient is the Object in the active sentence and that the active is the basic construction (see 3.1), while the Patient (or non-Agent) is the Subject and the Agent has peripheral status or is

117

absent in the passive sentence, that makes it possible to talk about the promotion of the Patient to Subject and the demotion or deletion of the Agent.

As already argued, the passive must have some formal marking, and it seems generally true that there is marking on the verb. Haspelmath (1990: 26–7) argues that there are no passive constructions without passive verbal morphology, but, provided 'verbal morphology' is used widely to include clitics, this may be no more than a part of the definition of passive rather than an empirical observation. Traditionally the terms 'active', 'passive' and 'voice' (the grammatical category that subsumes both) have been used to refer to specific paradigms of classical languages, especially Latin and Greek. They have, that is to say been used morphologically, and there are many languages in which the passive is marked in the morphology of the verb, to create what Keenan (1985: 250ff.) calls 'strict morphological passives'. In others, however, it is marked by auxiliary verbs (Keenan's 'periphrastic passives'); these verbs, Keenan suggests (257–61) are of four kinds: (i) verbs of being or becoming, (ii) verbs of reception, (iii) verbs of motion and (iv) verbs of experiencing. He gives as examples of each:

German	Hans wurde von seinem Vater bestraft
	Hans became 'by' his father punished
	'Hans was punished by his father'
Welsh	Caffodd Wyn ei rybuddio gan Ifor
	got Wyn his warn + INF by Ifor
	'Wyn was warned by Ifor'
Hindi	murgi mari gayee
	chicken killed went
	'The chicken was killed'
Vietnamese	Quang bi (Bao) ghet
	Quang suffer (Bao) detest
	'Quang is detested (by Bao)'

A discussion of the historical origins of passives is to be found in Haspelmath 1990.

It would not be entirely unreasonable to suggest that the terms 'voice', 'passive' etc. should be restricted to morphological passives and not used to refer to the 'periphrastic passives' of English and other languages. This would, however, be purely a terminological point and would not suggest that only morphological passives should be the topic of study. The suggestion would be that the terms themselves should be restricted to the morphological categories and that some other, wider, terms should be used to include the periphrastic passives of English and other languages (as well as the morphological passives). This would be consonant with the use of the terms 'mood' and 'modality' (see Lyons 1977: 848, Palmer 1986: 21–4), by which 'mood' is restricted to the category expressed in the morphology of the verb, while 'modality' is used more widely, to include e.g. the category in English that is expressed by modal verbs. However, this is not a practicable suggestion, both because there is no alternative term available and because the terms are in regular use to refer to the category in English and other languages as well as Latin, Greek etc.

5.2 Promotion of Object

The prototypical promotion of Object to Subject in English by the passive was illustrated in the last section. In this section, some rather different and more controversial examples are discussed.

There are some verbs in English that do not appear to have passives, e.g. HAVE (in the sense of possession) and RESEMBLE.

> John has a lot of property
> *A lot of property is had by John

This is also true of CONTAIN in a stative sense, but not in a dynamic sense:

> This jar contains sugar
> *Sugar is contained by this jar
> The rebel forces contained the army
> The army was contained by the rebel forces

Equally, verbs such as WEIGH may passivize when their 'objects' refer to the items weighed, but not to the measurement:

> The shopkeeper weighed the potatoes
> The potatoes were weighed by the shopkeeper
> The potatoes weighed five kilos
> *Five kilos were weighed by the potatoes

It would appear that passivization is restricted to verbs with dynamic meaning – where some action is involved. Yet this is not entirely true; OWN has a passive, even though it differs little in meaning from HAVE:

> The church owns a lot of property
> A lot of property is owned by the church

One way of dealing with this problem is to say that the NP after the verb is not an Object. Apart from the lack of passivization, the arguments are not notionally patients, but locatives or terms of measurement (often called 'adjuncts'). However, that is not an entirely valid argument, since, as will be seen in 5.3, promotion by passivization is not a test of 'Object-hood'. It might be more appropriate to recognize another type of (grammatical) argument, which occupies the place of the Object with an active verb, yet is (a) not affected by passivization, and (b) does not have the notional role of patient.

However, if availability for promotion is taken to establish such NPs as Objects, there is considerable varition in languages in respect of the notional roles of the NPs that may function as Objects. Thus, in Arabic both temporal and locative NPs are marked morphologically as Objects and can be promoted to Subject by passivization (Davison 1980: 51–2):

> Ṣāma zaydun   ramaḍāna
> fasted Zayd + NOM Ramadan + ACC
> 'Zayd fasted (during) Ramadan'

> Ṣīma   ramaḍanu
> fasted + PASS Ramadan + NOM
> 'Ramadan was fasted'

> Jalasa zaydun   ʔamāma   al-amīri
> sat   Zayd + NOM front + ACC the-prince + GEN
> 'Zayd sat (in) front of the prince'

> Julisa   ʔamāmu   al-ʔamīri
> sat-PASS front + NOM the-prince + GEN
> '*The front of the prince was sat'

Similarly in Sanskrit (Davison 1980: 52):

> Ratho   grāmaṃ   gacchati
> cart + NOM village + ACC go + 3SG + PRES
> 'The cart is going (to) the village'

> Rathena   grāmo   gamyate
> cart + INSTR village + NOM go + PASS + 3SG + PRES
> '*The village is being gone to by the cart'

There would be nothing very strange about the passives, if it were accepted that the temporal and locative NPs are Objects in the active sentences.

In Kinyarwanda (Bantu) all kinds of notional roles may be similarly identified as Objects. Unlike their translational equivalents in English, the verbs 'have', 'weigh' etc. all have passives; 'have' is exemplified in (Kimenyi 1980: 127–8):

> Ishaâti i-ti-e   ibifuungo bibiri
> shirt   it-have-ASP buttons   two
> 'The shirt has two buttons'

> Ibifuungo bibiri bi-fit-w-e   n'îshaâti
> buttons   two   they-have-PASS-ASP by shirt
> '*Two buttons are had by the shirt'

Similar, but more surprising, perhaps are the passives in (Kimenyi 1988: 361–2):

> Umugóre a-rwaa-ye   umútwe
> woman   she-be sick-ASP headache
> 'The woman has a headache'

> Umútwe u-rwaa-w-e   n'ûmugóre
> headache it-be sick-PASS-ASP by woman
> 'It is the woman that has a headache'

> Umugóre y-á-báa-ye   perezida
> woman   she-PAST-be-ASP president
> 'The woman became president'

> Perezida y-a-baa-w-e   n'ûmugóre
> president he-PAST-be-PASS-ASP by woman
> 'It is the woman who became president'

> Umugabo a-ra-geend-a   ijoro
> man   he-PRES-travel-ASP night
> 'The man is travelling in the night'

> Ijoro ri-ra-geend-w-a   n'ûmugabo
> night it-PRES-travel-PASS-ASP by man
> 'It is the man who is travelling in the night'

(Kimenyi does not explain why he uses the translations beginning with 'It is the woman/man who . . . '; the obvious implication is that the Agent is focused by passivization.) He notes that 'all semantic roles, patients, datives,

121

benefactives, manners, instrumentals, goals, locatives, temporals, attributives . . . , function as direct objects'.

Often a verb has what seem to be two Objects (including the types just discussed) and either may be promoted:

Umugóre a-r-éerek-a   ábáana amashusho
woman   she-PRES-show-ASP children pictures
'The woman is showing pictures to the children'

Abáana ba-r-éerek-w-a   amashusho n'ûmugóre
children they-PRES-show-PASS-ASP pictures   by woman
'The children are being shown pictures by the woman'

Amashusho a-r-éerek-w-a   ábáana n'ûmugóre
pictures   they-PRES-show-PASS-ASP children by woman
'The pictures are being shown to the children by the woman'

Umugóre a-kubis-e úmwáana urúshyi
woman   she-hit-ASP child   palm
'The woman has just slapped the child'

Umwáana a-kubis-w-e   urúshyi n'ûmugóre
child   he-hit-PASS-ASP palm   by woman
'The child has just been slapped by the woman'

Urúshyi ru-kubis-w-e úmwáana n'ûmugóre
palm   it-hit-PASS-ASP child   by woman
'A slap has just been given to the child by the woman'

Umugaanga a-ru-vuur-a   umugóre ínkôróra
doctor   he-PRES-cure-ASP woman   cough
'The doctor is treating the woman's cough'

Umugóre a-ra-vuur-w-a   ínkôróra n'ûmugaanga
woman   she-PRES-cure-PASS-ASP cough   by doctor
'*The woman is being treated the cough by the doctor'

Inkôróra i-ra-vuur-w-a umugóre n'ûmugaanga
cough   it-PRES cure woman   by doctor
'*The cough is being treated woman by the doctor'

Treating these in terms of constructions with two Objects entails the recognition of the construction Subject + Object + Object as well as the usual transitive Subject + Object. It might be claimed that these are not Objects but various kinds of oblique relations. There are two arguments against this: (i) they are not formally distinguished from Objects 'proper' in any way: word order provides no criterion, since word order is free, except in that new information comes last, and all can be represented by pronominal infixes in the verb (Kimenyi 1988: 355–6); (ii) Kinyarwanda has oblique relations (Dative, Instrumental and Locative) that are formally marked as such and can be also promoted to Subject (but see 6.6.2). There is equally no evidence to suggest that, when there are two Objects, they can be distinguished as primary and secondary Objects (2.4, but see 6.6.2).

Another language that has a construction with two Objects, either of which may be promoted, is Tigrinya (Ethiopian Semitic, personal research), but this occurs only with the verb 'give':

> Məsgənna nə-Bärhe   mäṣḥaf hibu-wo
> Mesgenna ANIM-Berhe book   gave + 3SG + MASC-3SG + MASC
> 'Mesgenna gave Berhe a book'

> mäṣḥäf nə-Bärhe   bə-Məsgənna tä-wähibu
> book   ANIM-Berhe by-Mesgenna PASS-gave + 3SG + MASC
> 'A book was given to Berhe by Mesgenna'

> Bärhe mäṣḥäf bə-Məsgənna tä-wahibu
> Berhe book   by-Mesgenna PASS-gave + 3SG + MASC
> 'Berhe was given a book by Mesgenna'

It might be thought that the first of the two Objects with its marker prefix *nə-* is, in fact, an Indirect Object/Dative, and that this is an example of promotion of Indirect Object/Dative (see 5.3), but this is not so. The verbal suffix *-wo* marks it as (third person masculine) Direct Object, while the corresponding marker of the Indirect Object would be *-llu*, as in:

> Məesgənna nə-Bärhe mäṣḥäf 'ädigu-llu
> Mesgenna ANIM-Berhe book sold + 3SG + MASC-to + 3SG + MASC
> 'Mesgenna sold Berhe a book'

Here only the Direct Object may be promoted:

> mäṣḥäf nə-Bärhe   bə-Məsgənna tä-'ädigu-llu
> book   ANIM-Berhe by-Mesgenna PASS-sold + 3SG + MASC-to
> + 3SG + MASC
> 'A book was sold to Berhe by Mesgenna'

123

Passive

There is no:

*Bärhe mäṣḥäf bə-Məsgənna tä'adigu
Berhe book by-Mesgenna PASS-sold + 3SG + MASC
'Berhe was sold a book by Mesgenna'

The nominal suffix *nə-* occurs with both Direct and Indirect Objects and is best seen as a marker of animacy.

There is another construction with two Objects in Tigrinya, but only one of them may be promoted. This is the construction in which the second Object indicates a part of the body and the first is marked as animate. Only the Object marked as animate may be promoted:

Məsgənna nə-Məḥrät gäṣ-a ḥarimu-wa
Mesgenna ANIM-Mehret face-3SG + FEM + POSS hit + 3SG + MASC-
3SG + FEM
'Mesgenna hit Mehret in the face'

Məḥrät bə-Məsgənna gäṣ-a tä-ḥarima
Mehret by-Mesgenna face-3SG + FEM + POSS PASS-hit + 3SG + FEM
'Mehret was hit in the face by Mesgenna'

(There is a similar construction in Korean – see 5.6.)

Rather different are the passives in English exemplified by (see Palmer 1987: 215ff.):

The daughter looked after the old man
The old man was looked after by the daughter

In the active *the old man* seems to be part of a prepositional phrase, but, obviously, *look after* is treated as a single verb with *the old man* as its object. This is not surprising with an expression like *look after*, which is idiomatic and cannot be treated as two semantically (or grammatically) separate words (it is a 'phrasal verb'). Similar passives are also possible with idioms such as *do away with, get rid of, put up with*. But passivization is possible with some combinations of verb plus preposition, even though there is no such idiomaticity:

This hat has been sat on
The bed has been slept in

Finally, it should be noted that even if a language has a passive, not all Objects/Patients can be promoted to Subject. Thus it was seen in 2.2 that in

Korean the passive Subject must be 'in general, animate and conscious'. Objects that do not have these characteristics cannot be promoted.

5.3 Promotion of oblique terms

Although the Patient-Object is the term most commonly promoted to Subject, in some languages terms other than Objects, oblique terms, may also be promoted.

The Beneficiary-Dative is often promoted (and it is relevant to note that the Beneficiary was often the promoted term in the double Object constructions of 5.2). An example from Japanese is (Song 1987: 75):

> John wa Mary ni   hon o   atae-ta
> John TOP Mary DAT book ACC give-PAST
> 'John gave a book to Mary'

> Mary wa John ni   hon o   atae-rare-ta
> Mary TOP John DAT book ACC give-PASS-PAST
> 'Mary was given a book by John'

Whether this is also true of English (as the translation given above might suggest) is discussed in 6.6.

More strikingly, Malagasy has a passive voice, but also a 'circumstantial' voice, which promotes both the Beneficiary-Dative and the Instrumental. Examples that were given in 1.4.1 (Keenan 1972: 172–3) are repeated here:

> Nividy   ny vary ho an'ny ankizy   ny vehivavy
> Bought + ACT the rice for the   children the woman
> 'The woman bought the rice for the children'

> Novidin'   ny vehivavy ho an'ny ankizy   ny vary
> bought + PASS the woman   for the   children the rice
> 'The rice was bought by the woman for the children'

> Nividianan'   ny vehivavy ny vary ny ankizy
> bought + CIRC the woman   the rice the children
> 'The children were bought the rice by the woman'

> Nividianan'   ny vehivavy ny vary ny vola
> bought + CIRC the woman   the rice the money
> 'The money was used by the woman to buy the rice'

The verb form indicates whether the Subject is the Agent, the Patient or one of the oblique terms, and the Subject appears in final position. The promoted Subjects ('the rice', 'the children', 'the money') also have the syntactic characteristics of Subjects in that they may function as pivots. They are used as heads of relative clauses, and it may be recalled that in Malagasy it is only Subjects that can be relativized (4.1.3 – the examples are repeated here):

> Ny vary izay novidin'   ny vehivavy ho an'ny ankizy
> the rice REL bought + PASS the woman for the   children
> 'The rice that was bought by the woman for the children'

> Ny ankizy   izay nividianan'   ny vehivavy ny vary
> the children REL bought + CIRC the woman   the rice
> 'The children for whom the rice was bought by the woman'

Similarly, one may assume, it is possible for the promoted Instrumental ('the money') to be the pivot, although Keenan does not give an example.

A very different language that can also promote either the Object or the Instrumental is Kwakwala or Kwakw'ala (Wakashan, British Columbia, Levine 1980: 241, Anderson 1985: 166). Examples are (the glosses are from Anderson, and notice that the suffixes on the NPs indicate the relation of the following NP):

> nəp'id-i-da   gənanəm-xa guk^w-sa   t'isəm
> throw-SUBJ-ART child-OBJ   house-INSTR rock
> 'The child hit the house with a rock by throwing' ('The child threw a rock at the house')

> nəp'id-suʔ-i-da   guk^w-sa   gənanəm-sa t'isəm
> throw-suʔ-SUBJ-ART house-INSTR child-INSTR   rock
> 'The house was hit by a rock thrown by the child'

> nəp'id-ayu-i-da   t'isəm xa guk^w-sa   gənanəm
> throw-ayu-SUBJ-ART rock-OBJ house-INSTR child
> 'The rock was what the child threw at the house' ('The rock was used for throwing at the house by the child')

As with Malagasy, there are two different types of passive, one for the promotion of the Object, the other for the promotion of the oblique with markers -*suʔ*- and -*ayu* respectively. Levine, in fact, argues against a passive interpretation in favour of one in terms of 'focus', but the constructions contain typical passive features, although it is, indeed, the case that there is

some similarity between the systems of Malagasy and Kwakw'ala and those
of 'topic' languages to be discussed in 6.4.

5.4   Impersonal and 'affected' passives

In a number of languages there are passives of intransitive verbs;
examples from Latin, German and Dutch are:

> Pugnatur   uno   tempore
> fight + 3SG + PRES + PASS one + SG + ABL time + SG + ABL
> omnibus   locis   (Caes. *B.G.* 7, 84)
> all + PL + ABL place + PL + ABL
> 'There is fighting at one time in all places'

> Es wurde   im   Nebenzimmer geredet
> it   became in the next room   talked
> 'There was talking in the next room'

> Er wordt   door de jongens gefloten   (Kirsner 1976: 382)
> it   becomes by   the boys   whistled
> 'There is whistling by the boys'

These are often referred to as 'impersonal' passives.

It is almost certain, however, that this type of passive is restricted to what
might be called 'agentive' verbs (see 3.5.4) or what Perlmutter (1978) calls
'unergative', where the single term S is an agent, as contrasted with
'unaccusative', where S is essentially a patient. Perlmutter and Postal (1984:
144) give an example from Welsh with the verb 'dance', but note that Welsh
does not permit the passivization of 'grow':

> Dannswyd gan y   plant
> was danced by   the children
> 'There was dancing by the children'

> *Tyfwyd   gan y   plant   yn sydyn
> was grown by   the children suddenly
> *'There was sudden growing by the children'

Perlmutter (1978: 168–9) also notes, for Dutch, the contrast between the
possible and impossible (see 3.5.4):

> In de zomer   wordt   er hier vaak gezwommen/*verdronken
> in the summer becomes it here often swum/*drowned

The simplest explanation for the fact that generally it is agentive intransitive verbs that are passivized may be found in Shibatani's suggestion (see the discussion in 6.7) that the primary function of the passive is 'defocusing' (which includes deletion) of the agent. Generally it is the Agent-Subject of transitives that is demoted or deleted; with intransitives, S is similarly deleted or demoted, but only if it is an agent. Alternatively, it might also be noted that these agentive verbs have unexpressed 'cognate' Objects ('fight a fight', 'dance a dance' etc), and that in English, one can 'have a fight/a whistle/a dance/a swim', but not '*have a grow/a drown'; notionally at least, these cognate objects might be considered to be the unexpressed Subjects of the passives ('(A fight) was fought' etc.); there is even some grammatical evidence for this in the constructions with the impersonal ('it') Subject, which might suggest the promotion of an unexpressed 'it' (the cognate object) in the active.

Impersonal passives are also found with verbs that have a second argument that is not marked as Object, but as an oblique term (the oblique term is not promoted, as in the examples of 5.3). Thus in Latin INVIDEO ('envy') is followed by the dative, not the accusative, but it has a passive (with the dative NP unchanged):

> invident   homines maxime
> envy + 3PL + + PRES + INDIC + ACT men   most
> paribus   aut   inferioribus (Cic. *de Or.* 2, 52, 209)
> equal + PL + DAT   or   inferior + PL + DAT
> 'Men most envy their equals or inferiors'

> illi,   quibus   invidetur   (Pl. *Truc.* 4, 32, 30)
> this + PL + NOM who + PL + DAT envy + 3SG + + PRES + INDIC + PASS
> 'Those who are envied'

The same is true of German:

> Seine Freunde halfen ihm
> his   friends helped him + DAT
> 'His friends helped him'

> ihm   wurde von seinen Freunden geholfen
> him + DAT became by his   friends   helped
> 'He was helped by his friends'

However, Latin has a number of active impersonal verbs, e.g. OPORTET ('must'), LICET ('is permitted'), all requiring the human or animate NP to be in the dative (*mihi oportet/licet* 'I must/am permitted') (see 2.5); there are also impersonal verbs in German that are followed by the dative (but others that are followed by the accusative). The impersonal passives fall into the same pattern.

It may seem less plausible to suggest that these too have 'cognate' Objects ('envy', 'help'), with the other NP as an Indirect Object/Dative peripheral relation, though that is not altogether impossible, in view of the possible interpretations 'envy was felt', 'help was given'.

There is a similar situation in Icelandic, where some verbs are followed by the dative, others by the genitive (Andrews 1982: 466–7):

þeir björguðu stúlkunni
they rescued   girl + DAT
'They rescued the girl'

stúlkunni var bjargað
girl + DAT was rescued
'The girl was rescued'

við vitjðum Ólafs
we visited   Olaf + GEN
'We visited Olaf'

Ólafs   var vitjað
Olaf + GEN was visited
'Olaf was visited'

Syntactically, the dative or genitive NP in the passive may function as a pivot, and is thus treated as another example of 'dative subject' (Andrews 1985: 122, but see the discussion in 4.3):

mér   var hjálpað
I + DAT was helped
'I was helped'

min   var vitjað
I + GEN was visited
'I was visited'

Ég vonast til   að vera hjálpað/vitjað
I   hope   towards to be   helped/visited
'I hope to be helped'

(But Andrews 1982: 467 says that the last sentence is 'questionable for many speakers'.)

The issue is made more complex by the fact that, in some languages, there appear to be impersonal passives of transitive verbs, in which the Patient remains in the Object position and is not promoted to Subject, e.g. in Irish (Keenan 1985: 275):

> Bhuail si   e
> hit   she him
> 'She hit him'

> Buaileadh (lei) e
> hit + IMPERS PASS (with her) him
> 'She was hit by him'

A similar example from North Russian (Timberlake 1976: 550) is:

> U mena bylo   telenka   zarezano
> at me   be + SG + NEUT calf + ACC + MASC slaughtered + SG + NEUT
> 'The calf was slaughtered by me'

There is a different situation in Japanese (but there are problems concerning both 'Subject' and 'passive', partly because the 'passive' suffix has a number of different, but possibly related functions (see 6.4), and partly because it is not wholly clear which of two particles, one of them usually referred to as 'the topic-marker', indicates the Subject). There are some interesting constructions, particularly that which has been called the 'adversity passive', where the apparent Subject of a verb with passive marking indicates the person adversely affected by the event. This is possible with both intransitive and transitive verbs (Kuno 1973: 23–4):

> Tuma ga   sin-da
> wife NOM die-PAST
> 'The wife died'

> John ga   tuma ni sin-are-ta
> John NOM wife by die-PASS-PAST
> '*John was died by his wife'

> Mary ga   piano o   hi-ita
> Mary NOM piano ACC play-PAST
> 'Mary played the piano'

> John ga   Mary ni piano o   hik-are-ta
> John NOM Mary by piano ACC play-PASS-PAST
> '*John was adversely played the piano by Mary'

These are the adversity passives of 'His wife died' and 'Mary played the piano', with John being adversely affected. In neither case, not even with the transitive, which has an Object in the active, is the Subject of the passive a grammatical relation that has been promoted. Rather, the adversity passive creates an additional argument – just as the causative does; an alternative treatment along these lines is suggested in 9.6. Other examples (Song 1987: 76, using slightly different glosses – the transcription has been modified) are:

> watasi ga doroboo ni zitensya o nusum-are-ta
> I NOM burglar DAT bicycle ACC steal-PASS-PAST
> 'I was subjected to a burglar stealing a bicycle from me'

> John wa ame ni hur-are-ta
> John TOP rain DAT fall-PASS-PAST
> 'John was rained on'

Slightly different is the passive (Song 1987: 75):

> Mary wa John no kao o tatai-ta
> Mary TOP John GEN face ACC hit-PAST
> 'Mary hit John's face'

> John wa Mary ni kao o tatak-are-ta
> John TOP Mary DAT face ACC hit-pass-PAST
> 'John was hit in the face by Mary'

Here it might seem that the possessive ('John's') has been promoted to Subject. But the possessive is not a term in the sentence – not a role or a relation. It would seem, then, that this, too, is best treated as an adversity passive, since a new argument has been created. Song notes that there is a similar construction in Korean, but with a difference in that in the active the possessor may be indicated either in the gentive or, apparently, as a second Object (see 5.2):

> John-ɨn ai-ɨi/lɨl son-ɨl jab-ŏssta
> John-TOP child-GEN/ACC hand-ACC catch-PAST
> 'John grasped the child's hand/the child by the hand'

> ai-nɨn John-ege son-ɨl jab-hi-ŏssta
> child-TOP John-DAT hand-ACC catch-PASS-PAST
> 'The child was subjected to John's grasping his hand' ('The child's hand was held by John'?)

131

Here it might appear that the passive is derived by simply promoting the second Object, but the first Object ('hand') cannot be similarly promoted, so that it may be simpler to treat this in the same way as the previous sentence, i.e. as an adversity passive.

5.5 **Passives and topicalization**

It is wise to exclude change of word order alone as a marker of the passive, even though word order is often the only formal distinction between Subject and Object (and in English it is the most important feature, and the only one that is always present). The reason for excluding word order is that in many languages it is used, independently of passivization, for the purpose of topicalization. Thus, even in English an Object may be placed in initial position for that purpose:

These books, I am giving away

This is not, however, restricted to Objects or even to NPs:

Intelligent, he is not
Yesterday, I was at home

In many languages, including Latin and modern Greek, the position of the arguments in the sentence is relatively free. This is clearly illustrated from Modern Greek (Philippaki-Warburton 1985: 113):

o janis filise ti maria
ti maria filise o janis
filise o janis ti maria
filise ti maria o janis
o janis ti maria filise
ti maria o janis filise
'John kissed Mary'

Here the Subject and the Object (and the verb) occur in all possible sequences, but there is no ambiguity because the Subject (*o janis*) and Object (*ti maria*) are marked morphologically and by their agreement with the verb, but not by word order. Neither the English nor the Greek examples provide examples of passives, but merely of the use of word order for topicalization. There are two points that distinguish such topicalization from passivization: first, the Object does not take on the grammatical markers of the Subject (its morphology and concord with the verb) and secondly, the form of the verb is unchanged. It may also be added that in Greek and English, it does not acquire pivot status. There are, however, marginal and debatable cases. For instance, it was seen in 4.1.1 that in Lango it is the topicalized NP that controls deletion in coordination, but this topicalization is not accompanied by any markers on the verb, and it is the Subject that controls reflexives (4.1.4). In any case, as was argued in 4.3, pivots should not be used as evidence for Subjects, and, a fortiori, they are not evidence for passivization. Another example of a construction about which there has been disagreement is to be found in Acehnese, to be discussed in 6.2.

A little more problematic is the situation in Kinyarwanda (Bantu, Kimenyi 1988: 357–8). This language has passives (discussed in 5.2 and 5.3), but it also has a device for interchanging Subject and Object, but with the additional point that the Object, when moved into Subject position, is the argument that agrees with the verb:

> abagóre ba-a-ri   bâ-teet-se   ibíshyíimbo
> women they-PAST-be they-cook-ASP beans
> 'The women were cooking beans'
>
> ibíshyíimbo by-aa-ri   bî-teet-se   abagóre
> beans   they-PAST-be they-cook-se women
> 'The beans were being cooked by the women'

Agreement with the verb is shown by the prefixes glossed by Kimenyi as 'they'; in the first sentence they are appropriate to the class that includes 'woman', in the second, to the class that includes 'beans'. Kimenyi translates the second as if it were passive, rather than as 'The beans, the women cooked', but it is better treated as a topicalization device rather than a passive, not only because Kinyarwanda has a quite different passive, but, more importantly, because there is, again, no passive marker on the verb. It was noted in 2.6 for Chichewa, another Bantu language, that even locatives may be placed in initial position and agree with the verb. Although agreement marking of topicalized arguments is typologically unusual, these sentences in Kinyarwanda are better treated as examples of topicalization than of passivization. Alternatively, perhaps, an absolute distinction between passivization and topicalization should not be drawn; these constructions of Kinyarwanda have one of the marks of the passive, but lack the more crucial passive marking on the verb.

Another problematic case is provided by Palauan (W. Austronesian, Foley and Van Valin 1985: 316–17). Here what appears to be a passive involves interchange of the positions of Agent and Patient and a set of special prefixes on the verb that agree with the passive Agent. (There is agreement with the Patient in both active and passive, but not, apparently, with the Agent of the active.) Examples are:

    a ʔad a mos-terir   a   ngalek
    ART man see-3PL + HUM ART child
    'The man saw the children'

    a   ngalek a le-bos-terir   a   ʔad
    ART child   PASS + 3SG-see-3PL + HUM ART man
    'The children were seen by the man'

Even oblique terms may, apparently, be promoted:

    a   ngelek-ek a smeʔer er   a   tereter
    ART child-my sick + INTR with ART cold
    'My child is sick with a cold'

    a   tereter a l-seʔer   er   ngiy a   ngelek-ek
    ART cold   PASS + 3SG-sick with 3SG ART child-my
    'With a cold is being sick by my child'

(A better gloss for the last might be 'A cold is being sick with by my child'.) However, these are more like examples of topicalization than of passive: the Patient-Object is unaffected and there is, therefore, no evidence that it is promoted to Subject, and it is not obvious that the special prefix signals demotion of the Agent, since with demotion agreement is usually lost, not gained – it may be that the function of the prefix is merely to make the status of the Agent-Subject explicit, because it has been moved from the usual Subject position.

    However, relativization on the Patient requires this 'passive':

    a   le-bos-terir   a   ʔad el   ngalek
    ART PASS + 3SG-see-3PL + HUM ART man REL child
    'the children which were seen by the man'

It is not possible to say:

    *a ʔad a mos-terir   el   ngalek
    ART man see-3PL + HUM REL child
    'the children which the man saw'

This rather looks like an example of passivization being used to promote the Patient-Object to Subject in a language which permits relativization on

Subjects only (see 4.6). Yet, this merely establishes a syntactic pivot and, as was argued in 4.3, pivots should not necessarily be equated with Subjects.

There is a rather different problem in Dinka (W. Nilotic, T. Andersen 1991), where there are two constructions, both of which have features of passives, as exemplified by (subscripted markers of creaky and breathy voice have been omitted):

> màriàal à-cé   màbòor yûup   (p.278)
> Marial DECL-PERF Mabor beat
> 'Marial has beaten Mabor'

> màbòor à-cîi   yûup è   màriàal
> Mabor DECL-PERF + PASS beat PREP Marial + GEN

> màbòor à-cíi   màriàal   yûup
> Mabor DECL-PERF + NTS Marial + GEN beat

The second example Andersen treats as a passive, and the third in terms of topicalization, with the gloss 'NTS' standing for 'non-topical subject'.

However, the NTS construction shares with the passive three typical features of passives in that (i) the verb forms are different from that of the active (notice the tone markers on the auxiliary elements), (ii) the Patient appears to be promoted in that it is moved to initial position and agrees in number with the verb and (iii) the Agent seems to be demoted, being marked by a preposition plus genitive or simply the genitive and no longer agreeing with the verb. Agreement of the Patient with the verb is not illustrated in the example above, but can be seen in:

> γɔk áa-kuέεl m   môc
> cows DECL + PL-steal + NTS man + GEN
> 'The man is stealing the cows'

Yet there are three differences: (i) only with the passive may the Agent be deleted, (ii) oblique relations and even adverbials such as 'today' may be topicalized (but still show agreement with the verb), (iii) with topicalization, there may be a pronoun coreferential with the Patient after the Agent. (ii) and (iii) are exemplified by:

> áakáal à-thέεt   tìik
> today DECL-cook + NTS woman
> 'The woman is cooking today'

γɔ́k   áa-kueén   dhɔ̀ɔk (kê)
cows DECL + PL-count + NTS boy   (3PL)
'The boy is counting the cows'

('Woman' and 'boy' do not have a distinct genitive form.)

Relativization is on topics, not Subjects, in that relativization on Patients requires the NTS construction, not the passive, as in:

mánh   cíi   jò   câam
child + AGT PERF + NTS dog + GEN eat + NON-FINITE
'The child that the dog has bitten'

This again (as in Palauan) looks very like promotion of Patient to Subject by passivization to meet the requirements for relativization.

The question whether the problematic constructions considered in this section are or are not passives is not one that can have a simple 'Yes/No' answer. The issue of languages with 'topic' systems, which are like passives in some ways, but may be treated rather differently, is the subject of 8.1.

5.6 Functions of the passive

There are several different reasons for the use of the passive in different languages.

(i) It promotes a non-Subject to Subject position to make it available as a syntactic pivot. This use has already been discussed in some detail (4.6).

(ii) Closely associated with this, especially with the use of pivots in coordination, is the promotion of a non-Agent for topicalization. We may compare:

The child ran into the road and was hit by a car
The child ran into the road. He was hit by a car

In the first sentence, there is the grammatical rule that, with coordination, only the Subject may be deleted. In the second, the use of the passive keeps 'the child' as the topic, but the difference is that there is no rule that says that only the Subject may be pronominalized – it would be possible to say:

The child ran into the road. A car hit him

However, the two features can be more closely related if it is said that Subjects are generally topics, so that promotion to Subject provides a new topic, and that it is as topics that Subjects are deleted in coordination.

(However, English has other topicalization devices that are not involved in the syntax of coordination, one of which was discussed in the last section.)

(iii) The passive is often used, with the Agent omitted, where the Agent is unknown, non-specific or unimportant, as in:

> He was killed in the war
> They were persuaded to come

It is for this reason that, as Quirk et al (1985: 166) say, 'it is notably more frequent in the objective, impersonal style of scientific writing and news reporting'. This is also the basis for Shibatani's claim that the primary function of the passive is the defocusing of the Agent (to be discussed in 6.7).

(iv) In some languages the passive is used because there are restrictions, in terms of animacy/agency etc., on the type of entity that may function as the Subject of an active verb. Thus, according to Trithart (1979 – see 4.6), passives are favoured in Bantu languages if they promote to Subject an NP higher on a scale involving human/animate/inanimate. Conversely, as was noted in 2.2, a strong preference for animate Subjects may block the passive in Korean, as in the example quoted by Song:

> John-in ki sakwa-lil mŏg-ŏssta
> John-TOP the apple-ACC eat-PAST
> 'John ate the apple'

> *ki sahwa-nin John-ege mŏg-hi-ŏssta
> the apple-TOP John-DAT eat-PASS-PAST
> 'The apple was eaten by John'

An extreme instance of restrictions upon Subjects and the use of a passive-like device to meet these restrictions is, perhaps, to be found in the inverse languages discussed in 8.2.

Klaiman (1988) argues that the issue in Korean is not one of animacy, but of control. She offers (p. 61), using a different transcription from that of Song, the examples:

> kI yAca-ka cA salamIi tIN-Il kIlk-Assta
> that woman-NOM that man's back + OBJ scratch-PAST
> 'The woman scratched the man's back'

> cA salam-Ii tIN-i kI yAca-eke kIlk-hi-Assta
> the man's back-NOM that woman-by scratch-PASS-PAST
> 'That man's back was scratched by the woman'

While the first sentence may mean that the woman scratched the man's back with or without him being willing, the second can only mean that the man let her scratch his back. In that sense he is in control of the action. However, notions of agency, control, and animacy are conceptually closely linked, and it may be that all or any of them are often involved.

5.7 Varieties of passive

English and other languages may be said to have more than one passive, of which only one is a 'true' passive, as shown by:

> They were married on Saturday
> They were married for many years

The second is a stative passive, expressing the meaning 'they were in the married state'. Similarly, as noted by Nedjalkov and Jaxontov (1988: 47) there is a difference in the two instances of *was shut*, in:

> When I came at five, the door was shut, but I do not know when it was shut.

English uses the same forms for the stative and 'true' passives, as does Russian (*byl zakryt*), but German uses SEIN 'to be' for the stative, but WERDEN 'to become' for the 'true' passive, as shown by their German translation of the English sentence:

> Als ich um fünf kam, war die Tür geschlossen, aber ich weiss nicht, wann sie geschlossen wurde.

P. K. Andersen (1991: 92–5) argues that the passive in English is not a 'passive', but an 'objective resultative', quoting Beedham (1982: 45) – 'the passive sentence portrays both the occurrence of an event and the state that arises from that event'. A difficulty with this claim is that there is no apparent difference, in terms of 'resulting state', between the active and the passive in English. If X killed Y or Y was killed, Y is equally dead. Andersen argues that the resulting state is merely a logical consequence of the event with the active, but that it is formally expressed by the passive, i.e. by means of the passive participle, but this is to extrapolate from the form to the meaning, which can be very misleading. It may be true that the form of the passive seems to contain (for historical reasons) an indication of the notion of state, while the active does not, but it does not follow that, in this respect, either (a) the active and passive differ in meaning or (b) that the passive in English is different from passives in other languages. The extent to which such extrapolation can mislead is illustrated by a quotation by T. Andersen (1991: 102) from Beedham (1982: 91), who suggests that *The house was painted by John* is nearer in meaning to *John has painted the house* than to *John painted the house*, because they 'share the most important semantic features, viz. those of action and state'. That is simply false: they share the formal feature of the participle, but semantically *was painted* corresponds to *painted*, and the passive of *has painted* is *has been painted*. Both the passive and the perfect are now grammatical idioms in English, and their meanings cannot be directly derived from their component parts, without independent semantic evidence.

The situation in German may seem a little more convincing, since the stative appears to say that the door 'was' shut, while the passive says that it 'became' shut. That merely means that the constructions are more transparent, less idiomatic, than the constructions in English. However, if the formal features are taken to be indications of the semantics, it is difficult to understand why the same form in English has two different meanings. What the English and German examples show is that a language may be said to have more than one passive (a 'true' passive and a stative passive in this case), and, further, that these passives may be expressed by the same construction as in English or by different ones as in German.

One meaning that is often accredited to the passive is that of 'potential'. An example from Hindi in Shibatani (1985: 828) is an impersonal passive of an intransitive:

larke se   cal-aa   nahĩĩ ga-yaa
boy INSTR walk-PCPL not   PASS-PAST
'The boy could not walk'

Haspelmath (1990: 33) adds:

(Kanuri)   hâm-ŋin   'I lift up'   háp-tè-skin   'I am liftable'
(Mwera)   com-a   'read'   com-ek-a   'be readable'

Shibatani also notes for Turkish:

Çevap yaz-mak için kâğıt-la   kalem kullan-ıl-ır
answer write-INF for paper-and pen   use-PASS-PRES
'Paper and pencil may be used to write the answer'

However, this is, perhaps, not a distinct type of passive but an implied use of it; even in English 'Paper and pencil are used to write the answer' would be understood as giving permission. An example from Japanese and some reflexive constructions in Spanish and Russian are also given by Shibatani as examples of 'potential' passives, but the Japanese example needs special consideration (in 6.4), while the reflexive constructions, though closely related to passives, are also best discussed separately (in 6.1).

Another possible type is the 'spontaneous' passive. Keenan (1985: 252–3) notes three types of passive in Malagasy (Madagascar):

> a-tsanga-ko   ny lai
> PASS-put up-by me the tent
> 'The tent is put up by me'
>
> voa-tsangana ny lai
> PASS-put up   the tent
> 'The tent is put up'
>
> tafa-tsangana ny lai
> PASS-put up   the tent
> 'The tent is put up'

The first is 'paraphrastic with the active', i.e. the passive proper, while the second is 'unequivocally perfective' and, thus, perhaps, to be regarded as a stative passive. The third, however, suggests that 'the putting up of the tent was almost spontaneous; the conscious activity of the Agent is down-played'. Spontaneity is also claimed by Shibatani for reflexives in Spanish, French, Russian and Quechua (see 6.1).

In theory all kinds of aspectual and other types of meaning may be associated formally-semantically with the passive. One set of such passives is noted by Keenan (1985: 268, quoting an unpublished manuscript) for Kampampangan (Malayo-Polynesian, Philippines), where three different affixes express an inceptive, a progressive and a past perfective passive (though these distinctions appear not to be made in the active); this is not directly relevant to the analysis of the passive. More interesting, perhaps, though still rather peripheral, is the fact that, in some languages, the availability of a number of different verbs to express the passive provides different shades of meaning. Thus Keenan (1985: 260–1) quotes for Vietnamese:

> Quang bi   (Bao) ghet
> Quang suffer (Bao) detest
> 'Quang is detested (by Bao)'
>
> Quang duoc Bao thuong
> Quang 'enjoy' Bao love
> 'Quang is loved by Bao'

A list of the main uses of passive morphemes and languages in which they occur is given by Haspelmath (1990: 36). These include 'passive', 'reciprocal', 'reflexive', 'anticausative', 'passive', 'potential passive' and 'fientive'.

6
Passive: related and problematic issues

The last chapter dealt with the most typical kinds of passive; in this chapter a number of other constructions will be considered.

6.1 Reflexives and indefinites as passives

Many languages have reflexive constructions, i.e. constructions in which the Object is indicated as being referentially identical with the Subject by means of a reflexive pronoun. Examples are the English *wash oneself*, and the equivalent French *se laver* and Russian *myt's'a*.

In a number of languages the same construction is also used as a passive. In Russian, for instance, the passive is formed by using the copula (the verb 'to be') with verbs in the perfective aspect, but by the reflexive form for verbs in the imperfective (Siewerska 1985: 247):

kalitka   byla otkryta   Olegom
gate + NOM was open + PERF + PAST PART Oleg + INSTR
'The gate was opened by Oleg'

kalitka   otkrylas'   Olegom
gate + NOM opened + IMPERF + REFL Oleg + INSTR
'The gate was being opened by Oleg'

In both cases the Object has been promoted to Subject, and is so marked by its morphology and by agreement with the verb, while the original Subject has been demoted to Instrumental.

Reflexives functioning as passives are also found in Romance languages, even though these also have passives formed with the copula, e.g. Spanish and Italian:

se   curó   a los   brujos
REFL cured + SG to the + PL sorcerers + PL
'The sorcerers were cured'

> si comprano due penne
> REFL buy + 3PL two pens
> 'Two pens are bought'

Unlike the Russian examples, however, these do not normally occur with an expressed Agent, although this is (rarely) possible in Italian, as in (Lepschy and Lepschy 1977: 213):

> Questo giornale si legge ogni mattina da
> This newspaper REFL read + 3SG + PRES each morning by
> moltissima gente
> very many people
> 'This paper is read every morning by lots of people'

The reflexive is also used, slightly differently, in a 'neuter' function, to produce an intransitive from a transitive verb, with the Patient as Subject (the term 'neuter' is traditionally used for the intransitive member of homophonous intransitive and transitive forms, such as 'break', 'open' in English). This use differs from the agentless passive in that it is not merely that no Agent is present, but also that no agency is even implied, and indicates what Shibatani (1985: 827) calls 'spontaneous occurrence' (see 6.4). Shibatani provides examples from Spanish, French, Russian and Quechua:

> se abrió la puerta
> REFL opened + 3SG the door
> 'The door opened'

> La porte s'est ouverte
> the door REFL + is opened
> 'The door opened'

> Lekcija načalas'
> lecture began + REFL
> 'The lecture began'

> Pingu-kuna-ka paska-ri-rka
> door-PL-TOP open-REFL-PAST + 3
> 'The doors opened'

(These constructions are also sometimes called 'mediopassives' and 'anticausatives' (Zubizarreta 1985: 259)).

However, sometimes the same construction is treated as if it were indefinite, with the reflexive pronoun acting as the Subject rather than as the Object, and so having the sense of 'someone'. This is so with Polish, as illustrated by (Siewierska 1988: 262):

> owe przesądy   dzisiaj inaczej   się   interpretuje
> these prejudices + ACC today differently REFL interpret
> 'These prejudices are interpreted differently today'

Here 'these prejudices' is treated as the Object (in the accusative case and not agreeing with the verb), while the Subject is a singular impersonal 'one'. A more literal translation would be 'One interprets these prejudices differently today'. This should be contrasted with the Russian example above and with the Czech (Siewierska 1988: 246):

> zivne   latky   se   pobleuji   filtrem
> nutritive substances + NOM REFL absorb + 3PL filter + INSTR
> 'Nutritive substances are absorbed by filter'

Here 'nutritive substances' is the Subject, agreeing with the verb, which is third person plural.

In Spanish, the two types of construction are found side by side (Shibatani 1985: 826):

> se   curó   a los   brujos
> REFL cured + 3SG to the + PL sorcerers + PL
> 'The sorcerers were cured'

> se   curaron   los   brujos
> REFL cured + 3PL the + PL sorcerers + PL
> 'The sorcerers were cured'

The literal meanings of these would seem to be 'One cured the sorcerers' and 'The sorcerers cured themselves' respectively.

Similar constructions are found in Italian (Lepschy and Lepschy 1977: 214–16):

> si   compra   due penne
> REFL buy + 3SG two pens
> 'One buys two pens'

> si   comprano due penne
> REFL buy + 3PL two pens
> 'One buys two pens'

Lepschy and Lepschy distinguish between a 'passive' and an 'indefinite' use of the construction, so that both constructions (with either the reflexive or the

Patient as Subject) can be indefinite, and add that the construction with the reflexive as Subject is less common. Undoubtedly, the two constructions are not always distinguishable: with a singular verb it would not be possible to decide between them:

> si   compra   una penna
> REFL buy + 3SG a   pen
> 'One buys a pen'

There is no grammatical way of establishing whether *si* or *una penna* is the Subject. There is a detailed discussion of the situation in Italian and other Romance languages in Cinque 1988.

Another type of blending is found in Quechua (Shibatani 1985: 845):

> runtu-kuna   caya-ku-sa-n
> egg-PL + NOM cook-REFL-CONT-3SG
> 'Eggs are being cooked/Eggs are cooking'

Here the Patient is in the nominative case and the verb is marked as reflexive, so that prima facie the Patient appears to be the Subject of a (reflexive) passive. Yet the verb is in the third person singular and so does not agree with it, but is essentially impersonal. This has some similarity to the impersonal passives of Irish and North Russian that were discussed in 5.4, where, however, the Patient was marked morphologically as the Object of the impersonal verb.

As noted in 5.7, the reflexive, like the passive, is also used in a potential sense (Shibatani 1985: 828), e.g. in Russian:

> Detjam ne spitsja
> children not sleep
> 'The children could not sleep'

Further reflexive-like constructions are discussed in 6.3.

6.2 Other passive-like constructions

Many languages use an indefinite 'they' or 'he'/'one' as a Subject to convey a meaning similar to that of an Agent-less passive. Thus in English 'they say . . .' has roughly the same meaning as 'It is said . . .'. Similarly, for Lakhota (N. America), Foley and Van Valin (1985: 334) quote:

         Mathó ki   ø-kté-pi
         bear   the 3SG-kill-3PL
         'They killed the bear'/'The bear was killed'

However, in some languages there are constructions that are very like these, but are treated as passive in that an obliquely-marked Agent may be added; examples from Kimbundu (Bantu, Givón 1979: 211) and Trukic (Micronesian, Jacobs 1976: 121) (both quoted in Shibatani 1985: 845) are:

         Nzua a-mu-mono kwa mame
         John they-him-saw by   me
         'John was seen by me'

         Waan re-liila-ø   ree-i
         John   they-him-killed by-me
         'John was killed by me'

There is only a slightly different situation in Ainu (Japan, Shibatani 1985: 823–4), where the forms for 'we' (-*an* with intransitives and *a-* with transitives) are used for (or identical with) the indefinite. Compare:

         Itak-an
         speak-1PL
         'We speak'

         Tampe a-e-kore
         this   1PL-2SG-give
         'We give you this'

         Tepeka paye-an yak Sat   ta paye-an
         here   go-INDEF if Saru to go-INDEF
         'If one goes there, one goes to Saru'

The same forms are used for what Shibatani calls the 'spontaneous' construction:

         Pirka   hawe a-nu
         beautiful voice SPON-hear
         'A beautiful voice is heard'

They also occur in what Shibatani simply calls 'passive', as in:

         kamui umma raike
         bear   horse kill
         'A bear killed a horse'

Umma kamui orowa a-raike
horse bear from PASS-kill
'A horse was killed by a bear'

Shibatani debates whether these examples are really passives. The Agent appears to have been demoted, but the only evidence for the Patient as Subject is its position in the sentence. However, Patients are marked as Objects (not Subjects) in the verb, as shown by an example from Classical Ainu:

kamui kat chasi upshorirke a-i-o-reshu
god build castle inside   PASS-1SG + OBJ-in-raise
'I was raised in a god-built castle'

It seems clear from these examples that the situation is very like that of Kimbundu and Trukic: there is a construction with an indefinite Subject, that, in terms of the oblique marking of the Agent, is treated as if it were passive.

More problematic are constructions that are simply described as passives, but in which the Agent remains in the case associated with the Object. Thus Shibatani (1985: 834) notes from Mojave (Arizona/California, Munro 1976: 241):

ny-tapiʔipay-ch-m
me-save-PASS-TNS
'I was saved'

He also quotes an example from Ute (SW USA, Givón 1979: 192). Givón has the pair of sentences:

ta'wóci   tu̱pu̱yci ti̱ráabi-kya
man + SUBJ rock + OBJ throw-PASS-PAST
'The man threw the rock'

tu̱pu̱yci   ti̱ráabi-ta-xa
rock + OBJ throw-PASS-PAST
'The rock was thrown'

However, for Ute at least, it seems more reasonable to treat the constructions as ones that have an indefinite Subject. Givón (1988: 419–20) presents as a passive in Ute a construction in which the Agent is omitted and the verb is marked:

> ta'wá-ci̱ sivá̱a̱tu-ci pa̱x̂a-x̂a
> man-SUBJ goat-OBJ kill-ANT   [ANTerior]
> 'The man killed the goat'

> sivá̱a̱tu-ci pa̱x̂a-ta-x̂a
> goat-OBJ kill-PASS-ANT
> 'The goat was killed'/'Someone killed the goat'

However, the Agent may be marked as plural in either construction, by a plural suffix on the verb:

> táata'wa-ci-u sivá̱a̱tu-ci pa̱x̂a-x̂a-qa
> men-SUBJ-PL goat-OBJ kill-PL-ANT
> 'The men killed the goat'

> sivá̱a̱tu-ci pa̱x̂a-ta-xâ
> goat-OBJ kill-PL-PASS-ANT
> 'The goat was killed (by some unspecified persons)'/'Some
> persons killed the goat'

This would strongly suggest that these sentences are not passives, but actives with indefinite or unspecified singular or plural Agents ('someone', 'they'/ 'some persons'), and that the 'passive' marker is a marker of the indefinite. Givón notes that various constructions can be 'passivized', e.g.:

> kaní-naa ̱g̱a̱ tu̱ká-ta-x̂a
> house-in   eat-PASS-ANT
> 'Someone ate in the house'

> tu̱u̱-tu̱ká-ta-x̂a
> well-eat-PASS-ANT
> 'Someone ate well'

These too are more easily interpreted as having indefinite Subjects than as passives.

Another construction that has been treated as passive is found in Acehnese (N. Sumatra, Lawler 1977: 225, Durie 1988: 104–5 – Durie's transcription and gloss):

> gopnyan ka   geu-côm lôn
> she   INCH 3 + kiss   I   [INCHoative]
> 'She kissed me'

lôn ka   geu-côm lé-gopnyan
I   INCH 3 + kiss   lé-she
'I was kissed by her'

If *le-* is treated as a 'by' type preposition, this would seem to be another passive-like construction, but with the passive marked only by a change in word order. However, change in word order can be seen as topicalization, and Durie argues that the *le-* prefix is merely an 'ergative marker', used when the Agent follows the verb.

There is a problem of a different kind with the putative passive in Chinese, which appears to be marked by the change in position of the Subject and Object and the demotion of the Subject by giving it peripheral status (marked by a preposition) as in (Hashimoto 1988: 330):

ta bei taita kanjian
he BEI wife see
'He is seen by his wife'

If *bei* is treated as equivalent to English *by*, there is no passive marker associated with the verb. However, Hashimoto argues that there are synchronic and diachronic reasons for treating *bei* as a passive marker, not a preposition. In that case there would be a passive marker, but no mark of the demotion of the Subject other than word order. In either case the construction is unusual, but more like a passive than an example of topicalization.

A rather different situation is found in Classical Greek, where a small number of verbs that are intransitive and active in form nevertheless appears to function semantically and, in one respect, grammatically as passives (see P. K. Andersen 1991: 37, 79). With these verbs the patient is the Subject, but the agent is marked by the preposition that is used to mark the Agent in the passive – the preposition HÝPO plus the genitive. Thus APOTHNÉːISKO: 'die' is often used instead of the passive of APOKTÉINO: 'kill' (which is not normally used in the passive in Classical Greek):

apéthane . . .   hypó Sámbullou
die + 3SG + AOR(ACT) by   Sambullou + GEN + SING
andrós)   Geló:iou   (Herod. 7. 154)
man + GEN + SING Geloan + GEN + SING
'He was killed by Sambullos, a Geloan man'

Other verbs that function in a similar way are PÍPTO: 'fall' and PHÉUGO: 'flee' ('be exiled'):

149

hyp' Atreíde:i   Agamémnoni

by   son of Atreus + GEN + SING Agamemnon + GEN + SING

pípte   kárena   (Hom. *Il.* 11. 158)

fell + 3SG + IMPERF(ACT) heads

'Heads fell (were made to fall) by Agamenmon, the son of Atreus'

ek   Náxou éphugon   ándres tó:n   pachéo:n hypó

from Naxos flee + 3PL + AOR(ACT) men   of the rich   by

tóu   dé:mou   (Herod. 5.30)

the + GEN + SING people + GEN + SING

'Men from among the rich were exiled from Naxos by the people'

6.3 The middle voice

It was seen in 5.1 that there are, in many languages, morphological passives. Often such passives belong to a two-term voice system of active and passive, but there are languages that are traditionally said to have a 'middle' voice; the two best-known examples are Classical Greek and Sanskrit. Although the middle contrasts morphologically with the active, unlike the passive it is not involved in the demotion or promotion of grammatical roles. As such, it is not central to the interests of this book, and will not be dealt with in detail, but it merits some discussion because of the ways in which it is related to the active (and the passive) as well as to the reflexives discussed in 6.1. (For a detailed discussion see Klaiman 1991, chapters 1 and 2, from whom many of the examples below are taken. Klaiman refers to this type of voice, which is not involved in 'role-remapping', as 'basic' voice , in contrast with 'derived' voice as exemplified by the passive, but the term is somewhat misleading, since neither is more basic than the other.)

The function of the middle is described by Lyons (1968: 373) in terms of the implication that 'the "action" or "state" affects the subject of the verb or his interest' and by Klaiman (1991: 92) in terms of 'situations having principal effects upon the . . . subject'. Not surprisingly, such vague characterizations allow a great variety of meanings to be included.

Most obviously, the middle is used to refer to actions that the entities represented by Subjects do to themselves (reflexives) or (often transitively) for themselves, e.g. in Sanskrit:

Devadattaḥ   kaṭam   karoti
Devadattah + NOM mat + ACC makes + ACT
'Devadattah makes a mat'

Devadattaḥ   kaṭam   kurute
Devadattah + NOM mat + ACC makes + MID
'Devadattah makes a mat for himself'

However, a number of different uses of the middle to express action to or for oneself can be distinguished in Greek:

loúomai	'I wash myself'
louómetha	'We wash one another'
porízimai khré:mata	'I get myself money'
paratíthemai deípnon	'I have a meal served to me'

The first can be characterized as reflexive, the second as reciprocal, the third as 'indirect' reflexive and the last as a causative indirect reflexive. In addition the middle voice is also used as a passive: Greek has only two morphologically distinct passive tenses, and the middle is used as passive for the rest.

In both languages the middle is used where part of the Subject's body is affected by the action:

(Sanskrit) āhati   śiraṃ
           he hits + MID head + ACC
           'He hits his own head'

(Greek)   eplé:ksato té:n   kephalé:n   (Herod. 3. 14. 7)
           struck + 3SG the + ACC head + ACC
           'He struck himself on the head'

The Greek example refers to striking one's head in grief. The verbs TÝPTO: 'beat' and KÓPTO: 'strike' are similarly used, in that in the middle they mean 'strike one's breast' and, therefore, 'mourn'; in that sense TÝPTO: can actually have an Object that refers to the person mourned:

týptontai . . .	pántes		kaí
beat + 3PL + PRES + MID	all + MASC + NOM + PL		and
pásai . . . ;	tón		de
all + FEM + NOM + PL	who + MASC + ACC + SG		but
týptyontai,	oú	moi	hósion	esti légein
beat + 3PL + PRES + MID	not	to me	permitted is	to tell

(Herod. 2. 61.1)

'All the men and women mourn, but it is not permitted for me to say who they mourn'

Slightly different is the use of the middle in Sanskrit as a neuter (see 6.2) as in:

so namati daṇḍam
he + NOM bends + ACC stick-ACC
'He bends the stick'

namate daṇḍaḥ
bends + MID stick + NOM
'The stick bends'

There are, however, other uses of the middle that are rather different. Klaiman (1991: 91) notes that some verbs in both languages are used in the middle where the object is brought nearer to or further from the subject's 'sphere':

Greek kalepó:s lambánesthaí tinos (Herod.2. 141. 4)
roughly take + MID + INF some-one + GEN
'To lay rough hands on someone'

Sanskrit vikrīṇīte
sells + 3SG + MID
'He sells (disposes of by sale) something'

In addition there is a lexical function of the middle in that certain verbs (so-called 'deponent' or middle-only verbs) have no active forms, but occur in the middle, e.g.:

Greek	HÉPOMAI	'follow'
	OÍOMAI	'think'
	BOÚLOMAI	'wish'
	HALLOMAI	'jump'
Sanskrit	LABH-	'receive'
	ĀS-	'eat'
	KṢAM-	'endure'

Klaiman (1991: 100) suggests that these express 'physical and mental attitudes and dispositions presupposing the control of an animate logical subject', and that it is this that makes their use consistent with the other middles, but admits that there are pairs of active-only and middle-only verbs that differ little in meaning such as (compared with the last two Greek examples):

Greek	ETHÉLO:	'wish'
	PE:DÁO:	'leap'

It should be mentioned that Latin, too, although it has no morphological middle voice, has 'deponent' verbs that occur only in the passive, but with active meanings, e.g.:

POTIOR	'obtain'
SEQUOR	'follow'

More surprisingly, perhaps, with some verbs in Greek, the present tense is morphologically active, but the future tense middle:

horó:	'I see'
ópsomai	'I shall see'
dákno:	'I bite'
dé:ksomai	'I shall bite'

This appears to be true of most, or all, verbs that express some kind of bodily activity, and Klaiman suggests that this shows the affinity of the middle with the 'temporomodal semantics of modality'. It is difficult to see precisely how this relates to the other functions of the middle.

Klaiman also discusses in some detail Fula (W. Africa), which is unrelated to Greek and Sanskrit, but has interesting parallels with them. There is a three-way contrast of an active-middle-passive type in (Arnott 1956: 130):

'o ɓorn-ii   mo ŋgapalkewol
he dress-PAST + ACT him gown
'He dressed him in a gown'

'o ɓorn-ake   ŋgapalkewol
he dress-PAST + MID gown
'He put on a gown'

'o ɓorn-aama   ŋgapalkewol
he dress-PAST + PASS gown
'He was dressed (by someone) in a gown'

The following examples are also similar to Greek examples (Arnott 1970: 137, 342–3):

'o res-ii   ɗum
he deposit-PAST + ACT it
'He deposited it on the ground'

'o res-ake   ɗum
he deposit-PAST + MID it
'He put it in deposit (for his own future use)'

moor-a
dress hair-ACT
'dress someone's hair'

moor-o
dress hair-MID
'get one's hair dressed'

However, a simple reflexive requires a further reflexive suffix; compare the last example above with:

moor-it-o
dress hair-REFL-MID
'dress one's own hair'

Fula has verbs that occur in any combination of the three voices: active only, middle only, passive only, active/middle, active/passive, middle/passive and active/middle/passive. Of most significance are those that occur only in the middle or middle/passive. These appear to be of five types (Klaiman 1991: 58):

mental actions: 'think', 'calculate', 'be sad'
speech with mental attitude: 'threaten', 'welcome'
bodily postures: 'sit', 'stoop', 'kneel'
bodily actions: 'swim', 'sniff', 'balance on head'
telic (goal-presupposing): 'arrive', 'approach', 'attack'

Klaiman describes these as 'deponent', i.e. as middles with active meanings, and says they express actions that 'presuppose the . . . subject's animacy and control, and relating to either physical state or attitude, or to mental disposition'. Unfortunately the notion of control is somewhat belied by the fact that the first group also includes 'know' and 'understand' and the fourth 'sneeze', 'smile', 'hear' and 'see'. Nevertheless, the similarity with the verbs of Greek and Sanskrit is obvious.

Comparison of Fula with Greek and Sanskrit suggests that it is reasonable to postulate a typological category of middle, with the notion of affectedness of the subject as the prototypical feature (although Klaiman sees control as the main factor, together with certain modal and aspectual features). It would, however, be helpful to have evidence from a much larger number of languages. Klaiman also discusses Tamil in this context, but, although the discussion may be relevant to her major interest in the notion of control, the situation in Tamil does not seem very relevant to the middle voice, but concerns rather degrees of transitivity and the causative; it is discussed in 9.3.4.

The way in which the semantics of middle and passive are often related is illustrated from Western Armenian (Haig 1982: 162–5); the same suffix -*v* is used for (i) the passive, (ii) reflexives and reciprocals and (iii) intransitive neuters ('anticausatives') such as 'open':

> Namag-ə kər-v-ets-av   Mari-e-n
> letter-the write-*v*-AOR-3SG Mari-ABL-the
> 'The letter was written by Mari'

> Vartan-ə   hak-v-ets-av
> Vartan-the wear-*v*-AOR-3SG
> 'Vartan dressed'

> Tur-ə   kots-v-ets-av
> door-the open-*v*-AOR-3SG
> 'The door opened'

The use of a single form for all three uses can, perhaps, be explained in terms of detransitivization, in that it is used for (i) the passive, which, with the demotion (or deletion) of the Agent, is intransitive, (ii) the reflexive and reciprocal, where the Patient-Object, being identical with the Agent-Subject, is unstated and (iii) those intransitives which differ from their corresponding transitives by the obligatory absence of an Agent and the occurrence of the Patient as Subject.

There is a similar situation with the so-called middle of Icelandic (Einarsson 1945: 147–8). First, it is used as a reflexive or reciprocal:

> klæðast   'dress oneself'
> þeir berjast   'they fight each other'

However, active forms with reflexive or reciprocal pronouns are also possible:

klæðast sig   'dress oneself'

Secondly, it provides intransitive neuters:

hefja e-ð	'begin something'	hefjast	'begin'
hræða e-n	'terrify someone'	hræðast	'be afraid'

Thirdly, it is used as a passive:

sjást	'be seen'
finnast	'be found'

In addition there are deponent verbs that occur only in the middle, e.g.:

ég eldist	'I grow old'
ég ferðast	'I travel'

However, this Icelandic middle is derived from the reflexive form (Einarsson suggests *klæða sik* > *klæðask* > *klæðast*), although the full reflexive form with *sig* also occurs. Klaiman argues that such derived reflexives do not provide evidence for the reflexive nature of the middle in other languages, but the similarities between the reflexives of 6.1, the 'middle' in Icelandic, the voice forms of W. Armenian and the middles of Greek, Sanskrit and Fula are so striking that it could well be argued that, typologically, they are essentially all the same grammatical category, with the notion of affected Subject as the linking feature. The association of the same forms with the neuter function and with the passive can, as suggested above, be explained in terms of detransitivization. Yet it must be recalled that not all middles are intransitive in Greek and Sanskrit. Similarly, there are transitive but reflexive forms in Swedish, e.g. (Klaiman 1991: 87):

jag avunda-s honom
I   envy-REFL him
'I envy him'

6.4 Multiple functions of passive markers

In some languages the marker of the passive has a number of other functions in addition to those considered in 6.2. The best-known example is Japanese, where the suffix *-(r)are-* has four functions that

Shibatani (1985: 822–3) glosses as 'passive, potential, honorific and spontaneous':

> Taroo wa sikar-are-ta
> Taroo TOP scold-PASS-PAST
> 'Taroo was scolded'

> Boku wa nemur-are-nakat-ta
> I   TOP sleep-POTEN-NEG-PAST
> 'I could not sleep'

> Sensei ga waraw-are-ta
> teacher NOM laugh-HON-PAST
> 'The teacher laughed (hon.)'

> Mukasi ga sinob-are-ru
> old time NOM think about-SPON-PRES
> 'An old time comes (spontaneously) to mind'

Shibatani suggests that what these have in common is the 'defocusing of the agent', which is what he sees as the primary function of the passive. However, this notion, as applied to these very heterogeneous Japanese examples, is far more vague than it is when used to refer to more obvious passive constructions with demotion or omission of the Agent, and it is to be noted that the 'potential' and 'honorific' constructions can be transitive, as in (Shibatani, personal communication):

> Sensei ga hon o kaw-are-ta
> teacher NOM book ACC buy-HON-PAST
> 'The teacher bought a book'

> Sono kodomo wa gohan o tabe-rare-nakat-ta
> that child   TOP meal ACC eat-POTEN-NEG-PAST
> 'That child could not eat a meal'

It may well be that there can be no real explanation, apart from a historical one, for the fact that the same form has such different meanings. Historical change often disguises or even removes the links that existed between different uses of a single form; the result is simple polysemy. Shibatani states that it is generally held that the spontaneous use was the original one and that the uses developed by 'taking advantage of the agent-defocusing effect of the suffix', but does not provide the evidence for it.

The striking point about the uses of the Japanese 'passive' morpheme is that three of its uses seem to have little or no connection with the passive

157

(*pace* Shibatani's comment about 'defocusing the agent'). The situation is different from that discussed in 5.7, where all the uses could, to some degree, be regarded as passive in meaning, though with other connotations. It may be noted in particular that the 'potential' use of the passive was discussed there, but in all cases, unlike the Japanese example, it was to be interpreted in a passive (as well as potential) sense.

6.5 Passives in ergative systems

If the passive is defined in terms of the promotion of non-primary terms to primary status and the demotion of primary terms, then some ergative systems have passives, but these 'passives' would be what are usually called 'antipassives' (though it might, indeed, be reasonable to call them 'passives' – see Jacobsen 1985). Alternatively the passive might be defined in terms of Agent and Patient, requiring the promotion of Patient and the demotion of Agent; in that case, there could not be passives in ergative systems, because, it is the Patient, not the Agent that is the primary term, and primary terms cannot be further promoted.

Shibatani (1985: 830) suggests that the passive should be defined solely in terms of the defocusing of the Agent (this is to be discussed in 6.7). In that case, passives are found in ergative languages; an example from Eskimo (Woodbury 1977: 323–4) is:

aŋut-ip   arnaq-ø   taka-vaa
man-ERG woman-ABS see-INDIC + 3SG + 3SG
'The man saw the woman'

arnaq-ø (aŋuti-mit) · taku-tau-puq
woman-ABS (man-ABL) SEE-PASS-INDIC + 3SG
'The woman was seen (by the man)'

Here the Agent 'man' is either demoted to the oblique status, marked by ablative case, or deleted, and Shibatani's condition is met.

It is worth noting, however, that it is often the case that where such passives occur, the language in question has other accusative features. Thus it was noted in 3.2 that Burushaski has ergative noun morphology, but accusative verbal agreement, in that S and A, not P, agree with the verb and, in this respect, act as Subjects. It has three constructions that might be regarded as passives, as exemplified by (Morin and Tiffou 1988):

ne   hir-é   cel   cá-m
the + MASC man-ERG water + ABS impound + PRET PTCP
bá-i
be-3MASC + SING + SUBJ   (p. 502)
'The man impounded the water'

cel   du-cá-m   duá
water + ABS PASS-impound-PRET PTCP be + 3SG + SUBJ
'The water was impounded'

ne   hir-é   phaló   bókum   bá-i (p. 500)
the + MASC man-ERG seed + PL + ABS sow + PRET PTCP be-
    3SG + MASC + SUBJ
'The man has planted the seeds'

phaló   bókum   b-icá
seed + PL + ABS sow + PRET PTCP be-3PL + SUBJ
'The seeds have been planted'

čúmu-sel-áŋ-e   jáa gaṭu-nc   xéša-m
fish-hook$_1$-PL-ERG my cloth$_2$-PL + ABS tear + PRET + PL-PTCP
    b-icá
    be-3PL$_1$ + SUBJ
'The fish-hooks tore the clothes'

čúmu-sel-áŋ-e   jáa gaṭu-nc   xéša-m
fish-hook$_1$-PL-ERG my cloth$_2$-PL + ABS tear + PRET + PL-PTCP
    b-ién
    be-3PL$_2$ + SUBJ   (p. 511)
'The clothes were torn by the fish-hooks'

Differences between the three constructions are (i) only the first has a passive marker on the verb, (ii) the first and second do not permit Agents – A is deleted, (iii) the third, which is called the 'pathetive', has only inanimate Agents and cannot have human patients. In all three there is one clear passive feature – it is the Patient that agrees with the verb, not the Agent as in the active construction. In terms of verbal agreement (which itself is accusative), then, these 'passives', operate within an accusative, not an ergative, system; however, the ergative-type marking on the nouns is unchanged even after passivization, the derived Patient-'Subject' still being marked as absolutive, not ergative, and (see the last example) the Agent remaining in the ergative. It may well be doubted whether the second two constructions, with no overt marker on the verb, should be considered passives, yet it is clear that they promote the patient to 'Subject' (in terms of verbal agreement) and either delete or demote the Agent.

Even more questionable is the suggestion that there is a 'passive' in Tongan that merely deletes the Agent, as suggested by Keenan (1985: 248) for examples from Churchward (1953: 67, 68):

> na'e tāmate'i 'e   Tevita 'a   Kōlaiate
> killed   ERG David ABS Goliath
> 'David killed Goliath'

> na'e tāmate'i 'a   Kōlaiate
> killed   ABS Goliath
> 'Goliath was killed'

There are two problems here: there is, again, no marking on the verb, and there is no verbal agreement (or any other feature) to suggest that the Patient has been promoted. Against this it can be said that the Agent has been 'defocused'.

Another possibility is that the language has ergative morphology, but accusative syntax in terms of pivots. This is the case with Tzotzil, first discussed in 4.2 (Foley and Van Valin 1985: 313):

> A   li   Petal e bat-em-ø   ta xobel
> TOP ART Peter   go-PERF-3SG + ABS to town
> s-max-ox-ø   li   Anton e
> 3SG + ERG-hit-PAST-3SG + ABS ART Anton
> 'Peter went to town and hit Anton'

> A   li   Petal e bat-em-ø   ta xobel max-bilø
> TOP ART Peter   go-PERF-3SG + ABS to town hit-PASS + 3SG + ABS
> yuʔun li   Anton
> by   ART Anton
> 'Peter went to town and was hit by Anton'

As was noted in 4.2, the verbal agreement is ergative: in the third person, A is marked with the prefix *s-*, while both S and P are unmarked (or marked as ø), but the rule for deletion in coordination involves A and S (i.e. the Subject of accusative languages). Since one function of the passive (see 4.6) is to provide pivots for deletion, it is hardly surprising that, where the pivot system is accusative, so is the voice system. As can be seen from the second example, the syntax requires the promotion of P to 'Subject' status for deletion, and this is precisely what a passive, not an antipassive, can do. It is not, therefore, really true that here we have an example of passive in an ergative system, since in terms of the relevant system (the syntactic system), Tzotzil is not ergative but accusative.

It is worth adding that just as in e.g. Tzotzil, an accusative (S = A) pivot system may require the passive, so an ergative (S = P) pivot system might be expected to require the antipassive. Indeed, Dixon (1979: 127) actually states that all languages with ergative (S = P) pivots have antipassives.

6.6   Promotion to object

Some languages have a device or a set of devices that involves promotion not to Subject, but to Object. This, like the passive (and, indeed, the causative – see chapter 9), changes the grammatical relations of terms in the construction, and, like the passive, can be considered to be a voice system. Strictly, it should merit a chapter on its own, but is discussed here because it has consequences for passivization.

6.6.1   *The applicative*

An example of promotion to Object is to be found in Chamorro (Austronesian, Baker 1988: 248, 237):

hu   tugi' i   kätta pära i   chelu'-hu
1SG + SUBJ write the letter to   the sibling-my
'I wrote the letter to my brother'

hu   tugi'-i   i   chelu'-hu ni kätta
1SG + SUBJ write-APPL the sibling-my OBL letter
'I wrote my brother the letter'

ha   punu' si Miguel i   bäbui päpra guahu
3SG + SUBJ kill   PN Miguel the pig   for   me [proper NOUN]
'Miguel killed the pig for me'

ha   punu'-i yu' si Miguel nu i   bäbui
3SG + SUBJ killed-for me PN Miguel OBL the pig
'Miguel killed the pig for me'

Similarly, for Indonesian Chung (1976: 41) offers:

> Mereka mem-bawa daging itu kepada dia
> they   TRANS-bring meat   the to   him
> 'The brought the meat to him'

> Mereka mem-bawa-kan dia gaging itu
> they   TRANS-bring-BEN him meat   the
> 'They brought him the meat'

> Ali mem-beli telefisi   untuk ibu-nja
> Ali TRANS-buy television for   mother-his
> 'Ali bought a television for his mother'

> Ali mem-beli-kan ibu-nja   telefisi
> Ali TRANS-buy-BEN mother-his television
> 'Ali bought his mother a television'

Promotion to Object is indicated both by the loss of the preposition and of a verbal marker, here glossed as 'for' and 'Beneficiary'.

In both set of examples the promoted term has a peripheral role (marked by a preposition) in the original sentence, but is given full relational status by the promotion. In the Chamorro examples there is a single preposition, but with the notional roles of recipient and beneficiary. In the Indonesian examples there are two different prepositions; the role in the second is clearly beneficiary, but in the first it is not, perhaps, simply recipient since motion is involved, though it is equally not simply locative. A possible term is 'goal'. In both cases, however, it is reasonable to identify the grammatical relation as Dative.

The device and resultant construction are generally referred to as 'applicative'. In some languages there is a single verbal marker, irrespective of the roles of the promoted items. An example is Kichaga (Bantu, Bresnan and Moshi 1990: 148–9):

> n-ắ-í-lyì-í-à   m̀-kà k-élyà
> FOC-1SUBJ-PRES-eat-APPL-FV 1-wife 7-food   [Final vowel]
>   (Numerals indicate noun class)
> 'He is eating food for/on (for the benefit/to the detriment of) his
>   wife'

> n-ắ-í-lyì-í-à   mà-wókɵ̀ k-êlyâ
> FOC-1SUBJ-PRES-eat-APPL-FV 6-hand   7-food
> 'He is eating food with his hands'

n-á-í-lyì-í-à   m̀-r̩ì-nyì   k-élyà
FOC-1SUBJ-PRES-eat-APPL-FV 3-homestead-LOC 7-food
'He is eating food at the homestead'

n-á-í-lyì-í-!á   njáá   k-élyà
FOC-1SUBJ-PRES-eat-APPL-FV 9 + hunger 7-food
'He is eating food because of hunger'

Applicatives are possible with intransitives:

n-á-í-zríc-í-à   mbùyà
FOC-1SUBJ-PRES-eat-APPL-FV 9 + friend
'She is running for a friend'

In other languages, there are different markers for the different relations that are established, although the maximum appears to be three – Dative, Instrumental or Locative. Baker (1988: 236) lists ('in order of decreasing commonness and syntactic regularity across languages') the roles of promoted terms across languages as dative-cum-goal, benefactive-cum-malefactive, instrument and locative, but generally, as the Chamorro and Indonesian examples show, dative-cum-goal and beneficiary-cum-malefactive are identified as the single grammatical relation Dative.

6.6.2 Applicatives and passivization

A striking characteristic of the promoted Objects is that generally they can be promoted to Subject through passivization. This is well documented for Kinyarwanda (Kimenyi 1988: 355–86), which will now be discussed in detail. Three types of construction in Kinyarwanda are of interest.

The first construction (and the simplest example of promotion to Object) is one in which an Instrumental can be promoted, this being signalled by the suffix -iish- on the verb (pp. 367–8):

Umugóre a-ra-andik-a   ibarúwa n'ííkarámu
woman   she-PRES-write-ASP letter   with pen
'The woman is writing a letter with a pen'

Umugóre a-ra-andik-iish-a   ibarúwa íkarámu
woman   she-PRES-write-INSTR-ASP letter   pen
'The woman is writing a letter with a pen'

The construction now contains two Objects; as was noted in 5.2, where there are two Objects, either can be promoted to Subject:

> Íkarámu i-ra-andik-iish-w-a   íbarúwa n'ûmugóre
> pen   it-PRES-write-INSTR-PASS-ASP letter   by woman
> 'The pen is being used to write a letter by the woman'

> Ibarúwa i-ra-andik-iish-w-a   íkarámu n'ûmugóre
> letter   it-PRES-write-INSTR-PASS-ASP pen   by woman
> 'The letter is being written with a pen by the woman'

Passivization of the first of the two active sentences above (without the *-iish-* suffix) allows promotion only of the Patient, not of the Instrumental, which is marked as a peripheral term by the preposition.

In the second construction to be considered, Locatives can also be promoted to Object, with locative marker being suffixed to the verb (pp. 368–9):

> Umwáalimu a-ra-andik-a   imibáre ku kíbáaho
> teacher   he-PRES-write-ASP maths   on blackboard
> 'The teacher is writing maths on the blackboard'

> Umwáalimu a-ra-andik-á-ho   ikíbáaho   imibáre
> teacher   he-PRES-write-ASP-on blackboard maths
> 'The teacher is writing maths on the blackboard'

This can then be passivized:

> Ikíbáaho   ki-ra-andik-w-á-ho   imibáre n'úúmwáalímu
> blackboard it-PRES-write-PASS-ASP-on maths   by teacher
> 'The blackboard is being used for writing maths on by the teacher'
> (Lit. '*The blackboard is being written maths on by the teacher')

However, there are two points in which the Locative differs from the Instrumental. First, once the Locative has been promoted to Object, it alone (and not the original Object) can be promoted to Subject by the passive. There is no:

> *Imibáre i-ra-andik-w-á-ho   ikíbáaho   n'úúmwáalímu
> maths   it-PRES-write-PASS-ASP blackboard by teacher
> 'Maths is being written on the blackboard by the teacher'

(Here it might well seem that the distinction between Primary and Secondary Object (2.4) might be useful – the Locative is promoted to Primary Object, while the initial Primary Object is demoted to Secondary Object: only Primary Objects can be promoted with the passive.) Secondly, the Locative can be directly promoted to Subject by passivization, i.e. without any evidence of promotion to Object – the preposition is still with the Locative, and there is no locative marker on the verb. (Similar promotion of Locatives, but without a marker of passivization, was noted in 2.6.) An example is:

> Ku kíbáaho ha-ra-andik-w-a imibáre n'úúmwáalimu
> on blackboard it-PRES-write-PASS-ASP maths by teacher
> '*The blackboard is being written maths on by the teacher'

The third construction of interest concerns the Benefactives. There is no preposition to mark these: they always function as Objects, but the verb requires the marker -*ir*, which Kimenyi glosses 'Applicative', though 'Benefactive' would be preferable in this context (pp. 373–4):

> Umukoôbwa a-ra-andika-ir-a umuhuûngu íbarúwa ku mééza
> girl she-PRES-write-APPL-ASP boy letter on table
> 'The girl is writing a letter for the boy on the table'

Presumably, either Object may be promoted to Subject by passivization, although this is not explicitly stated.

A sentence may have two of these markers of promotion to Object (including the applicative), but not normally three. Where there are two, however, there are restrictions on promotion to Subject with the passive. Thus if the applicative and locative promotion devices are used, both the original Dative and the original Locative may be promoted, but not the original Patient-Direct Object:

> Umukoôbwa a-ra-andika-ir-á-ho ámééza umuhuûngu
> girl she-PRES-write-APPL-ASP-on table boy
>   íbarúwa
>   letter
> 'The girl is writing a letter for the boy on the table'

> Umuhuûngu a-ra-andik-ir-w-á-ho ámééza íbarúwa
> boy he-PRES-write-APPL-PASS-ASP-on table letter
>   n'ûmukoôbwa
>   by girl
> 'The boy is being written a letter on the table by the girl'

Amééza a-ra-andik-ir-w-á-ho   umuhuûngu íbarúwa
table   it-PRES-write-APPL-PASS-ASP-on boy   letter
n'ûmukoôbwa
by girl
'*The table is being written a letter on for the boy by the girl'

not   *Ibarúwa i-ra-andik-ir-w-á-ho   ámééza umuhuûngu
letter   it-PRES-write-APPL-PASS-ASP-on table   letter
n'ûmukoôbwa
by girl
'A letter is being written on the table by the girl'

It is again (see above) possible to suggest that the initial Primary Object is demoted to Secondary Object (and so is not available for promotion to Subject), when the two peripheral relations are promoted to Object. There are, similarly, restrictions where there are other combinations of two promotion-to-Object devices; with both Locative and Instrumental promotion, for instance, only the original Locative (not the original Instrumental or Object) can be promoted to Subject with passivization.

Promotion to Object is common in Bantu languages, but Bresnan and Moshi (1990) suggest that these languages fall into two types, which they call 'symmetrical' and 'asymmetrical'. In the asymmetrical type, promotion to Subject is restricted to the Object promoted by the applicative construction and, in this sense, it is the only Object; in the symmetrical type there is no such restriction, as has been illustrated for Kinyarwanda. In this respect, then, in the asymmetrical languages only one Object has the characteristics of a prototypical Object, while in the symmetrical type other Objects share those characteristics. There are, moreover, other grammatical features that similarly distinguish the two types of language.

Kichaga, which was discussed in 6.6.1, is symmetrical. This can be seen in the passives of the first example here (Bresnan and Moshi 1990: 150):

ḿ-ká n-á-í-lyì-í-ò   k-èlyâ
1-wife FOC-1SUBJ-PRES-eat-APPL-PASS 7-food
'The wife is being benefitted/adversely affected by someone
eating the food'

k-èlyá k-í-lyì-í-ò   ḿ-kà
food 7SUBJ-PRES-eat-APPL-PASS 1-wife
'The food is being eaten for/on the wife'

In addition either Object may be expressed by an Object marker in the verb:

    n-á-í-m̀-lyì-í-à   k-élyâ
    FOC-1SUBJ-1OBJ-PRES-eat-APPL-FV 7-food
    'He/she is eating food for/on him/her'

    n-á-í-kì-lyí-í-à   m̀-kà
    FOC-1SUBJ-7OBJ-PRES-eat-APPL-FV 1-wife
    'He/she is eating it for/on the wife'

The Object markers even occur in the passive constructions (pp. 153–4):

    m̀-kà n-á-í-kì-lyí-í-ò
    1-wife FOC-1SUBJ-PRES-7OBJ-eat-APPL-PASS
    'The wife is being benefitted/adversely affected by someone
        eating it'

    k-á-í-lyì-í-ò
    7SUBJ-PRES-1OBJ-eat-APPL-PASS
    'It is being eaten for/on him/her'

By contrast, in an asymmetrical language such as Chichewa (Baker 1990: 266–7), it is only the promoted Object that is involved in any of these constructions. The other Objects are not involved in the passive or Object marking, as shown by the impossible starred forms in:

    kalulu a-na-gul-ir-a   mbidzi nsapato
    hare   he-PAST-APPL-ASP zebras shoes
    'The hare bought shoes for the zebra'

    mbidzi zi-na-gul-ir-idw-a   nsapato (ndi kalulu)
    zebras they-PAST-APPL-PASS-ASP shoes   (by hare)
    '?The zebras were bought shoes (by the hare)'

    *nsapato zi-na-gul-ir-idw-a   mdidzi (ndi kalulu)
    shoes   they-PAST-APPL-PASS-ASP zebras (by hare)
    'Shoes were bought for the zebras (by the hare)'

    amayi a-ku-mu-umb-ir-a   mtsuko mwana
    woman she-PRES-OBJ-mould-APPL-ASP waterpot child
    'The woman is moulding a water pot for the child'

    amayi a-ku-mu-umb-ir-a   mtsuko
    woman she-PRES-OBJ-mould-APPL-ASP waterpot
    'The woman is moulding a water pot for him'

> *amayi a-ku-u-umb-ir-a   mtsuko mwana
> woman she-PRES-OBJ-mould-APPL-ASP waterpot child
> 'The woman is moulding a waterpot for the child'

> *amayi a-ku-u-umb-ir-a   mwana
> woman she-PRES-OBJ-mould-APPL-ASP child
> 'The woman is moulding it for the child'

(The Object markers *mu* and *u* show agreement with 'child' and 'waterpot' respectively.)

There are similar features in other African languages. Thus in Fula (W. Africa, Arnott 1970: 355, 349), as in Kinyarwanda, there is an applicative suffix (glossed as DAT) to mark Beneficiaries as second Objects, and so make them, as well as the Patient, available for promotion to Subject:

> ɓe   kirs-an-ii-min   ŋgaari
> they slaughter-DAT-PAST + ACT us bull
> 'They slaughtered a bull for us'

> ŋgaari kirs-an-aama-min
> bull   slaughter + PAST + PASS-us
> 'A bull has been slaughtered for us'

> min-kirs-an-aama   ŋgaari
> we-slaughter-DAT-PAST + PASS bull
> 'We had a bull slaughtered for us'

There is another applicative for Instrumentals, with, again, two passives:

> wudere nden loot-ir-aama   saabunde
> cloth   DET wash-INSTR-PAST + PASS soap
> 'The cloth has been washed with soap'

> saabunde nde'e loot-ir-aama
> soap   DET   wash-INSTR-PAST + PASS
> 'The soap has been washed with'

(With the last example, however, the Patient ('cloth') has to be omitted – Klaiman 1991: 279, fn. 10.)

6.6.3   *The situation in English*

It has been suggested that an analysis similar to that suggested for Kinyarwanda may be used to account for the problem of the two Objects in English (with the roles of Patient and Beneficiary) that was discussed in 2.4. Consider again the two sentences:

> (a) Mary gave a book to John
> (b) Mary gave John a book

There are two possible passives:

> A book was given to John by Mary
> John was given a book by Mary

It is reasonable to suggest that these are, respectively, the passives corresponding to the two active sentences, with the promotion to Subject of *A book* in (a) and *John* in (b).

One way of dealing with this is to say that it is the Patient-(Direct) Object that is promoted in (a), and the Beneficiary-Dative/Indirect Object in (b). This is essentially the solution in traditional grammars, but it is unacceptable because it assigns the same grammatical relation to *to John* in (a) and *John* in (b); but while they have the same roles of Beneficiary, the formal marking shows that their grammatical relations are different.

Another solution is to say that there are two distinct constructions (a) with (Direct) Object and Indirect Object, (b) with Primary and Secondary Objects and that the (Direct) Object and Primary Object are promoted. This is the simplest solution, but there are two problematic issues. The first is that not all double Object constructions allow promotion of the first (Primary) Object. Thus in English, Beneficiaries marked with the preposition *for* also occur as Objects, but are not easily promoted to Subject. Consider:

> Mary bought a book for John
> Mary bought John a book

A passive is far less natural with the first than the second:

> ?John was bought a book by Mary
> A book was bought for John by Mary

The second problem is that the first Object, while identified as an Object by word order and morphology (*Mary bought him a book*) as well as by passivization, fails to exhibit fully many of the characteristics of (prototypical) Objects. Thus while the Object of (a) can quite naturally appear as the item questioned with a 'Wh' question, the first Object of (b) is far less natural in such a construction:

What did Mary give to John?
?Who did Mary give a book?

Hudson (1992: 257–64) discusses eleven properties to determine which of the two Objects has the characteristics of a single Object and concludes that it is in respect of passivization alone that the first Object has such characteristics. (However, four of the properties are essentially semantic and not strictly relevant; it is obvious, for instance, that the first Object is a Beneficiary, while single Objects are Patients.)

A third possibility, and one whose merit is that it parallels the analysis proposed for the Bantu languages, is to say that (b) is derived from (a) – that the Indirect Object in (a) is promoted to Object in (b) and that, in consequence, in both cases it is the Object that is promoted to Subject by passivization. However, English would be like the asymmetrical Bantu languages in that only the promoted Object may be further promoted to Subject, as seen by the possible and impossible (or very unlikely) passives:

Mary gave John a book
John was given a book by Mary
*A book was given John by Mary

However, this solution raises the same problems as the second, though it may be argued that it is not surprising if promoted Objects do not have all the characteristics of prototypical ones. In addition, there is the objection that there is no applicative or other marker to signal the promotion. There are, however, other languages in which there are alternative forms as in English, but no verbal marker to indicate a promotion device. A possible example from Southern Tiwa (New Mexico, Rosen 1990: 674) is:

bi-musa-wia-ban   'uide-'ay
1SG + B-cat-give-PAST child to   [B = marker for 'cats']
'I gave the cats to the child'

'uide tam-musa-wia-ban
child 1SG + B + A-cat-give-PAST   [A = marker for 'child']
'I gave the cats to the child'

A fourth (and converse) proposal is made by Dryer (1986). He argues that (*Mary gave John a book*) is the original or basic sentence and that *Mary gave a book to John* is derived from it by demoting *John* to peripheral status, which is marked by a prepostition – *Mary gave a book to John*. Two arguments are adduced in favour of this solution. First, with passivization, the demotion of a core relation to peripheral status is clearly marked by a preposition (*by*); there is, then, similar demotion here, also marked by a preposition. Secondly, this makes English much more like the languages with double Objects discussed in 2.4, especially where the Primary Object may be promoted to Subject. (A third solution, that a Dative/Indirect Object has been promoted to Object, is less plausible for these languages, since they do not have a construction corresponding to *Mary gave a book to John*; if there is such a rule of promotion, it would be obligatory for these languages, though optional for English.) Against this there is again the objection that there is no marker in the verb, and, more importantly, the objections against the second proposal are very much stronger, for, if the double Object form is considered basic, the first Object ought to have the characteristics of the single, prototypical, Object.

Finally, it should be noted that, although with two-Object constructions in English it is the (animate Beneficiary) first Object that is promoted, in some other languages with two-Object constructions it is only the (inanimate Patient) second Object that can be promoted. This is so in German (with the first Object demoted to Dative in the passive):

> Ich   lehre ihn   den   Tanz
> I + NOM teach him + ACC the + ACC dance + ACC
> 'I teach him the dance'

> Der   Tanz   wird   ihm   gelehrt
> the + NOM dance + NOM becomes him + DAT taught
> 'He is taught the dance'

It is not possible to say:

> *Er   wird   den   Tanz   gelehrt
> He + NOM becomes the + ACC dance + ACC taught
> 'He was taught the dance'

The same is true of Korean according to Shibatani (1977: 804).

6.7   Theoretical issues

So far the argument has proceeded largely by exposition with little theoretical discussion. That is fully justified in that theoretical issues cannot be usefully debated if the relevant facts are not first made apparent. It is now appropriate to consider the nature and the definition of the passive.

Jespersen (1924: 167–8) suggests that conditions for the use of the passive are:

(i) The active subject is unknown or cannot be easily stated;

(ii) The active subject is self-evident from the context;

(iii) There may be a special reason (tact or delicacy of sentiment) for not mentioning the subject;

(iv) Even if the active subject is indicated ('converted subject') the passive form is preferred if one takes naturally a greater interest in the passive than in the active subject;

(v) The passive may facilitate the connection of one sentence with another.

Shibatani (1985: 830) reduces these to three:

(i) Passives involve no mention of agent for contextual reasons;

(ii) Passives bring a topical non-agent into subject position;

(iii) Passives create a syntactic pivot.

It would be more illuminating, however, to say that there are just two devices involved, demotion of the Agent and promotion of a non-Agent (most commonly the Patient), but that there are two reasons for the non-Agent promotion – topicalization and use as pivot.

There is a problem, however, in the use of two quite distinct criteria for the definition of the passive, since they may not necessarily be related or dependent on each other, and Shibatani himself argues that the primary function of the passive is the defocusing of the Agent (which is not, therefore, a consequence of non-Agent promotion). His main argument is that there are passives of impersonal clauses and passives without promotion of a non-Agent; examples were discussed in 5.4 and 6.2 respectively, but are repeated here:

Latin   Pugnatur   uno   tempore
           fight + 3SG + PRES + PASS one + SG + ABL time + SG + ABL
           omnibus   locis
           all + PL + ABL place + PL + abl   (Caes. *B.G.* 7, 84)
           'There is fighting at one time in all places'

Welsh   Dannswyd gan y plant
           was danced by the children
           'There was dancing by the children'

Mojave   ny-tapiʔipay-ch-m
          me-save-PASS-TNS
          'I was saved'

Ute   tʉpʉ́yci   tɨráabi-ta-xa
          rock + OBJ throw-PASS-PAST
          'The rock was thrown'

The first two are passives of intransitives, but they do not provide good evidence for Shibatani's thesis for two reasons. First, they are fairly rare, and can be seen as merely formed by analogy with the more common and more regular passives of transitive verbs. Secondly, as Shibatani himself points out, Welsh allows passives only of 'agentive' intransitives, and, as suggested in 5.4, these might be dealt with in terms of cognate objects. The second two are, probably, not to be treated as passives but as constructions with an indefinite, unspecified, Subject (see 6.2).

One possible advantage of Shibatani's hypothesis is that it makes it easy to explain the apparent occurrence of passives in ergative systems. For, in such systems, the Patient cannot be promoted since it already has Primary (S = P) status, but the Agent can be demoted from Secondary status to oblique status. However, as argued in 6.5, where there are passives in what seem to be ergative systems, it is often the case that the language is only partially ergative, and that the relevant system is actually accusative. One problem, which was briefly discussed in 6.5, is whether mere deletion of the Agent, as in Tongan, should be treated as passive. If so it would seem to follow that deletion of the Patient ought to be a mark of the antipassive, and that this occurs in accusative systems, as in English *I read a book* and *I read*. This, in fact, has been suggested; it is discussed in 7.7.

Foley and Van Valin (1984: 149–68; 1985: 306–35) attempt to deal with the same issue by distinguishing between 'foregrounding' passives which 'permit a non-actor to occur as pivot' and 'backgrounding' passives, which 'serve to remove the actor from the core of the clause'. They again give examples of passives of intransitives and passives without Object promotion (1984: 325, 322):

Dutch   Er woorden   daar huizen gebouwd
          it became + 3PL there houses built
          'There were houses built there'

Finnish   Han-et jätettiin kotiin
          he-ACC was left at home
          'He was left at home'

173

It is easy to see why they treat these as backgrounding passives with arguments similar to those of Shibatani. Unfortunately, they use the distinction to categorize all passives as being of one type or the other. This is implausible because the passive in English and many other languages appears to be both foregrounding and backgrounding. They suggest that in German the passive with SEIN is backgrounding and the passive with WERDEN is foregrounding, as in (1985: 323):

> Mein Wagen ist (*von dem Mechaniker) repariert
> 'My car is fixed (*by the mechanic)'
>
> Mein Wagen wird (von dem Mechaniker) repariert
> 'My car is being fixed (by the mechanic)'

There are two differences between these passives; the first is a stative passive, as discussed in 5.7, while the second is a 'true' passive, and only the 'true' passive may occur with an Agent. Yet, with both, the Patient has been promoted to Subject and may act as a pivot, while the Agent has been demoted or deleted. It does not seem reasonable to argue that one is backgrounding, the other foregrounding.

Givón (1981: 168) adds a third function to passivization, that of detransitivization: passives are, that is to say, intransitives. This seems to be true of most or all familiar passives, since the promotion of the Patient and the deletion of the Agent or its demotion to an oblique position leaves the sentence with only one core argument, a Subject but no Object. However, it is not so obviously true when oblique relations are promoted to Subject, and the Object is unaffected, or where there are two Objects, only one of which is promoted, as in Kinyarwanda (6.6.2), although it might then be argued that there is at least a lowering of the transitivity. Whether there are any languages that have passives that merely exchange the status of Subject and Object is unclear. There are, of course, languages that merely change their position, but this is best treated as a matter of topicalization, not of passivization (see 5.5). More problematic are the 'inverse' systems that are to be discussed in 8.2.

Finally, it has been questioned, at various times by many different scholars, whether the passive should be regarded as directly derived from the active. This is largely a question concerning grammatical theory, and, in particular, whether Chomsky's original (1957) proposal about deriving passives from actives or (1965) deriving both from the same source is a valid assumption for a typological study. This is not a very important question for typology; what is important is the change (or simply the difference) in the grammatical relations of Agent and Patient or non-Agent. That change (or difference) is an observed fact, whatever the theoretical grammatical analysis. Talking about promotion and demotion seems the simplest way of dealing with it, and does not commit the investigator to a specific grammatical theory.

7
Antipassive

The antipassive in ergative systems appears to be the counterpart of the passive in accusative systems in that it is the Patient that is promoted and the Agent that is demoted. Yet there are many differences between the two, especially in the semantic functions of the antipassive.

7.1 Form of the antipassive

An example of an antipassive formation in Dyirbal was given in 1.4.1. A similar pair of examples from Yidiny (Australia, Dixon 1977a: 109) is:

> buɲa-:ɲ   wagu-ḏa wawa:l
> woman-ERG man + ABS see + PAST
> 'The woman saw the man'

> buɲa   waguḏa-nda wawa:ḏi:nu
> woman + ABS man-DAT   see + ANTIP + PAST
> 'The woman saw the man'

In both languages the Agent-Ergative is promoted to the Absolutive, while the Absolutive is demoted to Dative.

With a non-human animate Patient-Absolutive, however, demotion is either to the Locative or the Dative:

> ŋayu balmbiɲ   wawa:l
> I + NOM grasshopper + ABS see + PAST
> 'I saw the grasshopper'

> ŋayu   balmbi:ɲda/balmbi:nda   wawa:ḏiɲu
> I + NOM grasshopper + LOC/grasshopper + DAT see + ANTIP + PAST
> 'I saw the grasshopper'

With an inanimate Patient-Absolutive demotion is more commonly to the Locative:

> ŋayu   walba: wawa:ɟiɲu
> I + NOM stone + LOC see + ANTIP + PAST
> 'I saw the stone'

In Eskimo (Woodbury 1977: 322-3) demotion is to the Instrumental:

> miirqa-t   paar-ai
> child + ABS-PL take care of-IND + 3SG + 3PL
> 'She takes care of the children'

> miirqu-nik   paar-si-vuq
> child-PL + INSTR take care of-ANTIP-IND + 3SG
> 'She takes care of the children'

In Chuckchee (Kozinsky et al. 1988: 652, 663, 667) demotion is to Dative or Instrumental:

> ətləg-e   keyŋ-ən penrə-nen
> father-ERG bear-ABS attack-3SG + 3SG + AOR
> 'Father attacked the bear'

> ətləg-en   penrə-tko-gʔe   kayŋ-etə
> father-ABS attack-ANTIP-3SG + AOR bear-DAT
> 'Father ran at the bear'

> ətləg-e   təkečʔ-ən pela-nen
> father-ERG bait-ABS   leave-3SG + 3SG + AOR
> 'Father left the bait'

> ətləg-en   təkečʔ-a ena-pela-gʔe
> father-ABS bait-INSTR ANTIP-leave-3SG + AOR
> 'Father left the bait'

Slightly more surprising is the demotion of the Absolutive to the Ergative rather than to the Dative in Dyirbal, while the Ergative is, as usual, promoted to Absolutive (Dixon 1969: 37, cf. 1972: 65):

> njalŋga   yaɽa-ŋgu djilwa-n
> child + NOM man-ERG kick-PRES/PAST
> 'The man kicked the child'

> yaṛa   njalŋga-ŋgu djilwal-ŋa-nju
> man + NOM child-ERG   kick-ANTIP-PRES/PAST
> 'The man kicked the child'

This might seem like an instance of a simple reversal of the role-relation associations, which does not seem to occur with the passive (see 6.7). However, the Ergative and Instrumental (used in its basic function of indicating the notional instrument) have the same form in Dyirbal, and Dixon (1979: 62) states that demotion to the Ergative/Instrumental is rarer than demotion to the Dative (for which see the example given in 1.4.1).

The antipassive is formed, then, by (i) marking on the verb, (ii) promotion of the Agent-Ergative to Absolutive and (iii) demotion of the Patient-Absolutive to an oblique relation, especially Dative, Locative and Instrumental (or, as will be seen in 7.2.2, its deletion).

7.2 Functions of the antipassive

One of the functions of the antipassive is, like that of the passive, to promote a nonprimary term, in order for it to act as pivot (7.2.1). A second function is quite different – that of 'detransitivization' (7.2.2).

7.2.1 *Creation of pivots*

One function of the passive, as has been seen, is to make the Patient available to act as a syntactic pivot: since it is the Object in the active sentence, this Object has to be promoted to Subject for constructions in which Subjects are pivots. In an ergative system the corresponding device would be one that promotes the Agent-Ergative to Absolutive, since the Absolutive is the primary relation, if it alone can function as pivot (but see 6.5).

Promotion of the Agent-Ergative to make it available as a pivot is, of course, possible only in those languages that have syntactically ergative systems, i.e. in which the Absolutive, the primary relation P = S, functions as a pivot. A number of examples have already been given, but can usefully be repeated here.

The best-known example of such a language is Dyirbal. The use of the antipassive to provide pivots in coordination was shown in 4.1.1 (see also 1.4.1). Both the controller and the target must be Absolutive:

ŋuma;   banaga-ɲu yabu-ŋgu buṛa-n
father + ABS returned-PAST mother-ERG see-PAST
'Father returned and mother saw (him)'

ŋuma   yaba-ŋgu buṛa-n banaga-ɲu
father + ABS mother-ERG see-PAST returned-PAST
'Mother saw father and (he) returned'

It was noted that these could not mean 'Father returned and saw mother', 'Mother saw father and returned', because with those meanings the Agent 'father' in the second clause of the first sentence would have been the deleted target, while in the first clause of the second sentence the Agent 'mother' would have been the controller. But these meanings can be expressed by using the antipassive, since the Agent will then be promoted to Absolutive and available as target or controller respectively:

ŋuma   banaga-ɲu buṛal-ŋa-ɲu   yabu-gu
father + ABS returned-PAST see-ANTIP-PAST mother-DAT
'Father returned and saw mother'

yabu   buṛal-ŋa-ɲu ŋuma-gu   banaga-ɲu
mother + ABS see-ANTIP-PAST father-DAT returned-PAST
'Mother saw father and returned'

Similarly, in Dyirbal only P and S can be relativized. If A is to be relativized, it must first be promoted to the Absolutive by the antipassive:

ŋuma   yabu-ŋgu buṛa-ŋu   duŋgara-ɲu
father + ABS mother-ERG see-REL + ABS cry-PAST
'Father, whom mother saw, was crying'

ŋuma   buṛal-ŋa-ŋu   yabu-gu   duŋgara-ɲu
father + ABS see-ANTIP-REL + ABS mother-DAT cry-PAST
'Father, who saw mother, was crying'

In the both sentences 'father' is relativized (it is he who saw or was seen), but it is the Agent in the relative clause of the second sentence (he saw mother), and so must be promoted to Absolutive.

The creation of new pivots for a very similar purpose is found in Yidiny (Australia, Dixon 1977a: 325), but with one difference: in Dyirbal it is only the target NP, the NP that is relativized that must be Absolutive, but in Yidiny both coreferential NPs, controller and target, must be Absolutive. Examples presented in 4.1.3 (Dixon 1977b: 377–80) were:

wagu:ɖa maŋga:ɲ buɲa:ŋ   wuṛaɲunda
man   laughed   woman + ERG slapped + REL
'The man whom the woman slapped laughed'

buɲa   maŋga:ɲ waguɖanda wuṛa:ɟiɲu:n
woman + ABS laughed   man + DAT   slapped + ANTIP + REL
'The woman who slapped the man laughed'

buɲa   waguɖanda wuṛa:ɟiɲu   maŋgaɲunda
woman + ABS man + DAT   slapped + ANTIP laughed + REL
'The woman who laughed slapped the man'

In the first sentence, both 'man' and 'woman' are Absolutive (S and P respectively). In the second and third, the antipassive is required in order to promote an Agent 'woman' to Absolutive in the relative clause and main clause respectively.

Examples of similar use of antipassive in complementation are to be found in 4.1.2. It must, however, be said that there seem to be very few languages that are as fully ergative syntactically as Dyirbal or Yidiny. Even another Australian language that has antipassives (Warrungu, Tsunoda 1988) sometimes allows coordination of S and A without using the antipassive.

Rather different from any of these is the situation in Mam (Mayan, Guatemala and Mexico, England 1983: 1–4, cf. 1988: 532), where only the Absolutive NP can be focused, negated or questioned, and an Agent NP so treated must be promoted to Absolutive by the antipassive (see 4.1.4):

xiinaq x-ø-kub' tzyuu-n t-e qa-cheej
man ASP-3SG-DIR grab-ANTIP 3SG-OBL PL-horse
'The *man* grabbed the horses'

miyaaʔ xiinaq x-ø-kub' tzyuu-n t-e qa-cheej
NEG man ASP-3SG-DIR grab-ANTIP 3SG-OBL PL-horse
'It wasn't the man who grabbed the horses'

alkyee x-ø-kub' tzyuu-n t-e qa-cheej
who ASP-3SG-DIR grab-ANTIP 3SG-OBL PL-horse
'Who grabbed the horses?'

The antipassive in Mam has other uses, some of them like those discussed in the next section.

7.2.2   Detransitivization

In the examples discussed in 7.2.1 the effect of the antipassive was to promote A to the primary relation of Absolutive (associated with P in the active), while demoting P, in order to make A available as a pivot. In many systems, however, the function of the antipassive appears to be to 'detransitivize', i.e. to indicate that, in some sense, P is less of a patient and/or that A is less of an agent, or, to put it another way, to suggest that the actions of A less directly affect P. More precisely, it may be said that there is a lower degree of transitivity (see Hopper and Thompson 1980). The terms 'detransitivize' and 'transitivity' are, it should be noted, being used here in a semantic sense. There is also grammatical intransitivity: in all instances, P is omitted or demoted to oblique status while A is promoted to Absolutive and so assumes the status of S, since the resultant construction is intransitive. There would seem to be a number of possibilities.

(i) The Patient is unstated, although it is generally 'understood', in the sense that the verb is an action verb which operates on something, e.g. in Chuckchee (Siberia, Kozinsky et al. 1988: 667):

>ətlʔa-ta   məčəkw-ən təni-nin
>mother-ERG shirt-ABS   sew-3SG + 3SG + AOR
>'The mother sewed the shirt'

>ətla ine-nni-gʔi
>mother ANTIP-sew-3SG + AOR
>'The mother sewed'

A similar example from Yidiny (Australia, Dixon 1977a: 279) is (but see (viii) below):

>yiŋu   buɲa   buga:-ɖi-ŋ
>this + ABS woman + ABS eat-ANTIP-PRES
>'This woman is eating'

Dixon says that the corresponding basic sentence with an Ergative instead of an Absolutive would be 'decidedly awkward' and would require an explicit Patient. Foley and Van Valin (1985: 172) offer as the form with Patient:

>yiɲɖu:n buɲa:-ŋ   mayi   buga-ŋ
>this-ERG woman-ERG vegetables eat-PRES
>'This woman is eating vegetables'

In both instances, A is promoted to the status of S and P is omitted. Although there is no overt Patient in the antipassive constructions, it is clear that something was sewed, something was eaten.

This use of the antipassive to delete the Patient exactly parallels the use of the passive to delete an unknown or unimportant Agent in an accusative system (see 5.6).

(ii) The Patient is less directly affected by the action, as in Chuckchee (Kozinsky et al. 1988: 652):

ətləg-e   keyŋ-ən penrə-nen
father-ERG bear-ABS attack-3SG + 3SG + AOR
'Father attacked the bear'

ətləg-ən   penrə-tko-gʔe   kayŋ-etə
father-ABS attack-ANTIP-3SG + AOR bear-DAT
'Father ran at the bear'

In the second of these two sentences, 'father' has been promoted from Ergative to Absolutive, and 'bear' demoted from Absolutive to Dative; in addition the verb agrees with both nouns in the first sentence, but only with 'father' in the second (and there is a change of word order). There is also a change of meaning: the first sentence indicates that the bear was attacked, but the second that father merely ran at it or made an attack on it. Notionally, in the second sentence, the bear is not fully a patient, in that it does not fully undergo the effect of the action; this is indicated by the use of the antipassive, because its effect is to demote the Patient to the oblique status of Dative. The same kind of interpretation is, no doubt, to be given to the antipassive form that differs from the example in (i) only in the presence of the Patient:

ətlʔa   ine-nni-gʔi   məˇčəkw-a
mother + ABS ANTIP-sew-3SG + AOR shirt-INSTR
'The mother sewed the shirt'

(A comparable example discussed in 7.4 has the translations 'trying to sew', 'is sewing away at'.) Similar examples are found in several Caucasian languages, e.g. 'bite' vs. 'gnaw at' in Kabardian (Catford 1976).

Rather more subtle is the contrast in Chamorro (Eastern Oceanic, Cooreman 1988: 575):

un-hongge   i   lahi
2SG + ERG-believe the man
'You believe the man'

man-hongge hao nu i lahi
ANTIP-believe 2SG + ABS OBL the man
'You believe/have faith in the man'

ha-faisen i patgon nu i kuestion
3SG + ERG-ask the child OBL the question
'He asked the child a question'

Mamaisen gue' gi patgon nu i kuestion
ANTIP + ask 3SG + ABS LOC child OBL the question
'He asked the question from the child'

Note that 'man' is demoted to 'Oblique' (= Dative?) status in the first example, but 'child' to Locative in the second (which already has an 'Oblique' NP).

(iii) The antipassive may have an aspectual function, e.g. in Chamorro (Austronesian, Cooreman 1988: 583) to indicate iterative action:

Mang-galuti gue' ni ga'lagu
ANTIP-hit 3SG + ABS OBL dog
'He repeatedly hit the dog'

There is also an aspectual feature in the use of antipassive in Warrungu (Australia, Tsunoda 1988: 606), to distinguish 'see' from 'look for':

nyula nyaka-n wurripa
3SG + NOM see + P/P bee + ABS
'He saw bees'

ngaya nyaka-kali wurripa-wu katyarra-wu
1SG + NOM see-ANTIP + P/P bee-DAT possum-DAT
'I was looking for bees and possums'

The most relevant point here is that 'bee' is demoted from Absolutive to Dative with the antipassive; the (nominative) case of the pronouns was explained in 3.3.2.

(iv) Closely associated with the aspectual function is the use to indicate a partitive ('some of') Patient (cf. 2.7), as in Eskimo (A. C. Woodbury 1975: 26):

arna-p niqi niri-vaa
woman-ERG meat + ABS eat-INDIC
'The woman ate the meat'

arna   niqi-mik   niri-NNig-puq
woman + ABS meat-INSTR eat-ANTIP-INDIC
'The woman ate some of the meat'

So too in Chamorro (Cooreman 1988: 576):

In-chule'   i   litratu
1PL + ERG-take the picture
'We took the picture'

man-mañule ham   gi litratu
ANTIP-take   1PL + ABS LOC picture
'We took some of the pictures'

(v) The antipassive may indicate that the Agent does not act alone, as in Chamorro (Cooreman 1988: 580):

ha-yulang   si   Juan i   kareta
3SG + ERG-break UNM John the car   [UNMarked]
'John broke the car'

Man-yulang si   Juan gi kareta
ANTIP-break UNM John LOC car
'John took part in breaking the car'

(vi) For Chamorro, Cooreman (1988: 623) notes that the antipassive is obligatory when the Patient is indefinite, and that this is its most common use. Associated with this, perhaps, is the observation by Tsunoda (1988: 623) that in Warrungu the antipassive indicates topicality of the Agent, for that implies non-topicality of the Patient and non-topics are often indefinites.

(vii) The antipassive is used where the Patient is generic, as in Warrungu (Tsunoda 1988: 604):

nyula   manytya-ngku watyu-kali-yal
3SG + NOM food-INSTR   cook-ANTIP-P/P
'She cooks food'/'She's a cook'

Similarly, in Mam (Guatemala and Mexico) the antipassive is used for what England (1988: 534) calls the 'incorporating function', with generic Patient:

ma ø-b'iincha-n   qa-jaa
REC 3SG + ABS-make-ANTIP PL-house   [RECent past]
'He builds houses'

The term 'incorporating function' is intended to compare this construction with constructions in other languages in which the Patient is morphologically incorporated in the verb, together with a generic meaning. It may be relevant to note that Chuckchee (Kosinzky et al. 1988: 667) uses both an antipassive and an incorporating construction (see 7.5).

(viii) Finally, it may be noted that according to Dixon (1977a: 274–7) the antipassive marker -:ɖi-n in Yidiny has five functions:
(a) It marks the antipassive:

> wagu:ɖa   giba:ɖiɲu   buɲa:nda
> Man + ABS scratch + ANTIP + PAST woman + DAT
> 'The man scratched the woman'

(b) it marks a reflexive construction:

> wagu:ɖa   giba:ɖiɲu
> Man + ABS scratch + ANTIP + PAST
> 'The man scratched himself'

(c) The Agent, though still Ergative, is inanimate:

> ŋaɲaɲ ginga:ŋ   giba:ɖiɲu
> I + ACC prickle + ERG scratched + ANTIP + PAST
> 'A prickle scratched me'

(d) The Agent is human, but the result is accidental:

> ŋaɲaɲ bama:l   ɖaŋga:ɖiŋ   muguy
> I + ACC person + ERG grumble at + ANTIP + PRES all the time
> '(That) person keeps grumbling at me all the time'

(e) The action is continuous:

> ŋuŋu bama gama:ɖiɲu
> that   person vomit + ANTIP + PRES
> 'That person is vomiting'

Dixon suggests that these can all be explained as deviations from the transitive, active, constructions which have an Agent with volitional control and a single completed or anticipated action. (a) and (b) have no Agent, (c) and (d) have an Agent with no voluntary control and (e) does not refer to a completed action. Hopper and Thompson (1980: 276) suggest that the issue here is again one of transitivity – that the marker is a detransitivizing marker signalling lower transitivity with respect to volitionality, purposiveness and perfectivity. In the light of the other examples discussed in this section, this

185

has some merit, but it may be that grammatical polysemy of this kind cannot always be fully explained.

7.3 Promotion of oblique relations

The antipassives considered in 7.2 all involved promotion of the Agent-Ergative to Absolutive. However, in Chuckchee, the antipassive may be used to promote an oblique relation to Absolutive (Kozinsky et al. 1988: 667):

> ətləg-e təkeč-ən utkuč-ək pela-nen
> father-ERG bait-ABS trap-LOC leave-3sG + 3sG + AOR
> 'Father left the bait at the trap'

> ətləg-e təkeč-a utkuč-ən ena-pela-nen
> father-ERG bait-INSTR trap-ABS ANTIP-leave-3sG + 3sG + AOR
> 'Father left the bait at the trap'

In the first sentence 'bait' is marked as the Absolutive Patient, while 'trap' is Locative, showing where the bait was left, but in the second (antipassive) sentence 'trap' has been promoted to Absolutive, with 'bait' demoted to Instrumental. The promotion of 'trap' to the position occupied by the Patient in the active obviously suggests that it is notionally a patient, so that a better translation might be 'Father baited the trap with the bait'.

Notionally, this use of the antipassive is very like promotion to Object in accusative systems (6.6), but formally it is the counterpart of promotion of oblique relations to Subject with the passive (5.3), since in both cases promotion is to the primary relation – to Subject in the accusative system and to Absolutive in the ergative system.

It may be added, that, as with the construction discussed in 7.2.2 (vii), Chuckchee also has an incorporating construction that similarly promotes the Locative to the Absolutive, but incorporates the original Patient into the verb, instead of demoting it to Instrumental (see 7.5).

By analogy with Shibatani's view that the basic function of the passive is to defocus the Agent (6.7), it might be said that the basic function of the antipassive is to defocus the Patient. This would account for the example considered here as well as all the examples of 7.2. In most cases the antipassive promotes the Agent to Absolutive, but in the example discussed in this section it does not: A remains as Ergative, because, although the

Patient has been demoted, another term has been promoted to Absolutive and the construction remains transitive.

7.4 **Detransitives without antipassive**

Some languages with ergative systems have what seems to be a detransitivized construction, exactly like that of the antipassive discussed in 7.3, but with the crucial difference that no antipassive marker is present (though in spite of this they are often referred to as 'antipassives' – Rude 1988: 552, Estival and Myhill 1988: 459, Hopper and Thompson 1980: 268). The situation is that, in addition to the normal construction in which the Agent is marked as Ergative, there is another construction in which the Agent is marked as Absolutive, and/or the Patient is demoted to oblique status or omitted. Grammatically one construction is transitive, the other intransitive. There are various possibilities.

(i) The simplest case is where the Patient is merely omitted, and, since the resultant sentence is intransitive, the Agent is S and is marked as Absolutive. Comrie (1978: 358) quotes for Tongan (cf. Churchward 1953: 76–7):

> Naʻe inu ʻa e kava ʻe Sione
> PAST drink ABS the kava ERG John
> 'John drank the kava'

> Naʻe inu ʻa Sione
> PAST drink ABS John
> 'John drank'

This, of course, can be seen as simply a matter of a transitive/intransitive contrast, with the absence of a Patient making the second sentence intransitive and so requiring an Absolutive S. However, it is exactly parallel to the examples in 7.2.2 (i), where the antipassive was used.

(ii) The situation most obviously like that of the antipassive is one in which, in addition to a construction in which Agent and Patient are marked as Ergative and Absolutive, there is another construction in which the terms are marked as Absolutive and Oblique, and, as in the examples of 7.2.2, there is clearly lowered transitivity. Thus Anderson (1976: 221) quotes from Bzhedukh (W. Circassian):

> čʺaaλa-m čʼəgˆ°-ər ya-źˆ°a
> boy-ERG field-ABS 3SG-plough
> 'The boy ploughs the field'

čʺaaλa-r č'əgˈ-əm ya-żˈa
boy-ABS field-OBL 3SG-plough
'The boy is trying to plough the field'/'The boy is doing some
    ploughing on the field'

Anderson notes that there are many such pairs, and that the use of the detransitivized construction indicates that 'the action is carried out less completely, less successfully, less conclusively, etc., or that the object is less completely, less directly, less permanently, etc. affected'.

The construction may indicate that the action is incomplete, as in Kalkatungu (Blake 1982: 86):

tuka-yu tuar itʸayi
dog-ERG snake bite
'The dog bites/bit the snake'

tuku   tuar-ku   itʸayi
dog + ABS snake-DAT bite
'The dog is biting the snake'

Here there is lower transitivity in the sense that an incomplete action affects the Patient less.

Similarly, Catford (1976: 45) notes for Kabardian, though with the Patient being demoted to the Ergative, not to Oblique:

ħe-m   qʷɨpsħe-r jedza'qe
dog-ERG bone-ABS bite
'The dog is biting the bone'

ħe-r   qʷɨpsħe-m jewdza'qe
dog-ABS bone-ERG bite
'The dog is biting the bone'

The first construction is said to imply that 'the dog bites the bone right through to the marrow', and the second that 'the dog is merely gnawing at the bone'.

With rather different meaning contrasts, there are in Yukulta (Australia, Dixon 1979: 96) two constructions, one transitive with Ergative and Absolutive, the other intransitive with Absolutive and Dative. The transitive construction is used for statements of past facts and future intentions, and the intransitive construction for all other cases, including negatives and wishes. (But there is a complication in that the intransitive is further required if the Agent is third person and the Patient either first or second person, or if the

Agent is second person and the Patient is non-singular first person – the empathy hierarchy (2.2) is also involved.)

(iii) Sometimes the construction is marked, though not with an antipassive marker. Thus, with some verbs in Bzhedukh (Andersen 1976: 122), it has an explicit intransitive marker on the verb:

> p:śaśa-m c'əy-ər   ya-d-ə
> girl-ERG cherkesska-ABS 3SG(3SG)-SEW-PRES
> 'The girl is sewing the cherkesska'

> p:śaśa-r c'əy-əm   ya-d-a
> girl-ABS cherkesska-OBL 3SG(3SG)-SEW-PRES + INTR
> 'The girl is trying to sew/sewing away at the cherkesska'

As the earlier example showed, such marking is not always present.

In N. Baffin Island Eskimo (Kalmár 1979: 118), the intransitive construction is used with indefinite Patients, but the transitive and intransitive constructions are distinguished by 'Polypersonal' and 'Monopersonal' suffixes on the verb:

> inu-up   qimmiq   taku-v-a-a
> person-ERG dog + ABS see-INDIC-POLYP-3/3
> 'The/A person saw the dog'

> inuk   qimmir-mik taku-v-uq
> man + ABS dog-OBL   see-INDIC-MONOP + 3
> 'The/A man saw a dog'

A rather different kind of marking is that of the reflexive in Dyirbal (Dixon 1972: 90):

> balam   wuɖu   baŋgul   yaṛa-ŋgu ɖaŋga-ɲu
> CL + ABS fruit + ABS CL + ERG man-ERG eat-TNS
> 'The man eats fruit'

> bayi   yaṛa   ɖaŋga-mari-ɲu
> CL + ABS man + ABS eat-REFL-TNS
> 'The man eats'

(iv) In some cases demotion or omission of the Patient does not entail promotion of the Agent-Ergative to Absolutive (it remains in the ergative case). An example from Warlbiri (Australia, Hale 1973a: 336) is:

Antipassive

> njuntulu-ḻu npa-tju pantu-ṉu ŋatju
> you-ERG   2-1   spear-PAST me
> 'You speared me'

> njuntulu-ḻu npa-tju-ḻa pantu-ṉu ŋatju-ku
> you-ERG   2-1-CLIT   spear-PAST me-DAT
> 'You speared at me/tried to spear me'

The second example raises a problem concerning the status of the construction. The presence of the ergative marker suggests that it is transitive, but the second term is clearly marked as dative, not absolutive, which suggests that it is intransitive. The best solution is to recognize this Ergative + Dative construction as neither transitive nor intransitive, but as in between the two and with lowered transitivity.

(v) There is detransitivization also in Nez Perce (N.W. USA, Rude 1988: 552), although this language does not, strictly, have an ergative system, but one with three distinct relations (see 3.4), since A, S and P are all marked differently, the case forms usually being called 'ergative', 'nominative' and 'accusative', though Rude used the term 'direct object' (DO) for the last. Even so, it is clear that there are two constructions, one fully transitive, the other essentially intransitive:

> háama-nm pée-'wiye   wewúkiye-ne
> man-ERG   3 + ERG-shot elk-DO
> 'The man shot an elk'

> háama hi-'wíye   wewúkiye
> man   3 + NOM-shot elk
> 'The man shot an elk'

Rude says that with the second construction, with the Agent marked as S and the Patient without its basic marking (as 'DO' with the accusative case) the Patient tends significantly to be less topical, animate and definite than the Agent.

There is a long discussion of the kind of features associated with antipassives and the related intransitive constructions in Tsunoda 1981. Interestingly, by comparing Ergative + Absolutive constructions with other constructions generally, he is able to include, in his discussion, the situation in which a language has an ergative system in one tense or aspect and an accusative system in another (3.3.1). He suggests that in both types of situation an Ergative + Absolutive construction distinctively marks such features as perfectivity, completion, punctuality, definiteness etc.

7.5 Incorporation

Alongside the antipassive, Chuckchee (Kozinsky et al. 1988: 667) has another device for detransitivization, that of 'incorporation', by which one of the arguments is 'incorporated' into the verb, i.e. becomes grammatically and usually phonologically (but see below) part of the verbal element. This is a feature found mostly with ergative systems.

Incorporation can be illustrated by the comparison of two examples repeated from 7.2.2 and 7.3 with examples exhibiting incorporation (the first of each trio is active, the second antipassive, while the third exhibits incorporation):

ətlʔa-ta   məčəkw-ən təni-nin
mother-ERG shirt-ABS   sew-3SG + 3SG + AOR
'The mother sewed the shirt'

ətlʔa   ine-nni-gʔi   məˇčəkw-a
mother + ABS ANTIP-sew-3SG + AOR shirt-INSTR
'The mother sewed the shirt'

ətlʔa   məčəkwə-nni-gʔi
mother + ABS shirt-sew-3SG + AOR
'The mother sewed the shirt'

ətləg-e   təkeč-ən utkuč-ək pela-nen
father-ERG bait-ABS trap-LOC leave-3SG + 3SG + AOR
'Father left the bait at the trap'

ətləg-e   təkeč-a utkuč-ən ena-pela-nen
father-ERG bait-INSTR trap-ABS ANTIP-leave-3SG + 3SG + AOR
'Father left the bait at the trap'

ətləg-e   utkuč-ən təkečʔə-pela-nen
father-ERG trap-ABS bait-leave-3SG + 3SG + AOR
'Father left the bait at the trap'

There are two types of incorporation here (see the discussion in Mithun (1984), who provides a wealth of examples): the first merely incorporates the Absolutive-Patient and thereby deprives it of its (relational) status, the other incorporates the Absolutive-Patient, but also promotes an oblique argument to the relational status of Absolutive, which is no longer held by the Patient.

A further example of the first type from Ponapaean (Micronesian, Sugita 1973: 401) is:

> I pahn doakao mwahmw-o
> I will spear fish-the
> 'I will spear the fish'

> I phan dokomwomw
> I will spear-fish
> 'I will engage in spear-fishing'

The second type with promotion of a peripheral argument to Absolutive is further illustrated by Mithun (1984: 858) from Yucatec Mayan:

> k-in-č'ak-ø-k   če' ičil in-kool
> INCOMP-I-chop-it-IMPERF tree in my-cornfield   [INCOMPletive]
> 'I chop the tree in my cornfield'

> k-n-č'ak-če'-t-ik   in-kool
> INCOMP-I-chop-tree-TRANS-IMPERF my-cornfield
> 'I clear my cornfield'

> k-in-wek-ø-k   ha'
> INCOMP-I-spill-it-IMPERF water
> 'I spill water'

> k-in-wek-ha'a-t-ik
> INCOMP-I-spill-water-TRANS-IMPERF
> 'I splash him'

It is not only the Absolutive-P, but also the Absolutive-S, that may be incorporated: incorporation involves, that is to say, the primary grammatical relation Absolutive. Thus in Onondaga (Iroquoian, USA, H. Woodbury 1975: 10) the following pairs of sentences are both possible:

> waʔhahninúʔ?   neʔ oyékwaʔ?
> TNS + he/it + buy + ASP DEF tobacco
> 'He bought the tobacco'

> waʔhayɛkwahni:nuʔ?
> TNS + he/it + tobacco + buy + ASP
> 'He bought tobacco'

kahihwí ne? ohsahé?ta?
it + spill + CAUS + ASP NOM.PART it + bean + SUFF [NOMinal PARTicle]
'The beans are spilled'

kahsahe?tahíhwi
it + bean + spill + CAUS + ASP
'Beans are spilled'

However, in Southern Tiwa (New Mexico, Rosen 1990: 680) there are restrictions on the incorporation of S in that it cannot be incorporated if animate, and must be incorporated if inanimate, as shown by the possible and impossible:

Musan i-k'euwe-m
cats B-old-PRES   [B = word class marker]
'The cats are old'

*I-musa-k'euwe-m

I-k'uru-k'euwe-m
B-dipper-old-PRES
'The dipper is old'

*K'uru i-k'euwe-m

Agents are never incorporated. There is then, as Rosen notes, no ambiguity in:

Seuanin ibi-musa-mũ-ban
men   B + B-cat-see-PAST
'The men saw the cats'

This cannot mean 'The cats saw the men'.

Often, incorporation is used to suggest an indefinite, non-referential sense, as is shown by an example from Chuckchee given by Comrie (1973: 243–4):

Tumg-e   nəntewatən kupre-n
friends-ERG + PL set   net-ABS + SING
'The friends set the net'

Tumg-ət   kopra-ntewatg?at
friends-ABS + PL net-set
'The friends net-set (set nets)'

However, where an oblique argument is promoted, the obvious purpose is to indicate that it is this that is most affected, e.g. in the example from Yukatec

Mayan, that the field is cleared of trees rather than that trees are cleared from the field.

Mithun (1984: 860–1) shows that incorporation is also used to 'background' old information, as shown in a conversation in Huatla Nahuatl (Uto-Aztecan, Mexico):

> A askeman ti-'-kwa nakatl
> never you-it-eat meat
> 'You never eat meat'

> B na' ipanima ni-naka-kwa
> I always I-meat-eat
> 'I eat meat all the time'

A rather special use of incorporation is that of 'classificatory noun incorporation' (Mithun 1984: 863–72) where a semantically more general noun is incorporated with a more specific noun as the Patient as in Gunwinggu (Australia, Oates 1964: 104):

> bene-dulg-naŋ mangaralaljmayn
> they + two-tree-saw cashew nut
> 'They saw a cashew tree'

Mithun (1984: 849–54) also treats as incorporation instances where there is 'juxtaposition' rather than 'morphological compounding', i.e. where the argument remains a separate word, e.g. in Tongan (Churchward 1953: 76, cf. Mithun 1984: 851):

> Naʻe inu ʻa e kavá ʻé Sione
> PAST drink ABS the kava ERG John
> 'John drank the kava'

> Naʻe inu kavá ʻa Sione
> PAST drink kava ABS John
> 'John drank kava ("kava-drank")'

This is similar to the examples considered in 7.4 ('detransitives without antipassive'), and the term 'incorporation' does not seem to be entirely appropriate, although the function is similar. Yet there is a problem with the status of the Patient 'kava', which appears to be unmarked for absolutive/ ergative, and that may suggest that it has lost its relational status, as it would have done through incorporation.

194

Also similar are constructions such as that in Hungarian where a non-referential Patient is placed before the verb, but a referential Patient after it (Hopper and Thompson 1980: 258):

> Péter újságot olvas
> Peter paper   reads
> 'Peter is reading a newspaper'

> Péter olvas egy újságot
> Peter reads a   paper
> 'Peter is reading a (specific) newspaper'

Here, however, it is reasonable to suggest that the Patient retains its grammatical relation of Object, and to make a distinction in terms of a grammatical category that involves specific/non-specific. There are, in other languages, different devices for distinguishing specific/non-specific Patients (although for Spanish the distinction involves a difference of grammatical relation – see 2.3.3).

7.6   Lexical issues

The constructions discussed in the previous sections of this chapter occur also not as grammatical, but as lexical, variants, i.e. determined by the choice of verb. The issue of transitivity is, naturally, central. There are three possibilities, but two other constructions that were not noted in the previous sections will also be considered.

(i) Many verbs simply have a single argument, S, like the examples in 7.2.2 (i); these are fully intransitive and too obvious to require exemplification.

(ii) Other verbs have two arguments, but the second is oblique, usually Dative. An example, from Bayungu (W. Australia, Austin 1982: 41–2) with the verb 'fear', is:

> yinha   kupu-ju pirungkarri-yu ngurnu   kaparla-ku
> this + NOM child-ABS fear-PRES   that + DAT dog-DAT
> 'This child fears that dog'

This Absolutive + Dative construction is, of course, the type most closely associated with the antipassive in 7.1 and 7.2. Similar (patientive + dative) constructions were also noted for Georgian (3.6.1) and Tabassaran (3.6.2).

(iii) The construction with ergative + dative marking, exemplified in 7.4 (iv), is similar to the agentive + dative construction noted for Tabassaran

(3.6.2) and the verbal agreement system of Chocktaw (3.5.1). In fact, for both languages, there are the three possibilities of agentive + patientive (the active, transitive, type), agentive + dative and patientive + dative. It is not surprising that some scholars have treated Georgian and Tabassaran as ergative, although, in both languages (as well as Choctaw), the situation is too complex for such a simple characterization.

There is an interesting situation with some verbs in Australian languages. In Bandjalung (Austin 1982: 38–9), some verbs occur with an ergative NP, but no explicit Patient:

> mali-yu dandaygam-bu yarrbi-ni
> that-ERG old man-ERG sing-PAST DEF
> 'That old man sang'
>
> mali-yu jajaam-bu jaluba-ni
> that-ERG child-ERG urinate-PAST DEF
> 'That child urinated'

Although these appear to be intransitive, the putative S is marked as ergative. It could be argued that the feature is one of agentivity (3.5), since other intransitives have Absolutive S (i.e. that S is either Agentive or Patientive). There is, however, a different explanation: that with verbs such as 'sing' and 'urinate' (and other verbs listed, such as 'yawn', 'dance', 'smoke') the construction is not strictly intransitive, but, as Austin suggests, that it has an unexpressed 'cognate object', an 'object' that is essentially part of the action described by the verb – 'sing a song', 'speak a language' etc. It is significant that, in Bandjalung, such constructions may have antipassives, which are generally associated with transitive constructions (Austin 1982: 38–9):

> ngay gala   juuma-le-ela
> I + NOM this + NOM smoke-ANTIP-PRES
> 'I here am smoking'

This would suggest that the apparently intransitive constructions with the single term marked as ergative are, in fact, transitive. In a similar way, the possible relevance of cognate objects to transitivity was also mentioned in the discussion of intransitives with passives in accusative systems – see 5.4.

The situation with similar verbs is very different in Diyari (Austin 1982: 40). Here, even if there is an explicit Patient, the marking is absolutive + absolutive:

> nganhi nhinha-ya yawada   yatha-yi
> I + NOM this-ACC   language + ABS speak + PRES
> 'I speak this language'

This may be contrasted with:

> ngathu nhinha-ya nganthi   thayi-yi
> I + ERG this-ACC   meat-ABS eat-PRES
> 'I eat this meat'

Here the relevant point is that 'I' is nominative, the case associated with S, in the first sentence, but ergative in the second.

It must be said that Diyari does not have an ergative system, but a system of three basic relations (see 3.4), and that a similar (absolutive + absolutive/ patientive + patientive) contrast was noted in an agentive system (3.5.1). Nevertheless, a comparison with the behaviour of verbs with cognate objects in Diyari and Bandjalung is illuminating. The two languages appear to deal with them in quite opposite ways: Bandjalung suggests that there is an Agent even when the sentence is overtly intransitive, while Diyari suggests that there is no Agent even when the sentence is overtly transitive. What, perhaps, explains this apparent paradox is that cognate objects, since they are essentially part of the action expressed by the verb, (a) can be omitted or 'incorporated', though still to be 'understood' and (b), even if expressed, are not fully patients. Because of (a) Bandjalung treats verbs with them as transitive, even if they are not explicitly expressed, and because of (b) Diyari treats verbs with them as of lowered transitivity (with no Agent-Ergative), even if they are overtly expressed.

7.7   Antipassives in accusative systems

If a device in an ergative system language for demoting or deleting A is regarded as a passive (6.5), it should follow that a device in an accusative system for demoting or deleting P is an antipassive. However, if a basic requirement is that such a device is explicitly marked (usually in the verb), it seems unlikely that there are, in fact, any languages with accusative systems (in their morphology of the noun and/or verbal agreement) that also have antipassives. This would, indeed, be in accordance with the suggestion made in 4.2 that there is an implication that if a verb has accusative noun morphology and/or verbal agreement, it will have accusative syntax.

If, however, there is no requirement of explicit marking, so that the constructions in 7.4 are considered to be antipassives, as some scholars suggest, then it can equally be argued that there are passives in accusative systems. This would be so for English, as Heath (1976: 203) actually suggests, with:

He drinks

Speed kills

Since it has been argued here that the constructions in 7.4 are not antipassives, and, more importantly, that omission of the Agent in an ergative system is not an indication of a passive (6.5), Heath's suggestion is not accepted.

Foley and Van Valin (1985: 344) suggest a similar analysis for Kusaiean (Austronesian):

> nga ɔl-læ   nuknuk ɛ
> I   wash-PERF clothes the
> 'I washed the clothes'

> nga owo nuknuk læ
> I   wash clothes PERF
> 'I wash clothes'

> nga owo læ
> I   wash PERF
> 'I washed'

In the first sentence the verbal form *ɔl-* is transitive, while in the second and third *owo* is intransitive. The only problem here is why the intransitive form is used with the second where 'clothes' is indefinite. The most plausible explanation is that this is like the examples of incorporation discussed in 7.5, especially the Hungarian examples; alternatively, it can be argued that there is lowered transitivity when the Patient is indefinite, and that it is that that determines the use of the intransitive form. There is little clear justification for calling this antipassive.

There is another construction in accusative systems that might be considered antipassive – the construction in which an oblique term (Dative, Instrumental or Locative) is promoted to Object (see 6.6). This looks, prima facie, like the counterpart of the use of the antipassive that promotes oblique relations as discussed in 7.3. However, there is, perhaps, an important difference, in that, although an oblique term is promoted in the accusative systems, it is not wholly obvious that the Patient is demoted, since it generally remains as a second Object. If defocusing of the Patient, on the analogy of Shibatani's (see 6.7) defocusing of the Agent by the passive, is the primary function of the antipassive, it is not clear that this construction is an antipassive.

7.8   The typological status of ergative systems

It may be asked whether ergative languages and systems have an equal status with that of accusative ones, or whether they are less common, less typical or less natural.

Languages with ergative systems are scattered in many parts of the world, as a list of just a few languages will show – Basque (Western Europe), Tabassaran (the Caucasus), Hindi (India), Dyirbal (Australia), Tongan (the Pacific), Eskimo (North America), Mam (Central America) etc. Africa seems to be the only major area where there are no languages with an ergative system. There are, moreover, many such languages – over two hundred – in Australia. In terms of numbers and geographical spread, ergative systems are by no means unimportant or untypical of the languages of the world. On the other hand, there are very few languages that are fully ergative. Many 'ergative languages' have ergative systems of noun morphology or verbal agreement, or both, but accusative syntax (4.2). Warlbiri even has ergative noun morphology, but accusative agreement (3.2). In addition, some have passives, which seem more appropriate to accusative systems, although, in contrast, languages with accusative systems do not normally have antipassives (7.7).

The issue of naturalness may be relevant, for there are constructions that are, for semantic reasons, likely to follow accusative lines. The most obvious ones are the imperative (which generally follows an accusative pattern even in Dyirbal) and its associated subordinate jussive (4.4). It may also be argued that even coordination most naturally follows accusative, rather than ergative lines. In coordination Agents rather than Patients are usually topics, and in discourse the topic often remains the same over several sentences, and need not be repeated. It is natural, therefore, to omit A rather than P. (There might seem to be a counterargument in Du Bois (1987), who talks of the 'discourse basis for ergativity', but his arguments do not relate directly to the point at issue, since his 'ergativity' relates to the lexical expression of S and P, not their availability for deletion.)

There is another point. Ergative morphology is often not only restricted to noun morphology, but also consists solely of marking A, while leaving P and S unmarked. There is motivation for marking either A or P, in order to distinguish them in a transitive construction, but there is no motivation for marking S, because it is the sole (primary) term of the intransitive. Because of this, the identity of S with P often consists solely of the absence of marking, such identity being a consequence of the fact that A is marked. The identity (in terms of absence of marking) may thus be seen as accidental or, at least, of little significance. A number of 'ergative languages', then, may be ergative only in this rather trivial sense.

For these reasons, it might well be suggested that a typological study should be basically in accusative terms, treating ergative systems as a variation from the norm, and in many cases, merely an issue of morphological marking (cf. Anderson 1976 and the very different solution of Johns 1991). This would simplify the basic overall pattern, and, in particular, would also have the advantage of making the terms 'Subject' and 'Object' available for all languages. However, it would lead to some distortion of the facts for a fully ergative language such as Dyirbal and, to a lesser extent, to the analysis of other patterns such as those of agentive systems, as well as the 'inverse' systems and 'topic' systems that are to be discussed in the next chapter.

8
'Topic' and inverse systems

In this brief chapter two systems that appear to involve voice, but cannot easily be interpreted in terms of either passive or antipassive, are considered.

8.1 'Topic' systems

There are languages which might be interpreted as having devices that are like the passive and the antipassive in that they promote secondary or oblique terms to primary status, yet are not easily identified as either passive or antipassive. This is especially characteristic of most of the languages of the Philippines.

8.1.1 *Morphology*

In Tagalog (Schachter 1976), there are four arguments that Schachter identifies as A ('agent'), G ('goal'), B ('beneficiary') and D ('direction'). In the discussion here, for consistency with the rest of this book, 'Patient' (P) will be used instead of 'goal', 'Dative' (D) instead of 'beneficiary' and 'Locative' (L) instead of 'direction'. (The term 'goal' has been used in at least two other senses by other scholars.) Any of these four can be independently marked as 'topic' by (i) being preceded by the particle *ang* and (ii) specific forms of the verb, these forms being identified as AT ('Agent topic'), PT ('Patient topic'), LT ('Locative topic') and DT ('Dative topic'). In the translations give below the 'topic' is shown in italics:

> Magsalis ang babae ng bigas sa sako para sa bata
> AT + will take out TOP woman PAT rice LOC sack DAT child
> '*The woman* will take the rice out of the sack for the child'

Aalisin   ng babae ang bigas sa sako para sa bata
PT + will take out AGT woman TOP rice LOC sack DAT child
'The woman will take *the rice* out of the bag for the child'

Aalisan   ng babae ng bigas ang sako para sa bata
LT + will take out AGT woman PAT rice TOP sack DAT child
'The woman will take the rice out of *the sack* for the child'

Ipagsalis   ng babae ng bigas sa sako ang bata
DT + will take out AGT woman PAT rice LOC sack TOP child
'The woman will take the rice out of the sack for *the child*'

A similar system is recorded for Ga'dang (Philippines) by Walrod (1976), although Walrod talks about 'passives'. Here, given a sentence like 'I tied the pig to the post with a rope for the old man', different forms of the verb allow not only Agent ('I'), Patient ('the pig'), Locative ('the post') and Dative ('the old man'), but also Instrumental ('a rope') to become 'Subjects'/topics.

It might seem to be reasonable to deal with the Tagalog examples in the same way as the Malagasy examples discussed in 5.3, i.e. to suggest that there are four voices, an active with the Agent as Subject, a passive with the Patient-Object promoted to Subject, and others that promote Datives and Locatives to Subject. In that case, more illuminating translations would be:

'The woman will take the rice out of the sack for the children'
'The rice will be taken out of the sack by the woman for the children'
'The sack will have the rice taken out of it by the woman for the children'
'The children will have the rice taken out of the sack for them by the woman'

However, some scholars reject the notion of 'Subject' here and prefer to deal with the issues in terms of 'topicalization'. This would make the Tagalog system similar to that found in languages where a change in word order allows the Object (and other elements in the sentence) to be topicalized by being placed in initial position, e.g. in Greek (5.5). Indeed, Foley and Van Valin (1985: 328) specifically suggest that the Tagalog situation is 'exactly parallel' with that of Lango (East Africa) where Objects and Beneficiaries can be topicalized by being placed in initial position. The objection to this is that, unlike languages that exhibit topicalization, Tagalog specifically marks these topics not only by a specific morpheme preceding the topicalized NP, but also, like the passive and antipassive, by a marker on the verb. It is, therefore, reasonable to conclude that Tagalog has a device of the passive/antipassive type, i.e. that it is a system of voice, not of topicalization.

There are two reasons, however, that make it difficult to characterize the device as either passive or active, and the system as either accusative or ergative.

First, there is no indication in the marking on the noun or the marking on the verb to suggest whether the 'Agent topic' or the 'Patient topic' construction is the more basic. One argument for taking one of the sentence types as basic is statistical: the PT type is by far the commonest (Cooreman, Fox and Givón 1984: 17). Another is that often the Patient topic is unmarked. On that evidence, the Tagalog system would be ergative, and the voice system would be antipassive.

Secondly, comparison with intransitive sentences does not resolve the issue; the morphological system of nominals does not point to either an accusative (S = A) or ergative (S = P) system, because the intransitive structures are marked as either AT or PT/LT (Schachter 1976: 499):

> Magtatrabaho ang lalaki
> AT + will work TOP man
> 'The man will work'

> Papawisan   ang lalaki
> PT/LT + will sweat TOP man
> 'The man will sweat'

Shibatani (1988a: 103–4) shows a similar feature in another Philippine language, Cebuano:

> Ni-basa siy a   ug libro
> AT-read TOP (he) PAT book
> '*He* read a book'

> Gi-basa niya   ang libro
> PT-read AGT (he) TOP book
> 'He read *the book*'

> Ni-dagan siya
> AT-run   TOP (he)
> '*He* ran'

> Gi-kapoy siya
> PT-tired   TOP (he)
> '*He* got tired'

203

As Shibatani points out, this is reminiscent of an agentive system, but, since such systems are neither ergative or accusative, it gives no help in deciding whether the voice system is in terms of passive or antipassive.

It should be noted, however, that, although marking on the verb identifies S as having the grammatical roles of Agent, Patient or Locative, S is also marked as topic, exactly like one of the arguments in the transitive constructions. Topic thus has grammatical status like that of Subject or Absolutive: it is a grammatical relation and will be indicated as such by the use of an initial capital ('Topic'). The most reasonable conclusion is that, while the system in Tagalog and other Philippine languages is a voice system, it is unlike that of passive and antipassive in that it has no basic sentence type, any of the arguments being able to function as the primary relation Topic in transitive sentences, but with grammatical roles being differentiated in intransitive as well as transitive constructions, and with two different types of S in intransitives. It is neither accusative nor ergative, but neutral in terms of that distinction.

8.1.2 Syntax

The Topic is the pivot for relativization (Schachter 1976: 500); the voice system, like the passive and antipassive, is used to create new pivots:

> Matalino ang lalaking bumasa   ng diyaryo
> intelligent TOP man + LI AGT + read PAT newspaper   [LInker]
> 'The man who read a newspaper is intelligent'

> Interesante ang diyaryong   binasa   ng   lalaki
> interesting TOP newspaper + LI PT + read AGT man
> 'The newspaper that the man read is interesting'

Givón (1979: 154–5) provides, from Bikol, a related language, examples of relative clauses with Agent, Patient, Dative (D), Instrumental (I) and Benefactive as both Topic and pivot – notice that Dative (or 'Recipient' see 2.3) and Benefactive are distinguished:

> marái ʔang-laláke na   nag-taʔó ning-líbro sa-babáye
> good TOP-man   that AT-give PAT-book DAT-woman
> 'The man who gave the book to the woman is good'

marái ʔang-líbro na   na-taʔó kang-laláke sa-babáye
good TOP-book that PT-give AGT-man   DAT-woman
'The book that the man gave to the woman is good'
'The book given to the man by the woman is good'

marái ʔang-babáye na   na-ta'ó-hán kang-laláke ning-líbro
good TOP-woman that DT-give-DT TOP-man   PAT-book
'The woman to whom the man gave the book is good'
'The woman who was given the book by the man is good'

marái ʔang-lanséta na   pinag-putúl kang-laláke ning-tubú
good TOP-knife   that IT-cut   AGT-man   PAT-sugar cane
'The knife with which the man cut the sugar-cane is good'
'The knife used by the man to cut the sugar-cane is good'

marái ʔang-babáye na   pinag-bakal-án kang-laláke ning kandíng
good TOP woman that BT-buy-BT   AGT-man   PAT goat
'The woman for whom the man bought the goat is good'
'The woman that was bought (for) a goat by the man is good'

Givón makes the interesting observation (but in terms of 'Subjects') that it appears that, without exception, all languages that mark verbs to indicate which term is promoted to Topic status restrict relativization to the promoted term.

With deletion in complementation, however, the situation is more complex in Tagalog. Schachter (1976: 504) provides examples to show that it is the Agent (not the Topic) that is the pivot (and so is deleted):

Nagatubili   siyang   humiram   ng pera   sa bangko
AT + hesitated TOP + he + LI AT + borrow PAT money LOC bank
'He hesitated to borrow money from a/the bank'

Nagatubili   sayang   hiramin   ang pera   sa bangko
AT + hesitated TOP + he + LI PT + borrow TOP money LOC bank
'He hesitated to borrow *money* from a/the bank'

Nagatubili   siyang   hiraman   ng pera   ang bangko
AT + hesitated TOP + he + LI LT + borrow PAT money TOP bank
'He hesitated to borrow money from the *bank*'

Here change of topic does not affect the syntax: in all examples it is the Agent 'he', not the Topic, that is deleted in the complement clause. Translation into

English and interpretation in terms of passive and 'Subject' will illustrate the problem. The first sentence would correspond to *He hesitated [he] to borrow money from the bank*, with *he* deleted because (a) it is the Subject of the subordinate clause and (b) it is identical with the Subject of the main clause. In the second and third sentences, however, if the subordinate sentences were treated as passive, their Subjects would be *the money* and *the bank* and deletion would no longer be possible, since it would produce the impossible sentences *He hesitated money to be borrowed from the bank by him* and *He hesitated the bank to be borrowed money from by him*.

However, Shibatani (1988a: 124) points out that in Cebuano, although Agents may function as (deleted) pivots whether they are Topics or not, Patients may also be deleted, but only if they are Topics. Examples of deleted Agents are:

> Gusto ni Juan nga mu-tudlo ni Maria
> want AGT/PAT Juan LI AT-teach AGT/PAT Maria
> 'Juan wants to teach Maria'

> Gusto ni Juan nga tudlo-an si Maria
> want AGT/PAT Juan LI teach-PT TOP Maria
> 'Juan wants to teach Maria'

As the verbal markers (in the subordinate clause) show, the Agent 'Juan' is the Topic in the first, but not in the second of these sentences, where the Patient 'Maria' is the Topic. Deletion of a Patient-Topic is illustrated by:

> Gusto ni Juan nga tudlo-an sa Maestro
> want AGT/PAT Juan LI teach-PT AGT/PAT teacher
> 'Juan wants to be taught by the teacher/the teacher to teach him'

If the Patient is not the Topic, it cannot be the deleted pivot. The following sentence is possible, but not with the sense required:

> Gusto ni Juan nga mu-tudlo si Maestro
> want AGT/PAT Juan LI AT-teach TOP teacher
> 'Juan wants the teacher to teach (someone)'
> *not* 'Juan wants to be taught by the teacher/the teacher to teach him'

Here 'teacher' is the Topic and the sentence cannot mean 'Juan wants to be taught by the teacher' with deletion of the non-Topic 'Juan'.

It is only the Agent, however, that can control reflexivization (Schachter 1977: 292):

> nag-aalala ang lolo   sa   kaniyang sarili
> AT-worry   TOP grandfather LOC his   self
> '*Grandfather* worries about himself'

> inaalala   ang lolo   ang kaniyang sarili
> LT + worry AGT grandfather TOP his   self
> 'Grandfather worries about *himself*'

The voice system does not, then, change the term that controls reflexivization. Moreover, the reflexive itself can be the Topic (as above), but it cannot
be the Agent – as the impossibility of the following sentence shows:

> *inaalala   ang lolo   ng kaniyang sarili
> LT + worry TOP grandfather AGT his   self

In this last respect, it is again the Agent not the Topic that behaves like the
Subject of an accusative language, for, like the Agent in Tagalog, the Subject
in English cannot be the reflexive; the equivalent (impossible) sentence in
English would be '*Himself was worried about by grandfather'.
  The definition of 'Subject' in Tagalog was the theme of Schachter's (1976)
article, and there has been much discussion since (e.g. Shibatani 1988b). The
proper conclusion, however, is that the term is not appropriate, and equally
that the system cannot be characterized in terms of accusative/ergative or
passive/antipassive. The fact that both Topic and Agent function as pivots is
a little unusual, but there is something similar in Lango (4.1.1 and 4.1.4),
where Topics are pivots for coordination and Subjects are pivots for
relativization. It is, nevertheless, reasonable to suggest that Tagalog has a
voice system shown in the morphology of both verb and noun, which is used
to create pivots for relativization, but is only partly relevant to the syntax of
the complements and irrelevant for reflexives.

8.2 Inverse systems

It was noted in 2.2 and 5.6 that some languages use the passive to
meet restrictions on the type of NP that may function as Subject, the
restrictions generally depending on an animacy or (better) empathy
hierarchy. An extreme example of this type of restriction seems to be found
in languages that have what are called 'inverse' systems.

8.2.1 Basic systems

An inverse system can be illustrated from Plains Cree (Algonquian, Canada, Wolfart 1973: 24–5) by the following sentences:

> ni-sēkih-ā-enān atim   (→ nisékihānān)
> 1-scare-DIR-1PL dog
> 'We scare the dog'

> ni-sēkih-ekw-enān atim   (→ nisēkihikonān)
> 1-scare-INV-1PL   dog
> 'The dog scares us'

Morphologically the only difference between these two is that the first is marked as 'direct' (DIR), the second as 'inverse' (INV). The meaning difference results from the fact that there is a hierarchy in which first and second person NPs rank higher than third person NPs, and direct marking on the verb indicates that the higher ranking NP ('we') is to be interpreted as the Agent, while inverse marking signals that the lower ranking NP ('the dog') is the Agent.

If both NPs are third person, one will usually be marked as 'proximate' (PROX) the other as 'obviate' (OBV), which indicate relative nearness of the relevant entities to the speaker (the proximate being the nearer). Proximate NPs are ranked higher than obviate ones, and similar rules apply:

> sēkih-ēw   nāpēw   atimwa
> scare-DIR + 3 man + PROX dog + OBV
> 'The man scares the dog'

> sēkih-ik   nāpēw   atimwa
> scare-INV + 3 man + PROX dog + OBV
> 'The dog scares the man'

In the direct construction, the proximate 'the man' is the Agent; in the inverse, the Agent is the obviate 'the dog'. If the proximate/obviate marking is reversed, so is the Agent/Patient relationship:

> sēkih-ēw   nāpēwa   atim
> scare-DIR + 3 man + OBV dog + PROX
> 'The dog scares the man'

> sēkihik   napēwa   atim
> scares-INV + 3 man + OBV dog + PROX
> 'The man scares the dog'

Only slightly different is the situation in Mixe (Mexico, Lyon 1967: 272) where the direct/inverse marking is combined with personal pronouns, but again indicates that Agent is the NP higher or lower on the hierarchy (though Lyon does not talk of 'direct' and 'inverse'):

> tə   əhc ha hɔɔʔy nwopy
> PAST I   the person hit + 1 + DIR
> 'I hit the person'
>
> tə   əhc ha hɔɔʔy šwopy
> PAST I   the person hit + 1 + INV
> 'The person hit me'
>
> tə   paat ha həyuhk twopy
> PAST Peter the animal hit + 3 + DIR
> 'Peter hit the animal'
>
> tə   paat ha həyukh wyopyə
> PAST Peter the animal hit + 3 + INV
> 'The animal hit Peter'

The hierarchy that governs the choice in Mixe is complex. It is stated by Foley and Van Valin (1985: 289) as:

> speaker > addressee > human proper > human common > other
> animate > inanimate

A language of this type that has been much discussed (Hale 1973b, Shayne 1982, Witherspoon 1980, Klaiman 1988, 1991) is Navaho (Apache, S.W. USA). Here a Direct/Inverse contrast is made in the alternation of two prefixes *yi-* and *bi-*, which Witherspoon (1980: 5) treats as third person object markers, with *-z-* as the subject prefix:

> hastiin łíí'   yi-z-tal
> man   horse it + DIR-it-kicked
> 'The man kicked the horse'
>
> hastiin łíí'   bi-z-tal
> man   horse it + INV-it-kicked
> 'The man was kicked by the horse'

Here the direct marker indicates that it is 'the man' that is the Agent, the inverse marker that it is 'the horse'. However, it appears that word order is also relevant: Hale (1973b: 300) talks of 'subject-object-verb' order, while Shayne (1982: 391) explicitly states that word order is relevant in San Carlos

Apache. Where two NPs are equal on the hierarchy, this is certainly the case: with direct marking it is the first NP that is identified as the Agent, while with inverse marking it is the second. Witherspoon illustrates this with four sentences in which the two NPs are of equal status:

> łíí' dzaanééz yi-ztal
> horse mule   DIR-kick
> 'The horse kicked the mule'

> łíí' dzaanééz bi-ztal
> horse mule   INV-kick
> 'The horse was kicked by the mule'

> dzaanééz łíí' yi-ztal
> mule   horse DIR-kick
> 'The mule kicked the horse'

> dzaanééz łíí' bi-ztal
> mule   horse INV-kick
> 'The mule was kicked by the horse'

Where the two NPs are not of equal status, word order is, according to Witherspoon still relevant, in that direct marking still shows the first NP as the Agent, and inverse marking the second NP, but there is the restriction that the first NP (the 'subject') cannot be lower on the hierarchy than the second. Both of the following sentences are unacceptable:

> *łíí' hastiin yi-z-yal
> horse man   it + DIR-it-kicked
> ('The horse kicked the man')

> *łíí' hastiin bi-z-tal
> horse man   it + INV-it-kicked
> ('The horse was kicked by the man')

However, Shayne (1982: 385) reports (from an unpublished abstract) examples to suggest that where the NPs are not equal on the hierarchy, word order is not relevant:

> łíí' John yi-ztal
> horse John DIR-kick
> 'John kicked the horse'

łíí'   John bi-ztal
horse John ɪɴᴠ-kick
'the horse kicked John'

Here the hierarchy alone appears to establish Agent and Patient. With *yi-* the second, but higher, argument is the Agent, while with *bi-* it is the first, lower, argument that is the Agent. This contrasts with the examples discussed previously.

Witherspoon argues that what determines the choice of prefix is 'control' because it is not possible to say:

*awééł' hastiin yi-z-tał
baby   man   it + ᴅɪʀ-kicked
'The baby kicked the man'

What is required is:

hastiin awéé' bi-ztał
man   baby   it + ɪɴᴠ-it-kicked
'The man let the baby kick him'

The reason, Witherspoon argues, is that the man has greater control than the baby, as his translation (rather than 'The baby kicked the man') is intended to suggest. However, if the hierarchy is one of empathy rather than animacy, it may not be surprising if babies are lower on the scale than men.

8.2.2   *Inverse systems and passives*

Witherspoon (1980: 3) notes that, while Hale (1973b: 300) says that Navaho has 'a syntactic rule which is similar to the passive' other scholars have simply treated the data in terms of active and passive. The first NP is considered to be the Subject and the second to be the Object, and *bi-* is taken as the passive marker, which simply inverts the Subject + Object sequence. There are, however, two objections to this.

First, as with the topic systems of 8.1, neither of the two constructions (direct and inverse) seems to be more basic than the other, and there is no independent indication (i.e. other than by the verb markers) that the Patient has been promoted or the Agent demoted. Moreover, in all the passive constructions considered so far, the Agent is demoted to Oblique, not to Object, if it is not deleted. In Navaho, on a passive interpretation, it would be demoted to Object. It would seem that there is no promotion and demotion, but merely an alternation between the functions of the two NPs, 'direct' indicating Agent + Patient, and 'inverse' Patient + Agent.

Secondly, a passive interpretation disguises the crucial importance of the empathy hierarchy. In itself this is not a conclusive argument, because, as noted in 2.2 and 5.6, there are rules based on the hierarchy that restrict passivization in other languages. Taken with the first point, however, it is an important issue, for it helps to explain the absence of any clear demotion of the Agent; this is especially so if there is no fixed word order for Agent and Patient ('Subject' and 'Object'), as Shayne suggests for Navaho, or where, if the NPs are of equal status, they have to be distinguished in terms of proximate/obviate, as in Plains Cree, in order to provide an indication of the hierarchical ranking. It is for this reason that Klaiman (1991: 185) suggests that direct/inverse pairs, unlike active/passive pairs 'do not preserve propositional content'. This is clear from the translations of the Cree examples quoted in 8.2.1 ('We scare the dog'/'The dog scares us'), as compared with the active/passive pair in English ('We scare the dog'/'The dog is scared by us').

Yet the issue is not clear cut. Obviously, if there is fixed word order to determine which is Agent and which is Patient, the inverse construction is more passive-like than if the distinction rests wholly on the hierarchy; in the 'horse'/'mule' examples of Navaho the hierarchy plays no part, while in the 'man'/'horse' examples, it is not the only indication of Agent and Patient, and appears to have the blocking of unacceptable sentences as its prime purpose. On the other hand, if there is no fixed word order, the hierarchy is crucial, and the inverse construction is very unlike the passive.

Even more passive-like is the construction in Wakashan (Canada). Here there is a hierarchy in which first and second persons are higher than third, and in one pair of examples there is no independent evidence of demotion of the Agent (Jacobsen 1979: 126, 123):

da·sas   tq̓ʷasıq   χ̓icuxʷadi
see + INDIC + 1SG sit on the ground + ART person
'I see the one sitting on the ground'

da·saʔits   tiq̓ʷasıq
see + PASS + INDIC + 1SG sit on the ground + ART
'The one sitting on the ground sees me'

Yet in another pair of examples, there is an indication of demotion of the Agent (Jacobsen 1979: 120):

bačil   ʔaλi·tqʷał q̓idi·liq   ʔu·yuq
bite + + MOM + INDIC + 3 bear   dog + ART OBJ   [MOMentary]
'The bear bit the dog'

bačiλit   q̓idi·liq   ʔaλi·tqʷał-x̣it
bite + MOM + PASS dog + ART bear-REL + PASS
'The bear bit the dog'

(Jacobsen glosses -*x̣it* as 'relative-passive'; this Whistler (1985: 238) interprets as 'by'.)

It is clear, then, that languages exhibit features of both passive and inverse systems in varying degrees, but that does not invalidate the decision to distinguish them. In extreme cases the strategies of the two devices are different; in particular, in inverse systems the Agent is not overtly demoted or deleted and the empathy hierarchy plays a crucial part, while in passive systems there is demotion or deletion and the hierarchy is of little or no significance.

9
Causatives

Many languages have grammatical or semi-grammatical devices for expressing the general notion of causing someone to perform a certain action. It is such devices that are referred to as 'causatives'. A simple example from Italian (Lepschy and Lepschy 1977: 114–15, 203–6) is:

> Ada scrive una lettera
> Ada writes a   letter
> 'Ada writes a letter'

> Faccio scrivere una lettera a Ada
> I make to write a   letter to Ada
> 'I make Ada write a letter'

Like the passive, the causative can be seen as derived from a simple active sentence (but see 9.1) and as a device that changes the grammatical status of the arguments in the predication. Unlike the passive, however, it does not promote a term, but adds a new argument that represents the notional causer, which can be considered as having the (new) grammatical role of Causer, placing it in Subject position, while demoting the original Subject to oblique or peripheral status.

9.1   Forms of the causative

There are many languages that form their causatives morphologically, i.e. that have specific causative forms of the verb, just as many languages have morphological passives. An example from Tigrinya (Ethiopian Semitic, personal research, see 5.3) is:

> Bärḥe mäṣḥaf rə'iyu
> Berhe book   saw + PAST + 3SG
> 'Berhe saw the book'

Məsgənna nə-Bärḥe mäṣḥaf 'a-r'iyu-wo
Mesghenna ANIM-Berhe book CAUS-see + PAST + 3SG-him
'Mesghenna showed Berhe the book'

(For 'show' as 'cause to see', i.e. as the causative of 'see', see 9.3.2.)
In Tigrinya, the causative is a regular and productive grammatical
formation, in the sense that causatives can be formed from any verb by the
addition of the prefix 'a-, with other minor but regular changes, and with the
simple meaning of causing someone to perform the relevant action. In other
languages, however, the causative is not equally regular and productive. This
can even be seen in a language related to Tigrinya, Amharic (Hetzron 1976:
379), where there are two causative forms of BÄLLA 'eat', with prefixes a- or
as-, and meanings that are far from predictable, as the following examples
show:

ləǧu səga bälla
the boy meat eat + PAST + 3SG
'The boy ate meat'

abbat ləǧu-n səga a-bälla
father the boy + OBJ meat CAUS-eat + PAST + 3SG
'The father fed the boy meat'

abbat ləǧu-n səga as-bälla
father the boy + OBJ meat CAUS-eat + PAST + 3SG
'The father forced the boy to eat meat'

abbat ləǧu-n səga baškär as-bälla
father the boy + OBJ meat by servant CAUS-eat + PAST + 3SG
'The father had the servant make the boy eat'

abbat səgaw-n bawre as-bälla-w
father the meat + OBJ by beast CAUS-eat + PAST + 3SG-it
'The father let the beast eat the meat (through carelessness)'

(For 'let' as a causative, see below and 9.5.)
The lack of precise correlation between morphology and meaning is usually
taken to be a sign of 'derivation' rather than 'inflection', the term 'inflection'
being used for the regular formation of tense, mood, voice, etc., while
'derivation' is used for (morphologically and semantically) less regular
formations such as *organize/organization*, *choose/choice*, *perform/performance*
etc. However, it must be said that the formation of the causatives in Amharic

and other Ethiopian languages belongs to the same over-all system as the
passive, which is generally completely regular:

active   bälla
passive   täbälla
causative   abälla

All these 'derived forms', as they are usually termed, have the same range of
person, number, gender and tense forms as the simple active. Another
indication of derivation is the possibility, in some languages, for verbs to have
double or even triple causatives (see 9.4).

Like the passive, the causative may be either purely morphological, as in
the examples above, or 'periphrastic', using a specific verb of causation, e.g.
the verb FARE 'to make/do' in Italian, as illustrated in the first pair of
examples in this chapter. The combination of FARE with the following verb
can, nevertheless, be considered to be the grammaticalized form of the
causative, because it forms a single grammatical unit in that it cannot be
interrupted by any other form. This is not the case with other verbs in Italian
(with one exception – see below). This can be seen in the contrast with
VEDERE 'to see', which has alternative constructions:

Faccio scrivere Ada
I make to write Ada
'I make Ada write'

Ho   visto Ada scrivere
I have seen Ada write
'I have seen Ada write'

Ho   visto scrivere Ada
I have seen write   Ada
'I have seen Ada write'

There is, however, no:

*Faccio Ada scrivere

Pronouns generally precede the whole verb complex with both FARE and
VEDERE:

Gliela   faccio scrivere
To her + it I make write
'I make her write it'

Gliela   ho   visto scrivere
To her + it I have seen write
'I have seen her write it'

However, there is, again, a difference in that it is also possible, though less acceptable, to place the pronominal Object of the second verb after that verb with VEDERE, but not with FARE:

La   ho   visto scriver-la
Her I have seen write-it
'I have seen her write it'

(*La faccio scriverla)

There is one other verb in Italian that behaves like FARE – LASCIARE 'to permit/let/allow' (and it was noted earlier that one of the constructions in Amharic has the 'let' meaning). This too, should be treated as a causative, so that Italian can be said to have two causatives, one of 'making', the other of 'permitting'; there is further discussion in 9.5.

English uses the verbs MAKE, GET, HAVE and CAUSE to express causation, but none of these appears to have any specific grammatical features that would distinguish it from all the other verbs that occur in similar combinations (the 'catenatives' – see Palmer 1987: 172ff). English does not, therefore, appear to have a grammaticalized causative construction.

It appears, then, that there are degrees of grammaticality with both morphological and periphrastic causatives, but the effect of causatives on the grammatical status of arguments in predications still makes a brief account of them worthwhile in a study of grammatical roles and relations.

There is one theoretical issue that may be discussed briefly here. It is reasonable to talk about causatives as being 'derived' from non-causative constructions, just as passives may be said to be derived from active constructions, but this need mean no more than that a set of formal rules may be given to relate the passive and the causative to basic (active, non-causative) sentences. In several theories it is held that the basic or underlying structure of all causatives is like that of periphrastic ones, i.e. as consisting of two clauses, one subordinate to the other. Thus the example from Tigrinya at the beginning of this section would have an underlying structure of the type *Mesghenna caused (Berhe see the book)*. In a theory that was popular in the 1970s ('generative semantics'), this analysis was applied even to 'lexical causatives' such as KILL which was interpreted as 'cause to die'. Less controversially, some versions of Relational Grammar postulate that constructions with morphological causatives are 'biclausal' rather than 'monoclausal', i.e. that they consist of two clauses, rather than just one (see e.g. Davies and Rosen 1988). Although this view makes morphological causatives look similar to periphrastic ones, there is no need to accept it. All that needs to be said about causatives is that there is (i) marking on the verb (whether morphological or periphrastic), (ii) the addition of the Causer in Subject position, (iii) demotion of other arguments and (iv) a causal meaning. At a purely formal ('surface') level, constructions with morphological causatives are monoclausal, while those with periphrastic causatives appear to be biclausal in that they contain two predicators, yet often have syntactic features that make them more like monoclausal constructions.

9.2   The 'paradigm case'

In an influential article Comrie (1976) argues that there is a 'paradigm case' for causative constructions, involving the hierarchy of grammatical relations:

subject > direct object > indirect object > oblique constituent

In a causative construction, he suggests, the original Subject is demoted to the first position on the right that is not already occupied. This is illustrated by the causatives of intransitives, transitives and transitives with Indirect Objects.

With intransitives, it is predicted that the Subject will be demoted to (Direct) Object, as shown by the Hungarian and Italian examples:

a tanulók váratjak a tanár-t	(p. 267)
the pupils wait + CAUS the teacher-DO	
'The pupils make the teacher wait'	

Gianni lo fa venire	(p. 266)
Gianni him(DO) makes to come	
'Gianni makes him come'	

With transitives the prediction is that the Subject will be demoted to the status of Indirect Object/Dative. This can be illustrated from Turkish and French:

Dişçi mektub-u müdür-e imzala-t-tɨ	(p. 268)
dentist letter-DO director-IO sign-CAUS-PAST	
'The dentist made the director sign the letter'	

> J'ai   fait   manger la   pomme à   Claude
> I have made to eat   the apple   to Claude
> 'I made Claude eat the apple'

With transitives with Indirect Objects, the Subject would be demoted to oblique status, as illustrated from Turkish and Italian:

> Dişçi   Hasan-a   mektub-u müdür   tarafından göster-t-ti   (p. 270)
> dentist Hasan-IO letter-DO   director by   show-CAUS-PAST
> 'The dentist made the director show the letter to Hasan'

> Ho   fatto   scrivere una lettera a Paolo da Maria
> I have made   to write a   letter to Paolo by Maria
> 'I made Maria write a letter to Paolo'

Comrie provides a number of examples and lists of other languages for which examples could have been given. He could have given a full set of the three possible examples from a single language, if he had added, for Italian, the example of the causative of a transitive given at the beginning of this chapter (*Faccio scrivere una lettera a Ada*).

The paradigm case proposal is neat, but there are many exceptions which, admittedly, Comrie attempts to account for. Song (1991: 66) sees as 'the major disadvantage of the theory . . . the fact that very few languages, if any, conform to his paradigm case', but in fact it appears to account for a fair number of the data, and is, at least, a useful starting point.

Perhaps the strongest argument against Comrie's proposal is the fact that, even for a single type of basic construction, there may be as many as three different causative constructions. This can be illustrated from Xhosa (Bantu, Cooper 1976: 314):

> Ndi-bon-is-e   umfundisi iincwadi
> I-see-CAUS-PAST teacher   books
> 'I showed the teacher the books'

> Nidi-theng-is-e   iincwadi k-umfundisi
> I-buy-CAUS-PAST books   LOC-teacher
> 'I sold books to the teacher'

> Ndi-lum-is-e   umtana nge-nja
> I-bite-CAUS-PAST child   INSTR-dog
> 'I made the dog bite the child'

None of these is consistent with the paradigm case, except possibly the second, if the locative is taken as the marker of the Indirect Object. In the first sentence, the Subject is apparently demoted to Direct Object, although a Direct Object is already present. This is clearly an exception to the paradigm case, which actually predicts that the Subject will not be demoted to a position that is already occupied. Another example, given by Comrie is from Mongolian:

> xeden mal-ā   day-ā   dav-ūlax   (p. 275)
> small herd-DO pass-DO cross-CAUS
> 'He made the small herd cross the pass'

Similarly, the Subject is sometimes demoted to Indirect Object, even though there is already another Indirect Object. Comrie has examples from Punjabi and Italian:

> bənde ne   maṣṭər num̀ kàṇi mwṇdyam̀ num̀ swṇ-vā-i (p. 277)
> man SUBJ teacher IO   story boys   IO   tell-CAUS-PAST
> 'The man made the teacher tell the story to the boys'

> Ho   fatto scrivere a Maria una lettera a Paolo   (p. 278)
> I have made to write to Maria a   letter to Paolo
> 'I made Maria write a letter to Paolo'

Comrie calls this 'syntactic doubling'. He notes that double Direct Objects are quite common in non-causative constructions, but are rare elsewhere.

In the third of the Xhosa examples above the Subject is demoted to oblique status, although no Indirect Object is present. There is a similar situation with periphrastic causatives in French. Examples similar to the second and third of the Xhosa sentences, with the subject demoted to either Indirect Object or Instrumental are noted by Comrie (1976: 271):

> Je ferai   manger une pomme à Claude
> I will make to eat   an apple to Claude
> 'I will make Claude eat an apple'

> Je ferai   manger une pomme par Claude
> I will make to eat   an apple by Claude
> 'I will make Claude eat an apple'

(French also allows doubled Direct Objects – see 9.3.2.)

The situation in Hungarian (Hetzron 1976: 392–6) is even more inconsistent with the paradigm case. With transitive verbs, the Subject is demoted to the Instrumental, but not to the Indirect Object, as the paradigm case would suggest:

> levelet irattam a fiúval (*fiút)
> letter + ACC I + CAUS + write the boy + INSTR (*a boy + ACC)
> 'I made the boy write a letter'

With intransitives, the Subject may be demoted either to Indirect Object or Instrumental:

> köhögtettem a gyerekkel
> I + CAUSE + cough the boy + INSTR
> 'I had the boy cough'

> köhögtettem a gyerekket
> I + CAUSE + cough the boy + ACC
> 'I induced the boy to cough'

Finally, it should be noted that the original Subject may be omitted, rather than demoted, as in Italian (Lepschy and Lepschy 1977: 205):

> Ho fatto scrivere una lettera
> I have made to write a letter
> 'I got a letter written'

These various exceptions to the paradigm case will be discussed in the next section.

9.3 Contrasting structures

Many languages have more than one causative construction, with, not surprisingly, different meanings.

9.3.1 *'Active' and 'passive' causatives*

The most positive and general proposal that has been made concerning different constructions in the same language is that the contrast between demotion to Indirect Object and Instrumental, noted in the last section, represents a difference between active and passive. In terms of the theory briefly mentioned in 9.1, this would mean that, for the construction with the Instrumental, there was passivization of the underlying subordinate clause before causativization. Thus Hyman and Zimmer (1976: 199–200) consider the French sentences:

> J'ai fait nettoyer les toilettes au   général
> I have made clean   the toilet to the general
> 'I made the general clean the toilets'

> J'ai fait nettoyer les toilettes par le général
> I have made clean   the toilet by the general
> 'I had the toilets cleaned by the general'

These, it is suggested, derive, respectively, from:

> J'ai fait (le général nettoyer les toilettes)
> J'ai fait (les toilettes etre nettoyées par le général)

With the first, 'I did something to the general', whereas with the second 'I wanted the toilets cleaned' and 'the general is more incidental to the task'.

This is an attractive solution, particularly because the Subject is not only demoted to Instrumental, but may also be omitted, as in the Italian example at the end of 9.2; both are characteristic of the passive. It is not, however, necessary to accept the generative theory assumed by Hyman and Zimmer in order to talk about 'active' and 'passive' type causatives, but to use the terms simply to identify the two different constructions (though with the meaning differences suggested by the terms). Moreover, there is evidence against this theory. Comrie (1976: 273) notes that Finnish has the 'passive' causative construction, although Finnish has no passive:

> Minä rakennutin talo-n   muurarei-lla
> I   build + CAUS house-DO bricklayers-INSTR
> 'I make the bricklayers build the house'

Similarly, Cole (1983: 129–30) notes that, in French, the agentive *par* phrase of the passive may be used with causatives of verbs that cannot undergo passivization and that, conversely, although verbs of perception can be passivized, the *par* phrase cannot be used with their causatives:

> Le capitaine lui a   fait tirer dessus par les gardes
> the captain   to him has made shoot on   by the guards
> 'The captain had guards shoot at him'

> *Il a   été tiré dessus par les gardes
> he has been shot on   by the guards
> 'He was shot at by the guards'

Le film a été vu par les enfants
the film has been seen by the children
'The film was seen by the children'

*Antoine fera voir ce film par les enfants
Antoine will make see this film by the children
'Antoine will make the children see this film'

Comrie (1976: 217) notes that many languages have this type of contrast, including Hindi. The situation in Hindi is discussed at length by Saksena (1981, 1982a, 1982b) who argues that there is both 'direct' and 'indirect' causation: with the dative + accusative ('active') construction, the dative marker *koo* indicates the Agent as the 'target' to whom the activity is directed (as 'recipient') and so as being affected, whereas with the instrumental + accusative ('passive') construction the Agent is non-target, not affected. However there are only a few verbs that allow either construction. One pair of examples quoted is (1982a: 827).

māī-nee raam-see/koo masaalaa cakh-vaa-yaa
I-subj raam-obj/instr spice taste-caus-past
'I had Raam taste the seasoning'

With *-koo* the tasting is for the agent's benefit, with *-see* it is for someone else's. Similarly, with 'read the book' there is a distinction between getting the agent to read the book and getting the book read.

The contrast between 'direct' and 'indirect' causation is also possible with intransitive verbs, e.g. in Japanese (Shibatani 1982: 109):

Taroo-ga Ziroo-o hasir-ase-ta
Taro-nom Ziro-acc run-caus-past
'Taro made Ziro run'

Taroo-ga Ziroo-ni hasir-ase-ta
Taro-nom Ziro-dat run-caus-past
'Taro got Ziro to run'

Here, however, while direct causation demotes the original Subject to Direct Object (as in the paradigm case), indirect causation demotes it to Dative, not Instrumental.

223

Causatives

9.3.2 'Single event' causatives

The analysis in 9.3.1 does not account for the 'syntactic doubling' discussed in 9.2, particularly the constructions with two direct objects. The contrast between this and the 'paradigm case' is seen in two examples from French:

> Je l'ai   fait   manger des   épinards
> I him(DO) have made to eat   of the spinach
> 'I made him eat spinach'

> Je lui   ai   fait   manger des   épinards
> I him(IO) have made to eat   of the spinach
> 'I had him eat spinach'

Hyman and Zimmer (1976: 194) suggest that the first might be used of a child forced to eat spinach against his will, while the second might be used of a hungry person being offered the only food available; this might be translated 'fed him spinach'.

There are, then, three types of causatives with meaning differences. In addition to 'active' (direct) and 'passive' (indirect) causatives, there is a third type, in which the causation and the action are closely associated, and can be seen as a single event, with the causer actually taking part in it, often with translations such as 'show', 'feed', 'dress', etc., all of them simple transitive verbs in English.

It should be recalled (9.1), however, there is the same three-way contrast in Amharic also (though there is also a fourth type), but this is only partly consistent with the French data:

> abbat ləǧu-n   səga a-bälla
> father the boy-OBJ meat CAUS-eat + PAST + 3SG
> 'The father fed the boy meat'

> abbat ləǧu-n   səga as-bälla
> father the boy-OBJ meat CAUS-eat + PAST + 3SG
> 'The father forced the boy to eat meat'

> abbat ləǧu-n   səga baškär   as-bälla
> father the boy-OBJ meat by servant CAUS-eat + PAST + 3SG
> 'The father had the servant make the boy eat'

The second and third of these clearly illustrate the 'active'/'passive' contrast, while the first, which uses a different prefix, has the more unitary meaning of

224

'feed' rather than 'cause to eat'. In contrast with French, however, the distinction between 'feed' and 'make eat' is not carried by a difference in the status of the demoted terms, but in the form of the causative marker on the verb. For this reason Cohen (1936: 222, 228) refers to the *a-* prefix as the 'causative', but the *as-* prefix as the 'factitive'.

Rather differently, again, Cole (1983: 117–19) discusses three constructions in Bolivian Quechua with the examples:

> nuqa Fan-ta   rumi-ta   apa–či-ni
> I   Juan-ACC rock-ACC carry-CAUS-1SG
> 'I made Juan carry the rock'

> nuqa Fan-wan   rumi-ta   apa–či-ni
> I   Juan-INSTR rock-ACC carry-CAUS-1SG
> 'I had Juan carry the rock'

> nuqa wawa-man yaca-či-n
> I   child-DAT know-CAUS-1SG
> 'I taught it to the child'

The accusative, he suggests, expresses direct, coercive causation and the instrumental noncoercive, indirect causation, while the dative is used with 'verbs of experience', whose Subjects are typically animate nonagents (the 'single event' causatives). However, as can be seen, with the single event causatives, which include 'show', 'reach', 'feed' and 'remind', the Agent is in the dative, the accusative being used for the 'active' causative (and the instrumental for the 'passive').

It was noted above that 'single event' causatives are often translated into English by simple transitive verbs. Shibatani (1976a) states that in Japanese morphological causatives are never 'single event', such causatives being, as in English, expressed by lexical verbs. He distinguishes between the two types in terms of 'manipulative' and 'directive' causation, 'manipulative' (lexical, single event) causation always implying the physical involvement of the causer. Thus he contrasts:

> Taroo ga   Ziroo o   tome-ta   (p. 17)
> Taro NOM Ziro ACC stop-PAST
> 'Taro stopped Ziro'

> Taroo ga   Ziroo o   tomar-ase-ta
> Taro NOM Ziro ACC stop-CAUS-PAST
> 'Taro made Ziro stop'

Taroo wa Ziroo o   taosi-ta   (p. 34)
Taro TOP Ziro ACC throw-PAST
'Taro threw Ziro down'

Taroo wa Ziroo o   taore-sase-ta
Taro TOP Ziro ACC fall-CAUS-PAST
'Taro made Ziro fall down'

There are similar pairs for 'dress'/'make (someone) get dressed', 'raise'/'cause to rise', 'move'/'cause to move' etc. He also notes that only 'manipulative', not 'directive', causatives can be used with inanimate Objects, because they obviously require the physical involvement of the causer. It is not possible to say:

*boku wa isu o   ugok-aseta   (p. 33)
I   TOP chair ACC move-CAUS-PAST
'I caused the chair to move'

9.3.3 *Periphrastic vs. morphological causatives*

Some languages have both periphrastic and morphological causatives, and these often correlate with the semantic contrast between the 'full' causatives and the 'single event' causatives discussed in the last subsection. Thus for Korean, Shibatani (1973: 287) compares:

emeni-nun ai-eykey os-ul   ip-key   ha-ess-ta
mother-TOP child-DAT clothes-ACC wear-COMPL do-PAST-INDIC
'The mother had the child put on the clothes'

emeni-nun ai-eykey os-ul   ip-hi-ess-ta
mother-TOP child-DAT clothes-ACC wear-CAUS-PAST-INDIC
'The mother put the clothes on the child'

With the first, the mother in some way made the child wear the clothes; with the second, she dressed the child – the act of causing and wearing are essentially one. (Shibatani refers to the formation with -*hi*- as 'lexical' because it is not productive, but as was noted in 9.1, causative formations are often more like derivational than inflectional features.)

Shibatani adds that, with the periphrastic causative, a time adverbial may refer either to the time of causation or to the time of the resultant action, whereas, with the morphological causative, it can refer only to the time of the combined causation and action, as shown by:

emeni-nun ai-eykey yelsi-ey   pap-ul mek-key ha-ess-ta
mother-TOP child-DAT ten o'clock-at rice-ACC eat-COMPL do-PAST-INDIC
'The mother had the child eat rice at ten o'clock'

emeni-nun ai-lul   yelsi-ey   pap-ul mek-hi-ess-ta
mother-TOP child-ACC ten o'clock-at rice-ACC eat-CAUS-PAST-INDIC
'The mother fed the child rice at ten o'clock'

He states that with the first ten o'clock it may be either the time at which the mother instructed the child or the time at which the child ate the rice, whereas with the second it can only refer to the feeding and eating. This is not unexpected, since the periphrastic causative contains two verb forms either of which may be modified adverbially, whereas the morphological causative contains only one (though, in contrast, as was seen in 9.3.2, morphological causatives in Japanese never refer to 'single events').

However, although this may be true of Korean, it is not universally true that morphological causatives do not permit a time adverbial to refer either to the causation or to the action. Cooper (1976: 323) notes for Xhosa:

Umfundisi ubal-is-a   abafana intsomi emini qha
teacher   write-CAUS-PRES boys   story   only during the day
'The teacher makes the boys write a story only during the day'

This, says Cooper is ambiguous: 'only during the day' may refer to either 'makes' or 'write'. By contrast there is no ambiguity in the morphological causative of another verb:

Ndibondisa   umfundisi incwadi emini qha
I-see-CAUS-PRES teacher   books   only during the day
'I show the teacher books only during the day'

These two examples differ, of course, in that, although they are alike morphologically, semantically the first is a 'true' ('directive') causative and the second a single event ('manipulative') causative; the differences in time specification would follow from that.

9.3.4 *Other issues*

Even when morphological causatives alone are considered, there are issues concerning the choice of construction in terms of the grammatical status of their arguments.

First, in the previous discussion it was generally assumed that choice of construction was determined by meaning. This is not wholly true; it is sometimes lexically determined in part, by the choice of verb. Thus in Tswana (Bantu, Cooper 1976: 314–16), with the verb 'see' ('show' with the causative), the Subject may be demoted to Object or Locative, but not to Instrumental, whereas with 'wash' it may be demoted to Object or Instrumental, but not to Locative:

> ke-bon-tsh-a   dibuka moruti
> I-see-CAUS-PRES books teacher
> 'I am showing the books to the teacher'

> ke-bon-tsh-a   dibuka go-moruti
> I-see-CAUS-PRES books LOC-teacher
> 'I am showing the books to the teacher'

> ke-tlhatšw-is-a   mosadi dipatlo
> I-wash-CAUS-PRES women clothes
> 'I am making the women wash the clothes'

> ke-tlhatšw-is-a   dipatlo ka-mosadi
> I-wash-CAUS-PRES clothes INSTR-women
> 'I am making the women wash the clothes'

It might be thought that the distinction between 'single event' and 'full' causative is relevant here, in that, with 'single event' causative there can be demotion to Object or Locative (with little or no difference in meaning?), while with the 'full' causative there can be demotion to Object or to Instrumental (with the semantic difference associated with 'active' and 'passive' causatives). However, with the 'full' causative of 'smell', only the 'passive' type is possible:

> ke-nkh-is-a   ntša ka-ngwana
> I-smell-CAUS-PRES dog INSTR-child
> 'I am making the child smell the dog'

Semantically this is unexpected, since the child would appear to be the target of the causation.

In fact, the situation is not very different in Hindi, briefly discussed in 9.3.1. Saksena (1981, 1982a, 1982b) provides plenty of semantically based arguments to explain the choice between 'active' and 'passive' constructions; it is clear that, for the vast majority of verbs, it is determined by the choice of verb itself, and there are very few verbs with contrasting structures. This lack of free choice between alternative constructions in Hindi and Tswana (but with a loose association with differences of meaning) is another indication of the derivational rather than inflectional nature of the causatives (see 9.1).

Secondly, the situation in Hungarian, first mentioned in 9.2, is different from any so far noted. With transitives the Subject is demoted only to Instrumental (the 'passive' type), but with intransitives, surprisingly, it may be demoted either to Instrumental or Direct Object. Here the contrast depends on the kind of causation in that the Instrumental is used when causation involves an instruction (the distinction between what Croft (1991: 166) calls 'affective' and 'inducive' causation). This is seen in the pair (Hetzron 1976: 394):

> Lemondattam vele az elnökségről (Instrumental)
> 'I had him resign from the presidency' (by instructing him)

> Lemondattam öt az elnökségről (Direct Object)
> 'I caused him to resign from the presidency' (by obstructing him)

Finally, the situation in Tamil, which was mentioned in 6.3, deserves discussion. Tamil has a contrast between what are called 'weak' and 'strong' forms of the verb, and these are discussed by Klaiman in the context of the middles of Sanskrit, Classical Greek and Fula, with the suggestion that the weak forms are comparable with the middles. However, of the eleven sets of contrasting examples offered by Klaiman (1991: 71–4, from Paramasivam 1979), in no less than seven, the strong form can be interpreted as a 'single event' causative, as shown by, e.g.:

> piḷḷai cōṟu uṇ-t-āṉ
> son-NOM rice eat-WEAK + PAST-SG + MASC
> 'The son ate rice'

> ammā piḷḷaikkuc cōṟu ūṭṭ-iṉ-āḷ
> mother + NOM son + DAT rice eat-STRONG + PAST-SG + FEM
> 'The mother fed the son rice'

The others are 'graze' (intransitive and transitive), 'grow up'/'raise', 'worship', 'submit'/'subjugate', 'divide' (intransitive)/'separate' (transitive), 'sit'/'seat', and 'join' (intransitive)/'collect' (transitive).

In three of the other examples the difference seems to be a matter of increased/reduced transitivity (see 2.3, 7.2.2, 7.4) in that the strong forms are used where the Object is more affected by the action:

> kuṭṭam   avaḷai   neruŋk-iṉ-atu
> crowd + NOM her + ACC approach-WEAK + PAST-SG-NEUT
> 'The crowd approached her'
>
> kuṭṭam   avaḷai   nerukk-iṉ-atu
> crowd + NOM her + ACC approach-STRONG + PAST-SG-NEUT
> 'The crowd pushed in on her'
>
> racikarkaḷ naṭikaiyai vaḷain-tu   koṇṭu āṭiṉārkaḷ
> fans + NOM actress + ACC surround-WEAK + PTCP take-PTCPL danced
> 'The fans surrounded the actress and danced'
>
> racikarkaḷ naṭikaiyai vaḷait-tuk   koṇṭu āṭittārkaḷ
> fans + NOM actress + ACC surround-STRONG + PTCP take-PTCP beat
> 'The fans surrounded the actress and beat her up'

The other pair of examples are translated 'The mother, embracing the child, wept'/'The mother, embracing the child, engulfed it'.

In only one example was there a distinction similar to that found in Greek and Sanskrit:

> kuẓantai   kālai   utai-kiṟ-atu
> child + NOM leg + ACC kick-WEAK + PRES-SG + NEUT
> 'The child is kicking its legs (in the air)'
>
> kuẓantai   eṉṉai   utai-kkiṟ-atu
> child + NOM me + ACC kick-STRONG + PRES-SG + NEUT
> 'The child is kicking me'

One of the reasons that Klaiman, following Paramasivam (1979), gives for not treating these as causatives is that Tamil has both morphological and periphrastic causatives, but this is not a convincing argument, since other languages have more than one causative, and strong forms of the morphological causatives in Tamil often clearly indicate 'single event' causation. The examples suggest that there are at least three meanings of the strong forms: 'single event' causation, increased transitivity and the non-reflexivity of body parts. Since other morphological categories, particularly those that mark the passive in Japanese and the antipassive in Dyirbal, show considerable polysemy, it is not surprising if the same proves true of a causative marker.

9.4 Double causatives

It was mentioned in 9.1 that some languages have double causatives and that this was more a derivational than an inflectional feature. The reason for saying that is that inflectional features such as tense, mood and voice are not normally accumulative in this way. Thus Hetzron (1976: 381) quotes double causatives for Hungarian:

ül	'sit'
ültet	'seat somebody'
ültettet	'make somebody seat somebody'

He even notes (1976: 383) triple causatives for Awngi (Ethiopian Cushitic):

zur-	'come/go back'
zurc-	'give/take back'
xurəcc-	'send back'
zurəccəcc	'make send back'

There are also double causatives in Oromo (Cushitic, Ethiopia and Kenya), but these appear to have three functions (Dubinsky et al. 1988: 484–5). First, they may be used for double causation as in:

aannan-ni daanf-e
milk-NOM boil-AGR
'The milk boiled'

terfaa-n   aannan daanf-is-e
Terfa-NOM milk   boil-CAUS-AGR
'Terfa boiled the milk'

gamteessaa-n terfaa aannan daanf-is-iis-e
Gamtesa-NOM Terfa milk   boil-CAUS-CAUS-AGR
'Gamtesa made Terfa boil the milk'

Secondly, they express an 'intensive' causative as in (p. 487):

terfaa-n   gurbaa raff-is-e
Terfa-NOM boy   sleep-CAUS-AGR
'Terfa put the boy to sleep (e.g. by rocking him)'

terfaa-n   gurbaa raff-is-iis-e
Terfa-NOM boy   sleep-CAUS-CAUS-AGR
'Terfa made the boy sleep (e.g. by giving him a sleeping pill)'

Thirdly, there is a lexical distinction between what they call 'unergative' and 'unaccusative' verbs (see 3.5.4), the latter having 'patient' Subjects and generally being non-volitional. Unergative verbs take double causatives as shown in the contrast between (p. 488):

> terfaa-n   Deekam-e
> Terfa-NOM be angry-AGR
> 'Terfa was angry'
>
> Gaanteessaa terfaa Deekam-s-iis-e
> Gamtesa   Terfa be angry-CAUS-CAUS-AGR
> 'Gamtesa made Terfa angry'
>
> terfaa-n   fayy-e
> Terfa-NOM be healthy-AGR
> 'Terfa was healthy'
>
> Gaanteessa terfaa fayy-is-e
> Gamtesa   Terfa be healthy-CAUS-AGR
> 'Gamtesa made Terfa healthy'

9.5 Related constructions

Causative constructions of the kind that have been discussed in this section are often closely associated, either formally or semantically, with other constructions in many languages.

One issue has already been mentioned: it was seen in 9.1 that in Italian LASCIARE ('let'/'allow') has the same grammatical characteristics as FARE 'make' and that it could, therefore, be argued that Italian has two causatives, one of 'making', one of 'letting'. This is true, to a less marked degree, of French LAISSER, as compared with FAIRE, which was briefly exemplified in 9.2. Slightly differently, in Amharic (9.1), the same form may have a 'cause' or a 'permit' interpretation, and this is true also of Bella Coola (see below). This linking of 'make' and 'allow' is also to be seen in the modal systems of many languages, including English, where the two most basic notions of the deontic modal system are the 'directive' 'must' of obligation and 'may' of permission (see Palmer 1986: 97–100).

In Tigrinya (personal research, Leslau 1941: 104), there is also an 'adjutative', with the meaning 'help to', that functions grammatically in the same way as the causative:

Bärḥe ṣäriḥu
Berhe work + PAST + 3SG
'Berhe worked'

Məsgənna nə-Bärḥe 'aṣriḥu-wo
Mesghenna ANIM-Berhe work + CAUS + PAST + 3SG-him
'Mesghenna made Berhe work'

Məsgənna nə-Bärḥe 'aṣṣariḥu-wo
Mesghenna ANIM-Berhe work + ADJ + PAST + 3SG-him
'Mesghenna helped Berhe work'

In Bella Coola (Salishan, British Columbia, Saunders and Davis 1982: 4–7), there is a 'benefactive' construction that is closely related to the causative. Thus the same form is used to express not only 'make' and 'let' causatives, but also 'benefactives':

tx-is ʔaleks tiq́lsxʷtx
cut-he/it Alex rope
'Alex cut the rope'

tx-a-tus   mat ʔaleks x-tiq́lsxʷtx
cut-INTRANS-he/him Matt Alex PREP-rope
'Matt made Alex cut the rope'
'Matt let Alex cut the rope'
'Matt cut the rope for Alex'

In Bella Coola the same form is used for causative and benefactive. In other languages forms that are different, but belong to the same system, are used. Thus, for Ngiyambaa, Donaldson (1980: 163–4) links the benefactive and causative markers together in that both add an argument to turn an intransitive into a transitive:

ŋadhu-na   bura:y ŋuraŋ-ga yuwa-y-miyi
I + NOM-3ABS child + ABS camp-LOC lie-CM-CAUS-PAST [conjugation
                                     MARKER]
'I laid the child down on the bed'

bura:dhu-nu   yuŋa-y-baṛa
child + ERG-2OBL cry-CM-TRANSITIVIZER-PRES
'The child is crying at you'

Similarly, Bartholomew and Mason (1980) recognize three affixes that increase transitivity in Guerrero Aztec, an 'affective causative', a 'compulsive causative' and a 'benefactive', with affixes -*a*, -*tia* and -*lia* respectively:

cualani	'he is angry'	qui-cualani-a	'he angers him'
choca	'he cries'	qui-choc-tia	'he makes him cry'
qui-pohua	'he counts it'	qui-pohui-lia	'he counts it for him'

Slightly differently, in Sierra Popoluca (Mexico, Lind 1964), causatives and benefactives (or what Lind calls 'referentials') may be combined, but within one morphological system (their combination showing their essentially derivational nature – see 9.1):

Transitive	ikocpa	'He hit him'
Referential Ditransitive	aŋkocaʔy	'I hit his thing'/'I hit it for him'
Causative Ditransitive	anakkoc	'I caused him to hit it'
Referential Tritransitive	aŋkocaʔyaʔ	'I hit his thing for another'
Causative Tritransitive	anakkocaʔy	'I caused him to hit another's thing'/'I caused him to hit it for another'

One possible explanation for the similarity between causative and benefactive constructions is offered in 9.7.

9.6 Adversity passives

There was a discussion in 5.4 of the so-called 'adversity passives' in Japanese; although these were treated as passives there, since they contain the passive marker, they might well be treated as similar to causatives. Examples were:

John ga   tuma ni sin-are-ta
John NOM wife by die-PASS-PAST
'*John was died by his wife'

John ga   Mary ni piano o   hik-are-ta
John NOM Mary by piano ACC play-PASS-PAST
'*John was adversely played the piano by Mary'

These are purportedly the adversity passives of 'John's wife died' and 'Mary played the piano'. If they are passives, they are of an unusual kind. There is no promotion to Subject of a non-Subject argument in the active, but rather the addition of an argument in Subject position.

Song (1987: 97) notes the grammatical similarity between the adversity passive and causative ('make' and 'let') constructions, which differ only in the form of the passive and causative markers:

> Mary wa John ni te   o   nigir-ase-ta
> Mary TOP John DAT hand ACC grasp-CAUS-PAST
> 'John made/let Mary hold his hand'

> Mary wa John ni te   o   nigir-are-ta
> Mary TOP John DAT hand ACC grasp-PASS-PAST
> 'Mary was subjected to John's grasping her hand'

It is interesting to note that there is something similar in English in the use of the lexical verb HAVE, as seen in the sentence quoted by Chomsky (1965: 21):

> I had a book stolen

This can mean either that I got someone to steal a book or that I suffered the loss of a book through stealing. The same verb is used for either causing an action or being adversely affected by it. The English construction, however, unlike the causatives of the type that have been considered, does not have any specific grammatical status, but is like that of other catenative verbs.

All of this strongly suggests that Japanese adversity passives should be treated not like the familiar passives of the type discussed in chapter 5, but like causatives. They too add an argument in Subject position, but with the difference that the additional argument represents the one affected by the action, not the cause of it, while the original Subject is demoted. It may also be relevant to note that the notions of causer and affected entity have much in common with the notions of agent and patient. From that it follows that the relationship between the Subjects of causatives and the Subjects of adversity passives have much in common with the relationship between the Subjects of actives and passives, these being Agent and Patient respectively.

There is a related, but rather different issue in Korean, in that the same marker (-*ki*-) may be used for both passive and causative (Keenan 1985: 262):

> ai-ka   emeni-eke caki mom-lɨl an-ki-ess-ta
> child-SUBJ mother-IO self body-DO embrace-CAUS/PASS-DECL
> 'The child had mother embrace him'

ai-ka   emeni-eke an-ki-ess-ta
child-SUBJ mother-IO embrace-CAUS/PASS-DCL
'The child was embraced by the mother'

However, it would be difficult to derive both of these from the basic sentence 'The mother embraced the child' with the addition of a 'causer' or 'affected subject', since they differ in that one has, but the other lacks, a reflexive and the second sentence exhibits the familiar passive construction. Yet the identity of the marker still suggests the relationship between causer and affected entity, and both could be roughly translated by the ambiguous English sentence 'The child had the mother embrace him'.

9.7 An alternative intepretation of causatives

The assumption throughout this chapter is that a causative construction can be seen as one that adds a new role, that of Causer, in Subject position and demotes the original Agent-Subject, the causee, to oblique status. Evidence from several languages suggests an alternative interpretation.

It will be recalled from 5.4 that Kinyarwanda (Kimenyi 1988: 381), like other Bantu languages, has devices for promoting oblique arguments to Object. One of these, marked by the suffix *-iish-*, promotes the Instrumental:

Umugóre a-ra-andik–a   íbarúwa   n'íikarámu
woman   she-PRES-write-ASP letter   with pen
'The woman is writing a letter with a pen'

Umugóre a-ra-andik-iish-a   íbarúwa íkarámu
woman   she-PRES-write-INSTR-ASP letter   pen
'The woman is writing a letter with a pen'

However, the same suffix appears to be used as a causative:

Abányéeshuûri ba-ra-som-a   ibitabo
students   they-PRES-read-ASP books
'The students are reading books'

Umwáalímu a-ra-som-eesh-a   abányéeshuûri ibitabo
teacher   he-PRES-read-INSTR-ASP students   books
'The teacher is making the students read books'

Prima facie, there is no reason why the same suffix should be used for both promotion to Object and the causative, but an explanation is possible. This is that in both constructions the Object represents the entity by means of which the action is achieved, either the instrument or the secondary agent/causee (the Causer being the principal agent). This implies that the causative constructions being considered do not add a new role, that of Causer, in the Subject position originally held by the Agent, but add a new role in the Object position, indicating the person by means of whom the action was achieved, the causee being, on this interpretation, a kind of instrumental (or, conversely, the instrumental being seen as a secondary agent or causee). On this interpretation, causative constructions are identical with the constructions that promote oblique relations to Object. Thus in the Kinyarwanda examples 'the woman' is the principal agent with 'the pen' as the instrumental/secondary agent, and 'the teacher' is the principal agent, with 'the students' as the secondary agent/instrumental. Exact paraphrases are not possible, but a literal translation that treats the secondary agent as an instrumental, and so shows the similarity of the causative to the construction with promotion to Object, would be 'The teacher is reading (causing reading of) the book by means of the students'. It then follows that the sentence translated as 'The teacher is making the students read the books' is not derived from 'The students are reading the books' with an added Causer ('the teacher') in Subject position, but from 'The teacher is reading the books' with an added role of Causee/Instrumental, 'the students' that has been promoted to Object.

There is a very similar situation in Yidiny (Australia, Dixon 1977a), although the grammatical structures are different because the system is ergative. Yidiny has an affix *-ŋal* whose main function is to convert an intransitive structure into a transitive one by promoting an oblique argument to Absolutive P, and the demotion of the original Absolutive S to Ergative (the reverse of the antipassive). This can be illustrated with an oblique argument marked by the comitative affix *-ɖi*:

        waguɖa   ɲinaŋ   wagal-ɖi   (p. 303)
        man + ABS sit + PRES/FUT wife-COMIT
        'The man is sitting with his wife'

        waguɖaŋgu wagal   ɲina:ŋal
        man + ERG   wife + ABS sit + PRES/FUT + ŋal
        'The man is sitting with his wife'

Dixon illustrates three other types of oblique arguments that are similarly treated by the affix, but adds that it has a fifth use, in which an argument is added ('the controller') in the ergative case (or, with pronouns, in the nominative – see 3.4); the original S is unchanged in its marking, but is now P (in a transitive construction), S and P both being Absolutive. An example is:

ɖugi   guɲɖi:ɲ
stick + ABS break + PAST
'The stick broke'

ŋayu   ɖugi   guɲɖiŋalɲu
I + NOM stick + ABS break + PAST + ŋal
'I broke the stick'

Apart from the grammatical differences that result from the contrasts between the ergative and accusative systems, the situation is the same as in Kinyarwanda: the construction that moves an oblique to the status of P and the 'causative' are identical. The semantics are less obvious than in Kinyarwanda, but in terms of principal and secondary agents, one might say that 'the man' is the principal agent with 'the woman' as secondary agent in the first example, and 'I' is the principal agent, with 'the stick' as the secondary agent in the second. (Dixon prefers 'controller' to 'causer', but the Yidiny construction is obviously very similar to causatives that have been discussed in this chapter.)

In both Kinyarwanda and Yidiny the causative appears to be (or to be closely related to) a construction that promotes an oblique argument to the status of the Patient. There is a simpler, but no less striking, situation in Bella Coola, which was discussed in 9.5. It was seen that there is triple ambiguity in:

tx-a-tus   mat ʔaleks x-tiq́lsxʷtx
cut-INTRANS-he/him Matt Alex   PREP-rope
'Matt made Alex cut the rope'
'Matt let Alex cut the rope'
'Matt cut the rope for Alex'

A possible explanation of the triple ambiguity would be in terms of an interpretation something like 'Matt achieved the breaking of the rope with an effect on Alex (by making him do it, by letting him do it or for his benefit)'. This is slightly different from the other examples: 'Matt' is clearly the principal agent, but if 'Alex' is seen as the secondary agent, it is either as the one who is caused or allowed to perform the action, or as the one who is secondarily involved as beneficiary.

Perhaps, the terms 'principal agent' and 'secondary agent' are not entirely appropriate. The vaguer notions of direct and indirect agency or even principal/direct and secondary/indirect involvement might account more plausibly for the similarities between the Kinyarwanda, Yidiny and Bella Coola data.

This kind of interpretation could also be used for Hungarian which has only the 'passive' causative construction (9.3.1), as in (Hetzron 1976: 392):

> Megcsináltattam   az órát   az órással
> I + CAUS + repair + it the watch + DO the watchmaker + INSTR
> 'I had the watchmaker repair the watch'

This could be interpreted as something like 'I repaired the watch through the services of the watchmaker', which would help to explain why Finnish has a 'passive' causative but no passive voice, an issue discussed in 9.3.1 with:

> Minä rakennutin   talo-n   muurarei-lla
> I   build + CAUS house-DO bricklayers-INSTR
> 'I make the bricklayers build the house'

This could be interpreted as 'I built (by proxy) a house through the bricklayers'; even in English it is possible to talk of someone 'building' a house for himself, without meaning that he did any of the actual work.

This interpretation could even be used, more generally, for all the 'passive' causative constructions that were discussed in 9.3, but it does not seem to be applicable to the 'active' ones. However, an interpretation somewhat along these lines has been suggested for all causatives, including periphrastic ones, by Kemmer and Verhagen (forthcoming), who argue against treating causatives as derived from biclausal structures.

9.8 Final observations

It is, perhaps, appropriate that the last two sections should have been concerned with alternative analyses of some of the data, for one of the assumptions of this book has been that there are no unique solutions to the problems that have arisen. An even more important issue was that discussed in 7.8 – whether the separate treatment of ergative and accusative systems should have been replaced by an overall accusative analysis. The use of the terms 'Subject' and 'Object' throughout would have resulted in a more coherent and simple analysis for much of the data, particularly for the languages that have more than one system. Yet it would have been a procrustean solution for some of the data, forcing them into a framework where they do not really fit; this is particularly so of the full ergative languages such as Dyirbal, for there seems to be no more reason for treating Dyirbal in an accusative system than for treating English in an ergative one.

The essential aim of this book has been to provide a framework, as clear and simple as possible, for the presentation of relevant information about grammatical roles and relations. It should be of value for those interested in theory, for, sadly most theoretical work has proceeded without fully taking into account the great diversity of systems that are to be found in the languages of the world, and, therefore, often forcing new data into an already established theory.

It does not, of course, claim to be in any way definitive, and it is obvious that there is a great deal of relevant material that has not been included, most of it not yet fully investigated and published, although the last ten years or so have seen a great increase in interest in typological studies, and in the research that is needed to make them possible. Yet there is a great deal of work still to be done.

GLOSSARY

(For the reader's convenience, this glossary provides a brief and somewhat rough indication of the *basic* uses of the main terms; it does not account for some problematic cases.)

Notional roles: agent, patient, beneficiary, perceiver, recipient, instrumental, locative, etc. Defined purely notionally.

Grammatical roles: (mainly) the single role of an intransitive construction (S), Agent (A), Patient (P), Beneficiary, Instrumental, Locative, Causer (in causative constructions). Defined by (language-specific) formal marking in basic, active, constructions. Marking changed by operation of passive, antipassive and causative, but meaning remains constant.

Grammatical relations: Subject and Object/Direct Object in accusative systems, Absolutive and Ergative in ergative systems, Agentive and Patientive in agentive systems, Dative/Indirect Object, Instrumental, Locative. Marking remains constant, but meaning (in terms of roles) changed by (i) formal identification of S and A in accusative systems and of S and P in ergative systems, (ii) operation of passive, antipassive and causative.

Accusative system: in which S is formally identical with A in the active construction.

Ergative system: in which S is formally identical with P in the active construction.

Agentive system: in which S is formally identical sometimes with A, sometimes with P.

Topic system: in which there appears to be no basic, active, construction, but a set of devices to indicate various relations as Topics.

Glossary

Inverse system: in which there are two constructions, indicating whether the Agent is higher or lower than the Patient on an empathy hierarchy.

Primary relation, term: Subject in accusative systems, Absolutive in ergative systems, not applicable to agentive systems.

Secondary relation, term: Object in accusative systems, Ergative in ergative systems, not applicable to agentive systems.

Oblique relation: relations other than primary or secondary.

Peripheral roles/relations: roles and relations marked with prepositions.

Active: the basic, unmarked, construction, unaffected by passive, antipassive or causative.

Passive: device that promotes a relation other than Subject to Subject and demotes or deletes Subject (and the name of the resultant construction).

Antipassive: device that promotes a relation other than Absolutive to Absolutive and demotes or deletes Absolutive (and the name of the resultant construction).

Applicative: device that promotes an oblique relation to Object (and the name of the resultant construction).

Causative: device that adds new role of Causer in Subject position and demotes or deletes Subject (and the name of the resultant construction).

Promotion: changing a non-primary relation into the primary relation, or an oblique relation into the secondary relation.

Demotion: changing a primary relation into an oblique relation.

Deletion: formal omission of a relation.

Pivot: a relation that is co-referential with another relation and involved in syntactic rules for coordination, complementation, relativization etc.

REFERENCES AND
CITATION INDEX

The numbers in italic following the references indicate citation in the text.

Aissen, J. L. 1983. Indirect object advancement in Tzotzil. In Perlmutter 1983: 272–303

1992. Topic and focus in Mayan. *Language* 68: 43–80. *104*

Allen, W. S. 1951. A study in the analysis of Hindi sentence-structure. *Acta Linguistica* 6: 68–86. *58, 59*

Andersen, P. K. 1991. *A new look at the passive. (Duisberg Papers on Research and Culture 11)*. Frankfurt am Main: Peter Lang. *138, 139, 149*

Andersen, T. 1991. Subject and topic in Dinka. *Studies in Language* 15: 265–94. *135*

Anderson, S. R. 1976. The notion of subject in ergative languages. In Li 1976: 1–24. *105, 110, 187, 189, 200*

1985. Inflectional morphology. In Shopen 1985 Vol. III: 150–201. *126*

Anderson, S. R. and Kiparsky, P. (eds.) 1973: *A Festschrift for Morris Halle*. New York: Holt, Rinehart and Winston

Andrews, A. 1982. The representation of case in Modern Icelandic. In Bresnan 1982: 427–503. *129*

1985. The major functions of the noun phrase. In Shopen 1985 Vol. I: 2–154. *5, 40, 41, 42, 43, 109, 110, 129*

Arnott, D. W. 1956. The middle voice in Fula. *Bulletin of the School of Oriental and African Studies* 18: 130–44. *153*

1970. *The nominal and verbal systems of Fula*. Oxford: Oxford University Press. *154, 168*

Austin, P. 1981a. *A grammar of Diyari, South Australia*. Cambridge: Cambridge University Press. *64, 106*

1981b. Switch reference in Australia. *Language* 57: 309–34. *95, 99*

1982. Transitivity and cognate objects in Australian languages. In Hopper and Thompson 1982: 37–47. *195, 196*

Bach, E. and Harms, R. T. (eds.) 1968. *Universals in Linguistic theory*. New York: Holt, Rinehart and Winston

Baker, M. 1988. *Incorporation: a theory of grammatical function changing*. Chicago and London: Chicago University Press. *161, 163, 167*

Bandhu, C. 1973. Clause patterns in Nepali. In A. Hale 1973: 1–20. *59*

Bartholomew, D. and Mason, D. 1980. The registration of transitivity in the Guerrero Aztec verb. *International Journal of American Linguistics* 46: 197–204. *234*

References and citation index

Beedham, C. 1982. *The passive aspect in English, German and Russian.* Tübingen: Gunter Narr. *138, 139*

Blake, B. J. 1982. The absolutive: its scope in English and Kalkatungu. In Hopper and Thompson 1982: 71–94. *188*

Boas, F. 1911. *Tsimshian.* (Handbook of American Languages 1) Washington, DC: Government Printing Offices. *61*

Bresnan, J. 1982. *The mental representation of grammatical relations.* Cambridge, MA: MIT Press

Bresnan, J. and Kanerva, J. 1989. Locative inversion in Chichewa. *Linguistic Inquiry* 20: 1–50. *46*

Bresnan, J. and Moshi, L. 1990. Object asymmetries in comparative Bantu syntax. *Linguistic Inquiry* 21: 147–85. *162, 166*

Brettschneider, G. 1979. Typological characteristics of Basque. In Plank 1979: 371–84. *54, 104*

Catford, J. C. 1976. Ergativity in Caucasian languages. *North Eastern Linguistic Society* 6. (*Montreal working papers in linguistics* 6): 37–48. *182, 188*

Chapin, P. 1970. Samoan pronominalization. *Language* 46: 366–78. *102*

Chomsky, N. 1957. *Syntactic structures.* The Hague: Mouton. *2, 174*

1965. *Aspects of the theory of syntax.* Cambridge, MA: MIT Press. *174, 235*

Chung, S. 1976. On the subject of two passives in Indonesian. In Li 1976: 57–98. *162*

1983. An object-creating rule in Bahasa Indonesia. In Perlmutter 1983: 219–71. *34, 102*

Churchward, C. M. 1953. *Tongan grammar.* Oxford: Oxford University Press. *160, 187, 194*

Cinque, G. 1988. On *si* constructions and the theory of *Arb. Linguistic Inquiry* 19: 521–81. *145*

Cohen, M. 1936. *Traité de langue amharique.* Paris: Institut d'ethnologie. (Travaux et memoires de l'institut d'ethnologie, Université de Paris 24). *225*

Cole, P. 1983. The grammatical role of the causee in universal grammar. *International Journal of American Linguistics* 49: 115–33. *222, 225*

Cole, P. and Sadock, J. M. (eds.) 1977. *Grammatical relations. (Syntax and semantics 8)* New York: Academic Press

Comrie, B. 1973. The ergative: variations on a theme. *Lingua* 32: 239–53. *193*

1976. The system of causative constructions: cross language similarity and divergencies. In Shibatani 1976b: 261–312. *218, 219, 220, 222, 223*

1978. Ergativity. In Lehmann 1978: 329–94. *54, 68, 107, 187*

1982. Grammatical relations in Huichol. In Hopper and Thompson 1982: 95–115. *37*

1988. Passive and voice. In Shibatani 1988b: 9–23. *15*

Cooper, R. 1976. Lexical and non-lexical causatives in Bantu. In Shibatani 1976b: 313–24. *219, 227, 228*

Cooreman, A. 1988. The antipassive in Chamorro; variations on a theme of transitivity. In Shibatani 1988b: 561–93. *182, 183, 184*

Cooreman, A., Fox, B. and Givón, T. 1984. The discourse definition of ergativity. *Studies in Language* 8: 1–34. *203*

Craig, C. G. 1976. Properties of basic and derived subjects in Jacaltec. In Li 1976: 99–123. *74*

Croft, W. 1991. *Syntactic categories and grammatical relations.* Cambridge: Cambridge University Press. *1, 25, 26, 27, 28, 30, 33, 38, 74, 111, 229*

Davies, W. D. and Rosen, C. 1988. Unions as multi-predicate clauses. *Language* 64: 52–88. *218*

Davison, A. 1980. Peculiar passive. *Language* 56: 42–66. *120*

DeLancy, S. 1981. An interpretation of split ergativity and related patterns. *Language* 57: 626–57. *59*

Dixon, R. W. M. 1969. Relative clauses and possessive phrases in two Australian languages. *Language* 45: 35–44. *177*

　1972. *The Dyirbal language of North Queensland.* Cambridge: Cambridge University Press. *12, 59, 112, 177, 189*

　1976. *Grammatical categories in Australian Languages.* Canberra: Australian Institute of Aboriginal Studies

　1977a. *A grammar of Yidin.* Cambridge: Cambridge University Press. *20, 46, 63, 91, 176, 179, 181, 185, 237*

　1977b. The syntactic development of Australian languages. In Li 1977: 365–415. *10, 90, 99, 179*

　1979. Ergativity. *Language* 55: 59–138. *10, 12, 13, 18, 30, 57, 59, 61, 65, 66, 68, 89, 94, 98, 111, 112, 115, 161, 178, 188*

　1980. *The languages of Australia.* Cambridge: Cambridge University Press. *112*

Donaldson, T. 1980. *Ngiyambaa: the language of the Wangaaybuwan.* Cambridge: Cambridge University Press. *233*

Dryer, M. S. 1986. Primary objects, secondary objects and antidative. *Language* 62: 808–45. *38, 39, 170*

Dubinsky, S., Lloret, M-R. and Newman, P. 1988. Lexical and syntactic causatives in Oromo. *Language* 64: 485–500. *231*

Du Bois, J. W. 1987. The discourse basis of ergativity. *Language* 63: 805–55. *199*

Durie, M. 1985. Control and decontrol in Acehnese. *Australian Journal of Linguistics* 5: 43–53. *67, 75, 76*

　1988. The so-called passive of Acehnese. *Language* 64: 104–13. *148, 149*

Efrat, B. S. (ed.) 1979. *The Victoria conference on Northwestern languages.* British Columbia Provincial Museum

Einarsson, S. 1945. *Icelandic: grammar, texts, glossary.* Baltimore: Johns Hopkins University Press. *155*

England, N. C. 1983. Ergativity in Mamean (Mayan) languages. *International Journal of American Linguistics* 19: 1–19. *61, 94, 103, 184*

　1988. Mam voice. In Shibatani 1988b: 525–45. *103, 180, 184*

Estival, D. and Myhill, J. 1988. Formal and functional aspects of the development from passive to ergative systems. In Shibatani 1988b: 441–91. *187*

Fillmore, C. J. 1968. The case for case. In Bach and Harms 1968: 1–88. *4, 28*

1971. Types of lexical information. In Steinberg and Jakobovits 1971: 370–92. *4*

Foley, W. A. and Van Valin, R. D. 1984. *Functional syntax and universal grammar.* Cambridge: Cambridge University Press. *6, 71, 91, 92, 115, 173*

1985. Information packaging in the clause. In Shopen 1985 Vol. I: 282–364. *6, 10, 54, 88, 89, 105, 115, 116, 133, 145, 160, 173, 180, 198, 202*

Fox, B. A. 1987. The noun phrase accessibility hierarchy revisited. *Language* 63: 856–70. *98*

Franklin, K. 1971. *A grammar of Kewa, New Guinea.* (*Pacific Linguistics*, Series C, 16). Canberra: Department of Linguistics, Australian National University. *49, 91, 92*

Fromm, H. and Sadeniemi, M. 1956. *Finnisches Elementarbuch.* Heidelberg: Winter. *48*

Givón, T. 1979. *On understanding grammar.* New York: Academic Press. *47, 144, 147, 148, 200*

1981. Typology and functional domain. *Studies in Language* 5: 163–83. *174*

1988. A tale of two passives in Ute. In Shibatani 1988b: 417–40. *147*

Goddard, C. 1982. Case systems and case marking in Australian languages: a new interpretation. *Australian Journal of Linguistics* 2: 167–96. *64*

Gregorez, E. and Suárez, J. A. 1967. *A description of colloquial Guaraní.* The Hague: Mouton. *67, 71*

Haig, H. A. 1982. Passivization in Modern Western Armenian. In Hopper and Thompson 1982: 161–76. *155*

Hale, A. 1973 (ed.) *Clause, sentence and discourse patterns in selected languages of Nepal, II, Clause.* Norman OK: Summer Institute of Linguistics

Hale, K. L. 1973a. Person marking in Warlbiri. In Anderson and Kiparsky 1973: 308–44. *35, 56, 189*

1973b. A note on subject-object inversion in Navajo. In Kachru et al. 1973: 300–9. *209, 211*

Hammer, A. E. 1971. *German grammar and usage.* London: Edward Arnold. *32*

Harris, A. C. 1981. *Georgian syntax: a study in relational grammar.* Cambridge: Cambridge University Press. *78, 79, 80, 81, 85*

1982. Georgian and the unaccusative hypothesis. *Language* 58: 290–306. *78, 80, 81*

Hashimoto, M. J. 1988. The structure and typology of the Chinese passive construction. In Shibatani 1988b: 329–54. *149*

Haspelmath, M. 1990. The grammaticalization of passive morphology. *Studies in Language* 14: 25–72. *118, 139, 141*

Heath, J. 1976. Antipassivization: a functional typology. *Berkeley Linguistics Society* 2: 202–11. *197*

1977. Chocktaw cases. *Berkeley Linguistic Society* 3: 204–13. *68, 69*

Hercus, L. A. 1976. Arabana and Wangganguru. In Dixon 1976: 263–6, 461–7, 740–2. *95*

Hetzron, R. 1976. On the Hungarian causative verb and its syntax. In Shibatani 1976b: 371–98. *215, 220, 229, 231, 239*

Hill, J. 1969. Volitional and non-volitional verbs in Cupeño. *Chicago Linguistics Society* 5: 348–56. *77*

Hope, E. R. 1974. *The deep syntax of Lisu sentences: transformational case grammar.* (Pacific Linguistics, B 34) Canberra: Department of Linguistics, Australian National University. *23, 24*

Hopper, P. J. and Thompson, S. A. 1980. Transitivity in grammar and discourse. *Language* 56: 251–99. *33, 181, 185, 187, 195*

(eds.) 1982. *Studies in transitivity. (Syntax and Semantics 15)*. New York: Academic Press

Hudson, R. 1992. So-called 'double objects' and grammatical relations. *Language* 68: 251–76. *170*

Hyman, L. M. and Zimmer, K. E. 1976. Embedded topic in French. In Li 1976: 189–211. *35, 222, 224*

Jacobs, R. 1976. A passive continuum in Austronesian. *Papers from the parasession on diachronic syntax.* Chicago: Chicago Linguistic Society. 118–25. *146*

Jakobsen, W. H. 1979. Nouns and verbs in Nootkan. In Efrat 1979: 85–153. *212, 213*
1985. The analog of the passive transformation in ergative-type languages. In Nichols and Woodbury 1985: 176–91. *44, 158*

Jespersen, O. 1924. *The philosophy of grammar.* London: Allen & Unwin. *172*
1909–49. *A modern English grammar on historical principles.* 7 vols. London: Allen & Unwin. *44*

Johnson, D. E. 1974. On the role of grammatical relations in linguistic theory. *Papers from the Tenth Regional Meeting. Chicago Linguistic Society:* 269–83

Johns, A. 1991. Deriving ergativity. *Linguistic Inquiry* 23: 57–87. *200*

Kachru, B. B., Lees, R. B., Malkiel, Y., Pietrangeli, A. and Saporta, S. 1973. *Issues in linguistics: papers in honor of Henry and Reneé Kahane.* Urbana: University of Illinois Press

Kachru, Y., Kachru, R. B. and Bhatia, T. K. 1976. The notion of 'subject'; a note on Hindi-Urdu, Kashmiri and Punjabi. In Verma 1976: 79–108. *42, 10, 108, 109*

Kalmár, I. 1979. The antipassive and grammatical relations in Eskimo. In Plank 1979: 117–44. *189*

Keenan, E. L. 1972. Relative clause formation in Malagasy (and some related and some not so related languages). In Peranteau et al. 1972: 169–89. *17, 25, 96*
1976. Remarkable subjects in Malagasy. In Li 1976: 247–301. *101*
1985. Passive in the world's languages. In Shopen 1985 Vol I: 243–81. *16, 100, 118, 130, 140, 160, 235*

Keenan, E. L. and Comrie, B. 1977. Noun phrase accessibility and universal grammar. *Linguistic Inquiry* 8: 63–99. *97, 98, 100*
1979. Data on the noun phrase accessibility hierarchy. *Language* 55: 333–51. *98, 100*

Kemmer, S. and Verhagen, A. Forthcoming. The grammar of causatives and the conceptual structure of events. *Cognitive linguistics. 239*

Kibrik, A. E. 1985. Towards a typology of ergativity. In Nichols and Woodbury 1985: 268–323. *26, 78, 82, 85*

Kimball, G. D. 1985. A descriptive grammar of Koasati. New Orleans: Tulane University dissertation. *74*

Kimenyi, A. 1980. *A relational grammar of Kinyarwanda.* (University of California Publications in Linguistics, 91) Berkeley: University of California Press. *121*
1988. Passives in Kinyarwanda. In Shibatani 1988b. 355–86. *10, 45, 121, 123, 133, 163, 165, 236*

Kirsner, R. S. 1976. On the subjectless 'pseudo-passive' in standard Dutch and the semantics of background agents. In Li 1976: 385–415. *127*

Klaiman, M. H. 1988. Affectedness and control: a typology of voice systems. In Shibatani 1988b: 25–83. *137, 209, 212*
1991. *Grammatical voice.* Cambridge: Cambridge University Press. *4, 78, 150, 152, 153, 154, 155, 156, 168, 209, 212, 229, 230*

Kozinsky, I. Š., Nedjalkov, V. P. and Polinskaya, M. S. 1988. Antipassive in Chukchee: oblique object, object incorporation, zero object. In Shibatani 1988b: 651–706. *19, 35, 177, 181, 182, 183, 186, 191*

Kuno, S. 1973. *The structure of the Japanese language.* Cambridge, MA: MIT Press. *29, 130*

Lawler, J. M. 1977. *A* agrees with *B* in Achenese: a problem for relational grammar. In Cole and Sadock 1977: 219–48. *148*

Lehmann, C. 1984. *Der Relativsatz: Typologie seiner Strukturen. Theorie seiner Funktionen, Kompendium seiner Grammatik.* Tübingen: Nar

Lehmann, W. P. (ed.) 1978. *Syntactic typology.* Austin: University of Texas Press. *100*

Lepschy, A. L. and Lepschy, G. 1977. *The Italian language today.* London: Hutchinson. *9, 27, 77, 143, 144, 214, 221*

Leslau, W. 1941. *Documents tigrinya (éthiopien septentrional): documents et textes.* Paris: Klincksieck. *232*

Levine, R. D. 1980. On the lexical origin of the Kwakwala passive. *International Journal of American Linguistics* 46: 240–58. *126*

Li, C. N. (ed.) 1976. *Subject and topic.* New York: Academic Press
1977. *Mechanisms of language change.* New York: Academic Press

Li, C. N. and Thompson, S. A. 1976. Subject and topic: a new typology of language. In Li 1976: 458–89. *23*

Lind, J. O. 1984. Clause and sentence level syntagmemes in Sierra Popoluca. *International Journal of American Linguistics* 30: 341–54. *234*

Lyon, S. 1967. Tlahuitoltepec Mixe clause structure. *International Journal of American Linguistics* 33: 25–45. *209*

Lyons, J. 1968. *Introduction to theoretical linguistics.* Cambridge: Cambridge University Press. *150*
1977. *Semantics.* 2 vols. Cambridge: Cambridge University Press. *119*

Matthews, P. H. 1981. *Syntax.* Cambridge: Cambridge University Press. *3*

McLendon, S. 1978. Ergativity, case and transitivity in Eastern Pomo. *International Journal of American Linguistics* 44: 1–9. *13, 68, 70, 73, 113*

Merlan, F. 1985. Split intransitivity: functional oppositions in intransitive inflection. In Nichols and Woodbury 1985: 324–62. *73, 75*

Milner, G. B. 1973. It is aspect (not voice) which is marked in Samoan. *Oceanic Linguistics* 12: 621–39. *58*

Mistry, P. J. 1976. Subject in Gujerati: an examination of verb agreement phenomena. In Verma 1976: 240–69. *58*

Mithun, M. 1984. The evolution of noun incorporation. *Language* 60: 847–94. *191, 192, 193*

1991. Active/agentive case marking and its motivations. *Language* 67: 510–46. *67, 71, 72, 74*

Mohanan, K. P. 1982. Grammatical relations and clause structure in Malayalam. In Bresnan 1982: 504–89. *101*

Mondloch, J. L. 1978. *Basic Quiché grammar. (Institute for Mesoamerican Studies Publication 2).* Albany, NY: Institute for Mesoamerican Studies. *30*

Morin, Y-C. and Tiffou, E. 1988: Passives in Burushaski. In Shibatani 1988b: 493–524. *56, 158*

Munro, P. 1976, *Mojave syntax.* New York: Garland. *147*

Nedjalkov, V. P. 1988. Resultative, passive and perfect in German. In Nedjalkov and Jaxontov 1988: 3–62. *138*

Nedjalkov, V. P. and Jaxontov, S. J. 1988. *Typology of resultative constructions.* Amsterdam: John Benjamins

Nichols, J. and Woodbury, A. C. (eds.) 1985. *Grammar inside and outside the clause. Some approaches to theory from the field.* Cambridge: Cambridge University Press

Noonan, M. 1985. Complementation. In Shopen 1985 Vol II: 42–180. *95*

1992. *A grammar of Lango.* The Hague: Mouton de Gruyter. *92, 101*

Oates, L. F. 1964. *A tentative description of the Gunwinggu language.* (Oceanic Linguistic Monographs 10) Sydney: University of Sydney. *194*

Olson, M. L. 1978. Switch reference in Barai. *Berkeley Linguistics Society* 4: 140–57. *92*

Palmer, F. R. 1986. *Mood and modality.* Cambridge: Cambridge University Press. *1, 5, 117, 119, 232*

1987. *The English verb.* (2nd edition) London: Longman. *124, 217*

Paramasivam, K. 1979. Effectivity and causativity in Tamil. *International Journal of Dravidian Linguistics* 8: 71–151. *229, 230*

Peranteau, P. M., Levi, J. N. and Phares, G. C. (eds.) 1972. *The Chicago which hunt.* Chicago: Chicago Linguistic Society. *100*

Perlmutter, D. M. 1978. Impersonal passives and the unaccusative hypothesis. *Berkeley Linguistics Society* 4: 157–89. *76, 77, 127*

(ed.) 1983. *Studies in Relational Grammar 1.* Chicago: University of Chicago Press

Perlmutter, D. M. and Postal, P. M. 1984. Impersonal passives and some relational laws. In Perlmutter and Rosen 1984: 126–70. *127*

Perlmutter, D. M. and Rosen, C. G. (eds.). 1984 *Studies in Relational grammar 2.* Chicago: University of Chicago Press

Peters, S. (ed.) 1972. *Goals of linguistic theory.* Englewood Cliffs, NJ: Prentice-Hall

Philippaki-Warburton, I. 1985. Word order in Modern Greek. *Transactions of the Philological Society* 1945: 113–43. *132*

Plank. F. (ed.) 1979. *Ergativity: towards a theory of grammatical relations.* London, New York: Academic Press

Quirk, R., Greenbaum, S., Leech, G. and Svartvik, J. 1985. *A comprehensive grammar of the English language.* London: Longman. *137*

Rabel, L. 1961. *Khasi, a language of Assam.* Baton Rouge: Louisiana State University Press. *38*

Radford, A. 1988. *Transformational grammar: a first course.* Cambridge: Cambridge University Press. *5*

Rognvaldsson, E. 1982. We need (some kind of) a rule of conjunction reduction. *Linguistic Inquiry* 13: 557–61. *41, 43, 107*

Rosen, C. 1990. Rethinking Southern Tiwa: the geometry of a triple-agreement language. *Language* 66: 669–713. *170, 193*

Rosen, C. and Kashi, W. 1988. Twin passives, inversion and multistratalism in Marathi. *Natural Language and Linguistic Theory* 7: 1–50. *36, 42–3*

Rude, N. 1988. Ergative, passive and antipassive in Nez Perce: a discourse perspective. In Shibatani 1988b: 547–60. *63, 187, 190*

Saksena, A. 1981. The source of causative contrast. *Lingua* 51: 125–30. *223, 228*
  1982a. Contact in causation. *Language* 58: 820–31. *223, 228*
  1982b. Case marking in semantics. *Lingua* 56: 335–43. *223, 228*

Saunders, R. and Davis, P. W. 1982. The control system of Bella Coola. *International Journal of American Linguistics* 48: 1–15. *233*

Schachter, P. 1976. The subject in Philippine languages. In Li 1976: 491–518. *201, 204, 205, 207*
  1977. Reference-related and role-related properties of subjects. In Cole and Sadock 1977: 279–306. *206*

Shayne, J-A. 1982. Some semantic aspects of *Yi-* and *Bi-* in San Carlos Apache. In Hopper and Thompson 1982: 379–407. *209, 210, 212*

Shepardson, K. N. 1981. Toward a structural definition of direct and indirect objects: support from Swahili. *Word* 32: 109–33. *46*

Shibatani, M. 1973. Lexical versus periphrastic causatives in Korean. *Journal of Linguistics* 9: 281–97. *100, 226*
  1976a. The grammar of causative constructions: a conspectus. In Shibatani 1976b: 1–40. *225*
  (ed.) 1976b. *The grammar of causative constructions (Syntax and Semantics 6).* New York: Academic Press
  1977. Grammatical relations and surface case. *Language* 53: 789–809. *171*
  1982. Japanese grammar and universal grammar. *Lingua* 57: 103–23. *49, 223*
  1985. Passives and related constructions. *Language* 61: 821–48. *40, 139, 140, 143, 144, 145, 146, 147, 157, 158, 172, 173*
  1988a. Voice in Philippine languages. In Shibatani 1988b: 85–142. *203, 206*

(ed.) 1988b. *Passive and voice*. Amsterdam and Philadelphia: Benjamins. *207*

Shopen, T. (ed.) 1985. *Language typology and language description*. 3 vols. Cambridge: Cambridge University Press

Siewerska, A. 1988. The passive in Slavic. In Shibatani 1988b: 243–89. *142, 144*

Silverstein, M. 1976. Hierarchy of features and ergativity. In Dixon 1976: 112–72. *18, 30*

Song, J. J. 1991. Causatives and universal grammar: an alternative explanation. *Transactions of the Philological Society* 89: 65–94. *219*

Song, N. S. 1987. Empathy-based affectedness and passivization. *Transactions of the Philological Society* 1987: 74–89. *30, 125, 131, 235*

Steinberg, D. D. and Jakobovits, L. A. 1971. *Semantics: an interdisciplinary reader in philosophy, linguistics and psychology*. Cambridge: Cambridge University Press

Sugita, H. 1973. Semitransitive verbs and object incorporation in Micronesian languages. *Oceanic Linguistics* 12: 393–406. *192*

Talmy, L. 1976. Semantic causative types. In Shibatani 1976b: 43–116. *26*

Timberlake, A. 1976. Subject properties of the North Russian passive. In Li 1976: 545–70. *130*

Trithart, L. 1976. Topicality: an alternative to the relational view of Bantu passives. *Studies in African Linguistics* 10: 1–30. *115, 137*

Tsunoda, T. 1981. Split case-marking in verb-types and tense/aspect/mood. *Linguistics* 19: 389–438. *190*

1985. Remarks on transitivity. *Journal of Linguistics* 21: 385–96. *48*

1988. Antipassives in Warrungu and other Australian languages. In Shibatani 1988b: 595-649. *53, 60, 106, 180, 183, 184*

Van Valin, R. D. 1985. Case marking and the structure of the Lhakhota clause. In Nichols and Woodbury 1985: 363–413. *66*

1990. Semantic parameters of split intransitivity. *Language* 66: 221–60. *77*

1991. Another look at Icelandic case marking and grammatical relations. *Natural Language and Linguistic Theory* 9: 145–94. *43*

Verma, M. K. (ed.). 1976 *The notion of subject in South Asian languages*. Madison: University of Wisconsin. (Publication Series 2)

Vincent, N. V. 1982. The development of the auxiliaries HABERE and ESSE in Romance. In Vincent and Harris 1982: 71–96. *77*

Vincent, N. V. and Harris, M. (eds.) 1982. *Studies in the Romance verb: essays offered to Joe Cremona on the occasion of his 60th birthday*. London and Canberra: Croom Helm

Walrod, M. R. 1976. Case in Ga'dang verbal clauses. *Papers in Philippine languages* 8: 21–44 (*Pacific Linguistics*, Series A, 46, Department of Linguistics, The Australian National University). *47, 202*

Watkins, M. 1937. *A grammar of Hichewa*. Philadelphia: Linguistic Society of America. (*Language* dissertation 24). *116*

Whistler, K. W. 1985. Focus, perspective and inverse person marking. In Nichols and Woodbury 1985: 227–65. *6, 213*

Witherspoon, G. 1980. Language in culture and culture in language. *International Journal of American Linguistics* 46: 1–13. *209, 210, 211*

Wolfart, H. 1973. *Plains Cree: a grammatical study. (Transactions of the American Philosophical Society, 65, Part 5.)* Philadelphia: American Philosophical Society

Woodbury, A. C. 1975. Ergativity of grammatical processes. University of Chicago Ph. D. thesis. *183*

  1977. Greenlandic Eskimo: ergativity and relational grammar. In Cole and Sadock 1977: 307–36. *45, 55, 158, 177*

Woodbury, H. 1975. Onondaga noun incorporation: some notes on the interdependence of syntax and syntax. *International Journal of American Linguistics* 41: 10–20. *192*

Yallop, C. 1977. *Alyawarra: an aboriginal language of central Australia.* Canberra: Australian Institute of Aboriginal Studies. *99*

Zubizarreta, M. L. 1985. The relation between morphophonology and morphosyntax: the case of Romance causatives. *Linguistic Inquiry* 16: 247–89. *143*

LANGUAGE INDEX

GENERAL INDEX

factitive 225
figure 28
fluid S 68, 77, 84
focus 100, 103–4, 126, 180
foregrounding 173–4

gender 7, 17, 58, 216
generic 18–5
genitive 40, 44, 48, 50–2, 98, 129, 131,
135–6, 149
goal 5, 162–3, 201
Goal 6, 33
grammatical relation 6, 11–16, 18–21,
22–52, 241, *passim*
grammatical role 4–6, 9, 14–16, 18–21,
22–52, 241, *passim*
grammaticalization 5, 22, 86, 217
ground 28

hierarchy 30, 65, 98, 115, 137, 189,
207–13, 218
historical 73, 118, 149, 157
honorific 157
human 40, 63, 65, 72, 74, 82, 116, 128, 137,
159, 185, 209

idiom 124, 139
imperative 76, 111–13, 199
imperfective *see* perfective
impersonal 41, 59, 69, 144–5, 172
impersonal passive 76, 127–32, 139, 145
implicative 95, 106
inanimate *see* animate
inceptive 140
inchoative 72
inclusion 95
incomplete 188
incorporation 21, 184–6, 191–5, 197–8
indefinite 63, 142–8, 173, 184, 189, 193,
198, *see also* definite
indirect causation *see* direct causation
Indirect Object *see* Dative
inflection 55
initiator 25–6
instruction 229
instrument, instrumental 5, 24, 28, 122,
163, 178, 225, 237
instrumental (case) 49, 58, 101, 108, 223
Instrumental 3, 6, 8, 10–11, 17, 19–20, 28,
44–6, 47, 50, 96–7, 108–10, 123, 125–6,
142, 163–4, 166, 168, 177–8, 186, 198,
202, 204, 220–2, 228–9, 236–7
intensive 231

intentional 78
interrogative 103
intransitive 3, 8, 10–13, 28, 56, 60, 65–7,
69–70, 72, 75–9, 84–5, 105, 113, 127–8,
130, 139, 143, 146, 149, 155–6, 163, 173,
181, 187–90, 196–9, 203–4, 218, 223, 229,
233, 237
intransitivizer 75–6
inverse 208–12
inverse system 21, 31, 56, 137, 174, 200,
207–13, 242
inversion 33
iterative 183

jussive 111–13, 199

kinship terms 73

lexical 195–7, 225, 228
lexical causative 217–18
locative 5, 29, 121, 120–2, 162
locative case, marker 46, 164–5
Locative 3, 5–6, 8, 10–11, 19–20, 44–6, 47,
123, 163–6, 176–8, 183, 186, 198, 201–2,
220, 228

main/subordinate 57, 61–2, 99, 105, *see
also* subordinate
malefactive 163
manipulative 225–7
manner 122
marking 6–8, 14, 16, 55, *passim*
meaning *see* semantics
mediopassive 77, 143
middle 150–6, 229
modal subject 40–4, 48, 101, 107–8
modal verb 42, 81, 119
mood, modality 86, 119, 153, 155, 215,
231–2
morphological causative 216–17, 225,
226–7, 230
morphology 7, 11, 14, 26, 44, 50, 53–8, 60,
63, 65, 69–70, 74, 77–8, 82–4, 91, 96,
104–7, 110–11, 113, 118–19, 132, 142, 145,
150-1, 153, 158, 160, 169, 185, 197,
199–200, 203, 207–8, 214–15, 234

names 64, 73
negative 103, 180, 188
neuter 76, 78, 143, 152, 155–6
nominative 7, 31, 42–3, 49–51, 55–6, 60,
63–4, 70, 78, 87, 91, 107, 145, 183, 190,
197, 238